Computers in Language Research

Trends in Linguistics
Studies and Monographs 5

Editor

Werner Winter

Mouton Publishers
The Hague · Paris · New York

Computers
in Language Research
Formal Methods

edited by

Walter A. Sedelow, Jr.
Sally Yeates Sedelow

Mouton Publishers
The Hague · Paris · New York

Sally Yeates Sedelow, Ph. D.
Professor of Computer Science and of Linguistics
The University of Kansas, Lawrence

Walter A. Sedelow, Jr., Ph. D.
Professor of Computer Science and of Sociology,
and in the Program for the History & Philosophy of Science,
The University of Kansas, Lawrence

ISBN 90 279 7846 8
© Copyright 1979 by Mouton Publishers, The Hague. All rights reserved, including those
of translation into foreign languages. No part of this book may be reproduced in any
form — by photoprint, microfilm, or any other means — nor transmitted nor translated
into a machine language without written permission from the publisher. Typesetting:
Walter de Gruyter & Co. Berlin. — Printing: Karl Gerike, Berlin. — Binding: Lüderitz &
Bauer Buchgewerbe GmbH, Berlin.
Printed in Germany

Contents

Language and people, modelling and science

Brain size; coordination of eye/hand (*cum* opposable thumb)/brain; the invention and use of tools; language — each of these has had its proponents in the great international 'accounting' contest. The accounting in question is that needed for the human species' remarkable relationship to the other species and to global ecology. No doubt each of those properties of humankind is an important entry in the account. It might even seem evident that each is critical, and, further, that it is the interaction among them that has — for better or for worse, for richer or for poorer — given us the Human System for relating to environment.

In this present series within a series, *Computers in language research*, we examine, *inter alia*, one of the most remarkable achievements of that Human System: through symbols modelling its own behavior and, notably, recently available techniques for modelling its own symbol behavior (e. g., modelling symbolic models). It is at least arguable that this human activity of symbolizing symbolism is the most quintessentially human — the distinctively, perhaps uniquely, human — of all behaviors, as it is also, at least potentially, much the most powerful. The mathematical logician's pen is mightier than the sword; in fact, it is now essential even to the production of those most contemporary swords of war: atomic energy devices, biochemical agents, and their weaponly peers. Similarly, new food plant strains, new ecological comprehension, new curative therapies, new symbolic forms increasingly depend on a preliminary symbolic mediating — and to a degree undreamt of even so recently as at the onset of modern physics a century ago. The experimental fraction of science, though ever more socially significant through the impact of critical experiments, is continually shrinking; the symbol-manipulative fraction, continually growing. Skills in the generation of formalisms come to occupy an ever more modal situs in scientific careers, and identity crises emerge, unclearly, as to the professional *personae* appropriate to the chemist, the geneticist, or even the geologist or botanist. All such scientific professional roles are by way of being partially transformed in generic, but profound, respects into those of linguists of a sort, and part of the time many of the best scientists are effectively specialized metalinguists. Scientific method, epistemology and metaphysics, paradigmatics, and even the traditional theory component of the sciences are in process of becoming 'linguistic' specializations: dialects within scientific linguae francae. These are providing us with a formalist science of science, with ways of modelling those dialects we call the sciences.

Through their respective processes of professional socialization or enculturation, each science approximates a replication of itself in each successor academic generation. The replication is only proximal for, as we well know with all languages and dialects, change pervades. And nowhere in language is change so pervasive and so rapid as in the science languages, except in those formal and quasi-formal languages developed and developing in conjunction with computer science and computer technics. Those languages which are most 'natural' — least self-conscious, least deliberately artifactual, least constructed — change most slowly. They are least well understood, partly because not cut to a pattern, partly because not used to achieve limited and well-specified objectives. Those languages which are most fully designed also are most logically coherent and hence most formally tractable. As it happens, the segment of reality which they address and symbolize, the computing machines — or, as we would prefer, the logic machine, the 'logic-er' rather than the computer — is also, as physical artifacts go, highly unstable, and very rapidly changing and developing in certain structural properties. Thus these languages which can be changed easily and systematically, do change easily and systematically partly because that is what is happening to the specific realities they are meant to give us control over.

It is, then, not surprising that as the sciences become increasingly (physical) computer-dependent and (physical) computer-implicated — not to mention abstract machine-implicated, abstract computer-implicated — their linguistic aspect evolves more rapidly. The language of science and the individual dialects of the individual sciences stand precisely between traditional, mundane natural language and the contemporary (quasi-) formal languages which are the artifactual by-products of computing machines and abstract concepts of such machines. The science languages, then, being a mix of the substantially unplanned evolution of everyday language and the substantially planned specialized symbolizations of the computerniks and their ilk, is it any surprise that their change rate is intermediate as between 'natural' languages and that of more formal languages?

Dichotomizing is one of the most profound, significant, consequential properties of Occidental cultures. It is a generic feature of most of our

Western languages. And it can be argued that the output, the payoffs, the tradeoffs from such dichotomizing have been very rewarding. Interestingly enough, one of the most salient realizations of that dichotomizing has been as to form/substance, spirit/matter and, in more recent centuries, the related pairings of symbolic/material, linguistic/physical. On grounds of modelling parsimony or, for that matter, of conceptual elegance, it might be urged, in abstracto, that there is a prima facie preferability for a 'uniformitarian' or monistic world-view, in which we didn't start with a physical/symbolical polarity. In the present context a possibly more compelling argument may emerge from the difficulties one sheds — and the advantages one gains — if there is no attempt to define 'language' in a fashion that cleanly separates it from the rest of reality. No available definitions which do so dyadicize are operationally robust, nor does there appear to be any reason for supposing subsequent attempts will be more successful in that respect. Rather, the contrary.

A preferable alternative would be to place instances of phenomena labelled 'language' on an energy transformation (dis)continuum. Language phenomena could then characteristically emerge as low-energy physical phenomena of exceptionally low entropy. The advantages of such an 'approach' relate to (i) a facilitation thus provided for extending in their application to language, models and techniques which already have shown some utility in this domain, (ii) a more thorough transport to language research of the advantages attendant on expectations and standards of scientificity well established in the mature, classical physical sciences, and (iii) the greater ease of making gains on the 'unity of science' front. As to (iii), but for that matter with reference to (i) and (ii) as well, one may be said, in another aspect, to be forwarding the cause of a further normalization of the language of science — an avoidance of unnecessary dialects and jargons (unnecessary linguistic 'specialization') impeding the flow of scientific dialogue and pedagogy.

It may, after all, be taken as axiomatic that 'the eye of the beholder' (and/ or in some many instances the ear of the beholder) is a necessary though not sufficient condition for the existence of lingual, or symbolic, phenomena. In the extreme — and uncommon case — we might have the limiting instance of a solipsist, or at least an isolate, who alone perceives as symbolic, or lingual, what are in one or more senses his 'own' expressions. Far more commonly, language is in additional senses a social phenomenon, with at least an appearance of standardization or statistical regularity to the language behavior of a network, usually (but not strictly necessarily), of people. Chimpanzees not yet at least having been shown to model communication behavior existentially, it is the case that any symbolization of symbolic behavior is a human function. And, it may be argued, the decisively human function and human 'differens'.

A great and simple disadvantage of attempting to cleave cleanly between the symbolized and the symbolic is that parts of nature or artifacts that are not conventionally included in symbolization or language may, in fact, 'speak' to some beholder or beholders. Actually, one should go much further, noting that *all* those elements in the world that are taken for symbolic by some are to the majority meaningless. And, also, one wonders whether there is any feature of nature or culture that has not been — or could not be — taken to speak to someone at some time. The striped rainbow and stripes on a melon, for examples, are instances where the 'projective' activity of humankind has ascribed symbolic significance, given meanings and even phenomenologically 'created' elements in a language. The anthropomorphizing that gives us English (or French) words from the 'songs'(!) of birds and hermeneutic readings of the Earth itself are, in this respect, all of a piece. With the importation of an appropriate filter there is nothing that cannot be perceived as a 'symbol'. At least since the eighteenth century that has been — in one way or another, albeit always in some measure fragmentarily — understood, as can be seen in the work of John George Hamann, especially in Bishop Butler, in Vico, even in Voltaire's *Candide*.

But it has remained for more recent decades to unpack more completely and to sort out more carefully the full extent and character of convention in the human invention of meaning (symbolism, language). In our retrospections it may almost seem as though we should, or in any case could, see important patterns in the intellectual life of the past millenium as prologue, and the Classical centuries as a preface to that prologue, for the computer as a symbol-analytic device. We believe that these past thirty years will come to seem only the beginnings as to the utility of the computer for statistical and analytical mathematics. But what we may not yet so clearly see is that, prospectively, the 'entelechy' of computing machines is only in small part mathematical manipulation, whether the mathematics be 'pure' or only business arithmetic. The computer (or better logic-er, or maybe best, symbolic-er), is the first instrumentation that offers us significant hope of doing effective scientific work on the symbolism that humans create. And, interestingly enough in light of the argument above as to the impracticality of trying to separate the artifactual from the physical or 'natural', the computer also has been necessary for our current 'quantum leap' in the understanding of physical processes.

In a profound sense of the idea of data reduction, it is that which we regularly strive for whenever we look for structure — whether, say, in statistics or in discourse. For all its faults, the great advantage of philosophical 'ideal-ism', whether Platonic or otherwise, is its strong impetus to pattern recognition of a high order. In advancing the ideal of a quest for order, idealism has been far more significant than in any of the specific structures it has projectively imputed to the orders of reality it has at one time or another addressed. The importance of that sublime pattern perception by way of computer-based information systems which is entailed in serious efforts at systematically understanding what we classify as symbolic, derives from properties of the human information processing apparatus. Relative to the scale of demands on the 'human computer' posed by changing total environmental adjustment requirements, at least in complex non-traditional societies, as well as in the less humanly congenial environments (the great deserts; the Polar regions), that organic machine requires means to minimize its external-world-model-building tasks and the processing done utilizing such models.

Speculatively one may add that the appeal to scientists of such a dictum re theoretical structure as L. J. Henderson's "As simple as possible, as complex as necessary" is probably analogous in its source to the appeal of a generic Classicism in the arts: the simpler the organizing paradigm, the less likely the human computer system is to being over-taxed, the shorter its processing queues, and the less work that has to be paged in and out in (a high-overhead) background mode. Personally, we are very skeptical concerning the explanations that have been advanced as to how it happens that Parkinson's Law seems to hold, where it does. It seems to us that it may, in effect, give a kind of index to a characteristic over-taxing that modern central nervous systems are exposed to; perhaps starting with early childhood most central nervous systems have more jobs to process than capacity allows for, so that work expands to fill available time in a bureaucracy as a result of largely non-bureaucratically-derived analyses of ambience being advanced, partially non-consciously, to a processing stage whenever the overt 'on-line' work-load falls below certain processing levels. It is difficult to find in contemporary biographical or autobiographical literature what look to be anything like approximations to persons whose processing requirements are so modest that they seem, daily, to approximate to having most of their processing work done. Even in the most plausible instances psychiatrically-based insights would lead us to suppose that queue-exhaustion is more illusion than reality. Take an ostensibly very non-ambitious person, give him resources such that he is not much involved in "getting and spending", find for him devoted others who tend to his mundane needs, provide means of buffering off unattractive incursions from an outside world — and you may have an image of Max Beerbohm, "The Incomparable Max". What's striking is how few such comparatively undertaxed people — undertaxed central nervous system processing units, that is — one encounters. Even at the end of a longish life perhaps not many people would be characterized as ready for death; when, not so often, one does encounter such a person, one could interpret that condition as signifying a more than usual state of completion of processing jobs taken on during a life-time. Presumably such people have had enough time for contemplation in their later years as to be able to handle each day's jobs rather expeditiously, so that there is time to get back to finishing up with some of the 'assignments' the body's computer was programmed for earlier in life. These work-load conditions are no doubt affected by a small number of distinct variable sets: properties of the lifetime workload given by experience to be 'understood' (whether or not the understanding is acted upon, or action is frustrated), and properties of the data-structuring affected by paradigms transmitted to the CNS by received culture and, comparatively rarely, auto-didactically.

Since symbol generation and recognition centrally mediate human experience, one might expect extended use of the computer to help in understanding the staggering complexity and quantity of man's symbolic experience. As this series of volumes will demonstrate, a number of promising starts have been made. But much remains to be done if, for those language-dependent roles we want it to take, the computer is to have sufficient richness of symbolic experience to function adequately. To answer questions about a broad range of data bases (as in a library), to serve as a preliminary sorter of data (as in an information retrieval system), to perform translations from one natural language to another, or from one symbol system to another, to serve as a teaching assistant (as in a computer-assisted instruction environment), to serve as a research assistant in any symbol-oriented environment — for each and any of these roles, the computer must be able to cope with various types of symbol systems much more adequately than it can today. For the computer to cope with such systems, human beings, in turn, must understand those systems more thoroughly than they now do. These volumes should contribute to the theory of symbol systems in ways which look to hold promise for the precision required in mapping that theory into computer-based systems. These volumes also contain statements concerning current efforts to use the computer for symbol-dependent tasks, at present more limited levels of knowledge.

We hope that these volumes will serve as points of departure for others working in this broad research domain and in ways such that there will be promise of the rigor and cumulativeness which must characterize any science, including the linguistic sciences.

Walter A. Sedelow, Jr.
Sally Yeates Sedelow

WALTER A. SEDELOW, JR. and SALLY YEATES SEDELOW

Graph theory, logic, and formal languages in relation to language research

The fate of nations hangs on notation. And nowhere more than with notation is it true that the medium itself speaks more loudly than any specific messages. Notation sets outer bounds, and an inner mesh, for what can be conveyed — and how effectively. And so too it opens up vistas of thought and accomplishment even more engaging and impressive than the vistas of Vitruvius. Cumulativeness in science — *traditio* in scholarship and the arts as well — depends upon overt, shared symbols. A scheme of notation — a character set, a set of elementary symbols — provides an 'alphabet' in which we say we communicate, and, in fact, cooperate, or, most pessimistically, at least interact. Notation gives us the counters to move in the various games of cultural life. Without notational units to see or hear or touch there can be no intellectual working together, no collaboration. But with such units, we can be symbolic artificers, artificers in symbols.

When used frequently enough we call such units of symbolic structure conventional. And what is there more valuable than comfortable conventions that do our symbolic bidding, conventions that we even can make do tricks, and possibly arabesques — whether as poets or mathematicians, as novelists or symphonists, as logicians or iconographers? Notation is the matrix of culture, the fragile web holding us together, the symbolic devices we have fabricated in reaching out to each other to cooperate and to cumulate.

Pyed type may be symbolic, but it's not symbolism. That is, randomness — disorder (or better, non-order), entropy — is the enemy. At least it is the antithesis of conventional symbolism. Notation is the minimum set of elements, the smallest group of smallest primitives, out of which we construct our symbolic forms — our logical proofs, our mathematical demonstrations, our prose, our poems, all our symbolic structures. The difference between pyed type and a poem is conventional — as the digits themselves, or an alphabet, or a syllabary, are conventional. Here, though, with a poem or a proof, the governing conventions are not as to the elements or symbolic particles —

what shall be the letters of an alphabet, the signs for an algebra? — but as
to how those elements are sequenced and grouped, how they are ordered.
That is, what shall constitute an order? What, a disorder? How are these
symbolic particles or elements to be 'molecularized', much less molarized?
What, generically, are to be their 'laws', the accepted patterns of cultural
combinations?

An order is, in effect, a game. These high-culture games, like games of
other sorts, we begin to learn how to move the counters in when we are
young, and sometimes learn to play in more refined ways — more purified
ways, in accordance with abstract concepts — when we grow a little older.
Formal education can and does later provide, with varying levels of precision,
approximations to formal models of what we earlier learn less rigorously.

Only in recent chapters of the human story have games — games in both
the restricted and the extended senses of the term — been invented con-
sciously and wholly, even though in another sense every such invention is
really only a modification, a comparatively minor variant, in arranging
inherited pieces of the cultural detritus. It is true that some raccoon is the
first in his set to learn to wash food, and others then imitate until there is an
animal cultural convention. And so, too, presumably, with the human species'
earliest cultural conventions called symbolism; sometimes there are great men,
sometimes they become cultural heroes and heroines, like the Cherokee
Sequoyah, who create an alphabet, but even they build on what's been done
before by a great collectivity, as for instance by those who've gone before
whose behaviors cumulated in that patterning of sounds we call Cherokee.
Every neologism has at least one neologist; but neologisms imply 'logisms',
and those are floated only by a collectivity through time, albeit every 'logism'
once was a neologism and had its own inventor or inventors. But for a creation
or invention to become an innovation it has well enough to fit what is already
being done to gain acceptance. So the neologist, like birds at apices, has to
look lively to be sure that he leads only where others are already following;
otherwise the neologist may be not certified by his culture, and may be labelled
not neologist, but schizophrenic. It is not only of military wars that victors
write the histories.

In these more recent generations, and notably within this past century,
there has been more whole cloth weaving, more getting close to starting *ab
initio*, more conversion of the assumptive into the explicit. Ironically — and
it shows us faults of our virtues, losses of our gains — it is precisely by burrow-
ing more deeply into the cultural silt (as with Hilbert, or with Whitehead
and Russell) that we are most powerfully inventive. Invention is inescapably,
ineluctably a cultural product — which is not easily made clear in a language
so opposites-prone as is ours — and the most powerful symbolic inventions,

innovations, are, paradoxically, those which unfold quintessential properties of what is regularly done, what is least innovative.

To invent is to discover, for all symbolic invention is in an important aspect decompositional, but to discover is to invent, for all symbolic discovery is in an important aspect constructive. In even the extreme case of the logical fundamentals of mathematics, the elicited internal logic is notation-dependent, in a sense even notation-invented. There is here, as in any quarrying deeply into a symbolic lode, an act of phenomenological creation. And what the symbol-heroic miner brings to this act by means of his non-numeric CNS computer is far more extensive (intensive, really) in implication, and more critical as well, than is the everyday life of the non-symbolism-specialist who these days is more usually the focus of phenomenological attention by the followers of Hilbert's Göttingen colleague Husserl. Ironically, Hilbert and Husserl were at odds as to what constituted philosophy — and Hilbert's own mathematical results had been denominated "metaphysics" by not ungifted mathematicians who, unlike Hilbert, couldn't descry the pattern in the plantations of trees of which their symbolic forests were composed. It was only later, and by a mathematician, Goedel, who had been literally of Hilbert's school (the Göttingen Mathematical Institute), that the lack of a wholly consistent architecture for even a simple arithmetic was detected, that the mathematical emperors' rapidly growing new house was seen to be in important features somewhat ramshackled. And is that any wonder? It had after all, been a-building for much more than a millenium, and by diverse hands, some Indian, some Arabic, and, latterly, many (West) European. And they were each mathematical craftsmen rather than architects, inheriting, as it were, rôles in the building of a vast cathedral of intellect, with sharp focus and intensity but with no plan and not much foresight. Each did the deed that was appealing, the mathematical act that he — and rarely, she — could see his way clear to. No one of them did an entire mathematical dance to the music of time, but each did take a few new steps — some pas de deux, occasionally de trois — beyond those of his brethren, but making in toto a pattern whose outer contour and repeated microstructures were not precisely discerned.

Only in these latter decades have we become so effective in designing mirrors of abstraction in which to look closely at the products of symbolic art as to be able to take apart ourselves in our acts of symbolism and — like the ultimately self-competent surgeon — reassemble, and on cleaner, clearer lines: the formalist's equivalent to the Bob and Ray "Do it yourself brain-surgery kit".

That is to say, the bounds of the mathematically, or formally, unexamined life have been repeatedly forced to retreat: fewer and fewer primitives are found necessary to bear the heat of the mathematical/formal day, and even those primitives are losing their innocence as the mathematical and logical sophisticates interact with them ever more closely, scrutinize them ever more carefully, no doubt producing phenomenological 'observer effects'.

In America professional architecture is comparatively recent; the first architect, Peter Harrison, did his great buildings (Christ Church; King's Chapel; Truro Street Synagogue; Redfern Library) in the century in which one of our great-grandfathers was born. Similarly with mathematical architecture ("foundations"); it, too, is comparatively new — that self-conscious awareness of elements, rules of usage, and the micro-structures and macro-structure of vast edifices of symbolism put together somewhat unwittingly — in that like the poems of Plato's poets — by many hands and brains. In these present decades, after Hilbert, after Whitehead, after Russell, after Goedel and the rest, we take and try to take more careful stock of the properties of our mathematical building blocks and the results of the conventional ways we use them, so that rather on demand we can produce new what's freshly needed as the occasion requires. Yet, even so, our most-used programming instructions are in languages which there is no promise of reducing to unflawed logical structure.

Beyond what was possible for Leibnitz and Newton in the time each had to travel from what was received to what he could get newly accepted, today we can see more copiously the place of any item of notation and each rule of accepted symbol-manipulative practice within larger matrices of possibility. And we can generate somewhat more informed surmises as to what are the likely symbolic consequences and potentialities of different choices and mixes of options among the symbolic elements and among possible rules of combination. A more ample combinatorics casts its spell over mathematical imaginations, and with more searching examinations of the implications of what we can do with what we have, we are better able to determine the likely limits of the possible for a notational set and any combination scheme for using the set.

Which may be said to bring us more directly to the matter at hand: graph-theoretic notation (and, in principle, matrix equivalents), logic, and formal languages, particularly in relation to the rigorous inspection of (non-numeric) symbol behavior, such as natural languages. It often has been observed that Western mathematics, especially in Anglophone countries, was dominated for several centuries — to a degree, is still dominated — by an exfoliation of the Newtonian calculus, to the comparative exclusion of other mathematical specializations. Not only at Cambridge did the long sorting out of conceptual tangles in the banyan-tree roots of analysis take place — tangles at first screened from view by the wonder Newton's intuitive leaps of genius induced in the eyes of scientific and philosophical beholders. The more extensive

efforts to develop formulations appropriate to furthering the physics he also
made possible defined scope for much mathematical knitting, a Kuhnian
everyday science growing within the usually closed system of a paradigmatic
womb of analysis.

As with every notational set and rules for its usage that come to be
established, and evolve, there are trade-offs. On the one side, certain latent
possibilities in the combination of set items — a sub-set of the possible combinations — come to pass, are realized and become legal. On the other, certain
combinational possibilities latent in other possible but non-existent sets
remain unrealized because these notation sets are not conceived — remain
unconceived (much less born and matured) in a Platonic world of possible
forms. Whatever grip on the world and its manipulations they might have
made possible for us as logics, languages, models, and theories are only, as in
these words, elegiacally present — so many mute Miltons and unsinging
Hampdens, as it were. The energies that could have given us the actualization
of these notational sets and usage rules from the infinitely possible set of sets
is deflected elsewhere to the notational sets that are, to their use, and to the
semantic effects they come to have. Alternative possible character sets and
their manipulation are latent, and at least for a time remain so.

But each embryonic mathematics, formal system, or quasiformal system
grows and after a time matures, puncturing its amniotic sac, its confining
paradigm. Then after the confused period of parturitic recovery a new notational scheme, out of all the possibilities inherent in a symbolic culture's
'genes', is conceived and grows up a little later than its predecessor, with its
own outer bounds and inner mesh (integument and cells) of strengths and
possibilities. Such is the case with graph theory, formal language theory, and
some parts of mathematical logic, among the younger cousins of analysis.
Meanwhile, many of the possible siblings of the Newtonian calculus remain
unborn, or, born, suffer from arrested development for want of nurturing.
Later an Abraham Robinson appears to lament the opportunities for work,
undone, that the maturation of certain non-standard forms of analysis — in
this case, Leibnitzean — would have made possible.

In this reflective light on language, incidentally, we see that the wisdom
of nature (where the world is seen as itself an information processing system,
that is) in prodigality of birth, here within a litter, but also in numbers of
litters, extends to nature's generation, with some cultures of the human species
as its instrument, of notational sets and their symbol systems and certain
specific instantiations. That is, just as multiple, independent invention/discov-
ery is the rule in particular cases (as with the Newtonian and Leibnitzean
calculi, the Darwinian and Wallacean evolution idiolects), as well as with
whole notational systems (such as in the set of the world's written 'natural'

languages), so multiple invention/discovery is itself but a specific instance of the more encompassing multi-birth pattern in nature. And the members of the set of newborn symbol sets then, appropriately enough, show signs of sibling rivalry; we see that comprehensively in the serious forms that competition takes among the world's languages and their embodying literatures. And we see it instantially in at least attenuated sibling rivalry where symbolic formulations are used to realize the dynamics in parental tensions when they are put forth on the stage of culture in dramas of priority conflict (as with the symbolical offspring of Darwin and Wallace, and so many others, not to mention the especially ironic case of Freud and his associates).

Even though it is true that statistics and other forms of discrete mathematics, not to mention mathematical logic, still have had heavy sledding as appropriate specializations for teaching, research, and degrees in departments of mathematics, especially during these past three decades the acceptability and volume of non-analysis mathematics have grown. Graph notation and theory — and their utilization in other specialties, as with automata theory, and its own subspecializations and applications — are a case in point. There is also more attention to the logical foundations of mathematics and some inroads into mathematics by specializations fostered through computer science.

Take the case of graph theory. With that notation and the 'rules' for its usage that have emerged much can be done — and comparatively easily intuitively apprehended owing to its analogality, its geometric analogality — that without it would be practically incomprehensible. So, too, of course, with other types of mathematics that extend the range of formalist sensibility, whether or not non-numeric — such as in the contiguous domain of matrices.

It is important to note here that if sometimes invention becomes the mother of necessity, in the case of graph theory it is the putative parents that are necessitous. For while graph theory has a discernible more remote ancestry among the bearers of mathematical culture, its immediate parents — or at least its fostering parents — are the computing machine (the logic machine) and its ghostly mate, the abstract machine (the machine of finite state sequential machine theory), including, of course, Turing machines.

As Walter Sedelow recently noted in an as yet unpublished talk given at the United States Naval Academy (Annapolis), it may be argued with reference to computers (logicers), as in our culture it is so regularly argued as to other developments, whether pragmatic primacy is to be accorded to physical realities or to their symbolic, less blatantly physical, doppelgängers. That is a part of the issue at stake as to how much credit should be accorded to Babbage, inasmuch as he didn't succeed in the full physical realization of his ideas. With the computing machines as hardware ever more blatantly surrounding us, it is perhaps at times difficult to gain credibility for saying that the symbolizing (the idea) of the machine may be — and yet even prove to be in the future — more potent than the 'reality'. The form may be — perhaps one should say, must be — more consequent than the matter.

But, as suggested in the Preface to these volumes, the symbol/material antithesis (as with the symbolic versus the material computer) is misleading; it is an artifact of certain instantiations of our Indo-European verbal symbol systems which are opposites-prone, as notably educted by Aristotle in his logical writings. In this patterning by opposites, and notably by negation as a type of dichotomizing (perhaps in some sense the most fundamental type), we may have located the basis for a Kuhnian paradigm shift at a more comprehensive cultural level than any so far attended to — each of which to date has been specific to a scientific sub-culture. If, indeed, it does come to pass that the "cramp" (of Kuhn's teacher Crane Brinton, in *The anatomy of revolution*) is too severe to be withstood, produces problems which can't be ignored and within the paradigm can not be solved, then we may find that we have the makings not of the 'political revolutions' Brinton studied, nor even of the 'scientific revolutions' Kuhn has studied, but of a 'cultural revolution' which in its own time might be sui generis — in that the shift in paradigmatic fundamentals would entail not merely (some of) the language and other processes of the subculture(s) of a science or sciences, or (some of) the language and other processes of a polity or polities, but (some of) the language and other processes of a whole culture or cultures. If that should come to pass, Peter Ramus (and his éclairateur Walter Ong), Alfred Korzybski (and his epigons of the School of General Semantics), not to mention the contemporary UC-Berkeley computer scientist Lotfi Zadeh (and his students) may, when the future is history, come to be hagiographed as so many John the Baptists.

When a speculum is wanted in which to see — i. e., model — more clearly the paradigm shift process itself (as in moving from building two-valued logics to building multi-valued logics, or in moving from informal structures to logic and formal languages in mapping the meaning of natural language), the materials for that mirror (if not the mirror all assembled) will be found in the distringuished and influential work on cognitive balance theory of our Kansas colleague Fritz Heider, who at Lawrence as earlier at Northampton (Smith College) and at Graz and elsewhere, worked out perhaps the most intellectually powerful of the types of Gestalt psychology. Baylyn et al. opine that of all the Central European emigrés of the 30's, among psychologists Heider's work is the most continuingly seminal. And Heider of himself says that it originated out of the interaction of symbolic factors (notably Spinoza) and experiential factors (necessarily mediated in some measure symbolically) generated by the social dislocation emanating from The Great War of 1914–1918. Again, a pairing of form with matter (as formally mediated).

In a talk at Dartmouth (September 1975) which inaugurated the International Advanced Research Symposium on Social Networks sponsored by the Mathematical Social Science Board, Heider articulated these themes. That talk soon will be in print, in conference proceedings edited by Samuel Leinhardt of Carnegie-Mellon University. What is especially notable here, and will also shine forth from those conference proceedings, is a fitting together, a 'Gestalt', if you will, relating directly back to the issue before us. For, impressively enough, it is Heider's own work which appears to be the principal eponymous factor in the personal equations accounting for setting in motion the whole vast apparatus of contemporary graph theory — where we see graph theory as one notation entailed in the paradigm shift to more formal methods in language research, as exemplified by these papers. The work of Frank Harary, as well as of Dorwin Cartwright, Richard Norman and others was given motion, motivated, by the need to formalize what Heider saw plain in the (psychological) dynamics of interpersonal linguistic interaction, but much less clearly as to the formalisms needed to phenomenologically create those relationships as a 'field' of study with greater rigor than the cognate topological psychology of his friend and colleague in Massachusetts psychology in the 30's and earlier 40's, Kurt Lewin.

In the exposition here of graph theory by Steven Hedetniemi and Seymour Goodman (University of Virginia) we have an unusually clear presentation of the basics of that theory, presented from the beginnings and so thoroughly that the linguist or other student of symbolic behavior can follow it. It is self-contained, so that the neophyte at this type of notation — these conventions of combination and some of their substantive implications — does not need to turn to other works of reference to understand how it is being done. Hopefully, he then can — and will — go and do likewise.

What is of importance monumental in scale here is that the domain of applicability of this methodology for directed-graph construction extends to both the computer and the study of language itself. Further, as also with the formal languages addressed by Benson, the computer as instrumentation can be, and is, studied with graph theory in an extremely comprehensive way: the hardware machine itself (as a set of switches, etc.), both statically and dynamically; the programmed software that runs on the machine, both statically and dynamically; and the interaction between the machine-software system and the coded information put into it. And with this methodology and its transformations into matrix representations the greatest rigor can be achieved in studying the computer as a logical device, as well as its in-puts,

through-puts, out-puts. It is also to the point to note that just as graph theory
is at the heart of computer science it also can be used advantageously (along
with set-theoretic notation, etc.) to study systems-theoretically or cybernet-
ically the more comprehensive systems within which a hardware-software
computer system is embedded, including the special case of any computer
in a computer-to-computer communications network. Further, and again as
also with the formal language apparatus discussed by Benson, both manually
and mechanically ('computer-wise') we can study the symbolic structures
of natural language, music, etc. with this same methodology. Not only are
the parsing trees of linguistics but special instances of directed graphs, it is
also the case that in analyzing the properties of a semantic space (e. g.,
through delineating the connectivity of *Roget's Thesaurus*) or of discourse
above the level of the individual sentence (whether in a folk tale or a motion
picture), we can profitably make use of graph theory. Other models of reality
beyond the symbolic also are addressed in this same way. The kernel notion
of looking at organic realities with mechanical concepts is not new; for
example, one school of 17th century anatomy was much taken with that idea,
and in the 18th century the idea was generalized, 'philosophized', for organisms
as wholes, including man, as we readily see in the work of d'Holbach and La
Mettrie. Philosophical and, later, technical manifestations of this kind of
orientation came to be dominant, even pervasive, in late 19th century physical
science. Characteristically, through, there was a tendency to hypostasis and
reification, as controversies swirling around Mach made evident. That amounted
to supposing that what we today would regard as imported utilitarian symbol
constructs (theories, models) had some sort of ultimate veridical status; or,
worse, they were not consistently and carefully kept separate from their
objects of study.

It is a major advantage which we have over our predecessors for moving
toward a new paradigm of greater power in the study of human symbol systems through methodological formality that graph theory is now so comparatively well developed and widely taught. It gives us a notation useful in certain
ways of studying language that we at present have no alternative for, and it
is a medium in studying the formative relationships and the transformational
processes presented in the work of Benson and of Bohnert and Backer. For
example, the re-writing systems that underlie the grammars of formal languages
are particular types of directed graphs.

There are many students of language — and, most likely, a rather rapidly
growing number — who feel that the adoption of Chomskyan vocabulary and
propositions about language as a means to a more adequate linguistics was an
instance of premature closure. Whatever one may conclude on that issue, it
certainly may be strongly argued that for those students of language who

are guided by a clear sense of scientificity in their aspirations the current scene leaves much to be desired.

The publication here of the studies by Bohnert (Michigan State University) and Backer and Benson (Washington State University) must be, then, an occasion for considerable rejoicing among those who would like to see, and contribute to, a much more scientifically adequate linguistics. Not only do they make available powerful additions to the range of ways of construing natural language formally, but they also point up specific research opportunities that would enable us to build securely on our current knowledge. Such a build-up would, of course, make use of graph theory, as explicated here by Hedetniemi and Goodman.

As Bohnert makes clear, the aspiration of getting a firmer grip on the logical strata in natural language is centuries old. But as is also evident, not much progress has been made toward formalizing that mode of understanding. That lack of progress may be due in part to the fashionability of other approaches to language research in recent decades, which en passant Bohnert and Backer also indicate. Since the approach taken by Bohnert and Backer starts at what in other contexts would be a 'deep level' and moves toward the surface of idiomatic English, it is at the moment somewhat 'counter-cultural'. While the great advantage of this approach is in the rigor and understanding it can directly add to our knowledge of languages, there is also a useful indirect effect produced by its largely tacit challenge to widely held assumptions embedded in other lines of attack that recently have been very modish.

It is worth underscoring that Bohnert and Backer argue not for a logical notation to make more tidy discussions of sentential deep structure, but rather to embody in that logical notation the structural properties themselves. Science is critically dependent on generality, and one of the attractive properties of the Bohnert et al. notation and its use is that it gives us a grammar quite independent of a variety of features imputed to languages as a by-product of a notational scheme derivative from the parochial studies of Latin grammarians. As with the Hedetniemi paper, the simplicity and clarity of presentation make this approach accessible to those without prior training in it, or even familiarity with it. The analytical apparatus is built out of the logistics of degree, grouping, quantification, and scope.

This formal approach, machine-implementable and machine-implemented, could be developed into a full-fledged program of research, perhaps eventuating in a new and useful paradigm for a science of language, or at least an important model within a science of language.

Benson's study is a richly significant and highly original examination of the theoretical issues implied by a formal approach to the analysis of language.

This intensive examination of the internal structure of the research literature on formal languages with a view to explicating its bearings on the formal study of language powerfully clarifies precisely what we know. Even more important, it calls attention to loci and types of theoretical investigation now needed to give us more coherent, more adequate, and more productive theory. He also suggests the possibility and at least implies the desirability of a redirection of research attention by compiler analysts to linguistic topics of such sort that they could effectively transfer their accumulated expertness, noting along the way that there are now opportunities when doing so for the formal language theorists to better link up syntactic understanding to the understanding of semantics.

In a way that would be paying a debt, since in the first instance basic notions of context-free and context-sensitive grammars came into formal language theory by way of a borrowing from Chomsky's linguistics. Now Benson feels that the future lies with research on the context-free grammars, whether in the original domain of linguistics or in the formal language study of compilers. Graph theory as realized in tree automata is the notation of choice for such research. And in such study of context-free grammars one source of ideas is to be found in the very foundations of computer science, more especially in the algebraic automata theory research of Hartmanis et al. One of the more significant ways in which, for example, the study of the algebraic decomposition of abstract machines has prospective importance is in the analysis of the structure of the formal systems used in the computer-based understanding of language. From such an approach might come an effective and rigorous way of breaking out into clean subsystems, the various components to an understanding of language. But the way is by no means clear, especially through the semantic thicket. One possible route, making use of graph theory for the study of general thesaurus connectivity properties, is to be found in the *Proceedings* of the current (1976) National Computer Conference: Sally Yeates Sedelow, "Analysis of 'natural' language discourse".

Taken together these papers are indeed a map for finding new and more satisfactory routes that will lead us further into the domain of language knowledge.

S. E. GOODMAN and S. T. HEDETNIEMI

A descriptive introduction to graph theory and some of its applications

1. Fundamentals

1.1 Graphs, points and lines

In this chapter we introduce, primarily by means of examples, a significant sampling of the terminology of graph theory.

A *graph* $G = (V, E)$ consists of a finite non-empty set $V = V(G)$ of *points* (Vertices) together with a finite (possibly empty) set $E = E(G)$ of unordered pairs uv of distinct points, called the *lines* (edges) of G. The graph $G_1 = (V_1, E_1)$ in Figure 1.1 consists of seven points, $V_1 = \{t, u, v, w, x, y, z\}$, and seven lines, $E_1 = \{uv, vw, wx, wy, wz, zv, vx\}$.

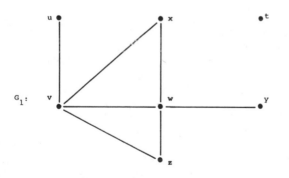

Figure 1.1

If uv is a line of a graph G, we say that points u and v are *adjacent* (sometimes written u adj v); if uv is not a line of G, we say that u and v are *not adjacent* or u and v are *independent*. In like manner, a set S of points in a graph G is *independent* if no two points in S are adjacent. The set $S = \{u, x, y, z\}$ is an independent set of points of G_1 in Figure 1.1.

The notions of adjacency and independence apply as well to the lines of a graph. We say that two lines are *adjacent* if they have a point in common, otherwise they are said to be *independent.* The lines uv and vw are adjacent, while uv and wx are independent in Figure 1.1.

If uv is a line of G, we also say that point u is *incident with* or *covers* line uv, and that line uv is *incident with* or *covers* points u and v.

Notice that we have said that lines consist of *unordered* pairs of *distinct* points. Thus, lines are *undirected* in the sense that uv and vu are considered to be the same line. Furthermore, lines of the form uu, called *loops*, are not allowed. We also do not allow *multilines* in a graph, i. e. the occurrence of two or more copies of a given line. When multilines are considered in a particular application, we refer to the graph as a *multigraph* (cf. Figure 1.2).

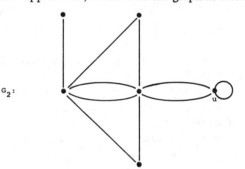

Figure 1.2 A multigraph with a loop at u.

If one changes the definition so that a graph consists of a finite set of points together with a set of *ordered* pairs (u, v) of distinct points, then one defines what is called a *directed graph* or *digraph*, cf. Figure 1.3, in which $V(G_3) = \{u, v, w, x, y, z\}$ and $E(G_3) = \{(u, v), (v, w), (v, x), (x, w), (w, y), (w, z), (z, v)\}$. When considering digraphs $D = (V, E)$ we will usually refer to the elements of V as *nodes* and the elements of E as *arcs*.

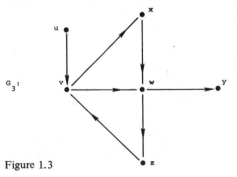

Figure 1.3

If (u, v) is an arc in a directed graph, we say that u is *adjacent to* v and v is *adjacent from* u.

1.2 Degrees

The *neighborhood of a point* v, N(v), consists of the set of points adjacent to v, i. e.

$$N(v) = \{u \mid uv \in E\} \, .$$

The *degree of a point* v, denoted d_v or deg(v), equals the number of points in N(v), i. e. $d_v = \deg(v) = |N(v)|$. Thus, if the points of G_1 in Figure 1.1 are ordered w, v, x, z, u, y, t, then their corresponding degrees are 4, 4, 2, 2, 1, 1, 0, i. e. $d_w = 4$, $d_v = 4$, $d_x = 2$, etc.

Using only the notion of the degree of a point, we are ready to prove our first graph theorem. Our proof is not the shortest one possible. We deliberately use mathematical induction to illustrate a standard technique for proving results in graph theory.

Theorem 1.1 Let G be a graph having q lines and points $v_1, v_2, \ldots, v_p$.

Then $\sum_{i=1}^{p} d_i = 2q$.

Proof: We proceed by mathematical induction on the number of lines q in G. Clearly, if q = 0 then every point in G has degree 0; hence $\Sigma \, d_i = 2q = 0$. Also, if q = 1 then exactly two points in G will have degree 1 and all other points will have degree 0; hence $\Sigma \, d_i = 2 = 2q$.

Assume that every graph having q = N or fewer lines satisfies the inductive hypothesis. Let G be a graph having q = N + 1 lines and let uv be an arbitrary line in G. By our inductive hypothesis, we know that the graph G′, which is obtained from G by removing line uv, satisfies $\Sigma \, d_i' = 2(q - 1)$, where d_i' denotes the degree of a point v_i in G′. But adding the line uv to G′ will increase by 1 the degrees of points u and v, and no other points. Thus, $\Sigma \, d_i' + 2 = \Sigma \, d_i = 2q$.

Corollary 1.1a In any graph G the number of points of odd degree is even.

As an application of Corollary 1.1a, consider a group of k persons which we will represent by k points V = $\{v_1, v_2, \ldots, v_k\}$. If two people, v_i and v_j, know each other, let us say that there is a line between them, $v_i v_j$. Corollary 1.1a tells us that in any group, the number of people who know an odd number of other people is even. It also follows from Theorem 1.1 that in any (finite) group there must exist two people who have the same number of acquaintances. The next corollary is a graph theoretic statement of this fact.

Corollary 1.1b In any graph G having points $v_1, v_2, \ldots, v_p$, there must exist an i and j, $i \neq j$, for which $d_i = d_j$.

In a directed graph $G = (V, E)$ the degree of a point v is divided into two components, its *in-degree*, $id_v = id(v) = |\{u\,|\,(u, v) \in E(G)\}|$, i. e. the number of points from which v is adjacent, and its *out-degree* $od_v = od(v) = |\{u\,|\,(v, u) \in E(G)\}|$, the number of points to which v is adjacent.

For the graph G_3 in Figure 1.3, $id(w) = 2 = od(w)$; $id(u) = 0$, $od(u) = 1$, $id(y) = 1$, $od(y) = 0$, and $id(x) = 1 = od(x)$.

If a point u in a graph has degree 0, we say that it is an *isolated point* (cf. point t in Figure 1.1), and if u has degree 1, we refer to u as an *endpoint* (cf. points u and y in Figure 1.1).

In a directed graph, a point of in-degree 0 and positive out-degree is called a *source* or a *transmitter* (cf. point u in Figure 1.3); a point having out-degree 0 and positive in-degree is called a *sink* or *receiver* (cf. point y in Figure 1.3).

A result similar to Theorem 1.1 can easily be established for directed graphs.

Theorem 1.2 Let G be a directed graph having q lines and points $v_1, v_2, \ldots, v_p$. Then

$$\Sigma\, id_i = \Sigma\, od_i = q .$$

1.3 Regular graphs

If G is a graph in which every point has the same degree, say k, then we say that G is a *regular graph of degree k*. Figure 1.4 illustrates all of the regular graphs which have 6 points.

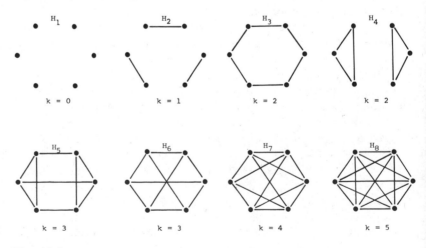

Figure 1.4

Regular graphs of degree 3 are referred to as *cubic graphs* (cf. H_5 and H_6 in Figure 1.4).

There are several interesting classes of regular graphs which have been studied in the graph theory literature. We mention a few of them here.

A graph G with n points is called *complete*, and denoted K_n, if every pair of points are adjacent, cf. the complete graphs in Figure 1.5.

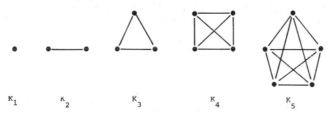

Figure 1.5

The reader will recognize the graph H_8 in Figure 1.4 as the graph K_6. One can readily observe that K_n is a regular graph of degree $n - 1$ which has $\binom{n}{2} = n(n - 1)/2$ lines (cf. Figure 1.6).

K_n	K_1	K_2	K_3	K_4	K_5	K_6	K_7	K_8	K_9	K_{10}
$\binom{n}{2}$	0	1	3	6	10	15	21	27	35	44

Figure 1.6

The *complement* of a graph $G = (V, E)$ is the graph $\overline{G} = (V, \overline{E})$, where two points u and v are adjacent in $\overline{G}$ if and only if they are not adjacent in G. The complement of the complete graph K_n is denoted $\overline{K_n}$ and is called the *totally disconnected graph on n points*.

It is easy to see that if G is a regular graph of degree k having p points, then the complement of G, $\overline{G}$, is a regular graph of degree $p - k - 1$.

A *bipartite graph* G is one whose points can be partitioned into two independent sets such that no line in G is incident to two points in the same set. This definition is readily generalized to *n-partite graphs* whose points can be partitioned into n independent sets. A *complete bipartite graph* $K_{m, n}$ consists of 2 independent sets of points, say S and T, having m and n points, respectively, and two points u and v are adjacent if and only if they belong to different sets. It is easy to see that the complement of $K_{m, n}$ consists of two complete, point-disjoint graphs K_m and K_n, i. e. $\overline{K}_{m,n} = K_m \cup K_n$. These definitions are illustrated in Figure 1.7.

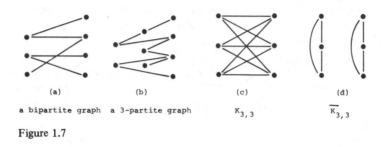

| (a) | (b) | (c) | (d) |
| a bipartite graph | a 3-partite graph | $K_{3,3}$ | $\overline{K}_{3,3}$ |

Figure 1.7

Another interesting class of regular graphs are found in coding theory, where one is interested in studying the set of all sequences of 0's and 1's of a fixed length, say n. The *n-cube*, denoted Q_n, is the graph whose points correspond one-to-one with the set of all n-tuples of 0's and 1's, and where two points are adjacent if and only if the corresponding sequences differ in exactly one digit. Figure 1.8 illustrates the n-cubes for $n \leqslant 3$.

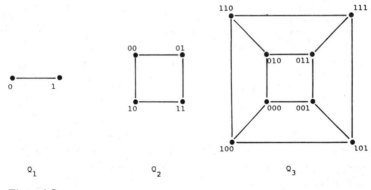

Figure 1.8

A counterpart in directed graph theory to a complete graph is a tournament. To be more precise, we say that a directed graph $G = (V, E)$ is an *oriented graph* if whenever $(u, v) \in E(G)$ then $(v, u) \notin E(G)$. A *tournament* is an oriented complete graph, i. e. for any two points u, v in T, either (u, v) or (v, u) is a line of T, but not both. Tournaments, as defined, represent what are usually called round-robin tournaments, in which every player must play every other player and no ties are allowed.

Figure 1.9 provides several examples of tournaments. Tournaments have been studied rather extensively by graph theorists, in fact a book has been written on this class of graphs (Moon 1968).

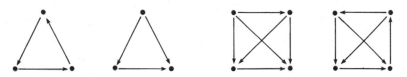

Figure 1.9 Examples of tournaments

1.4 Subgraphs

A graph $G' = (V', E')$ is a *subgraph* of a graph $G = (V, E)$ if $V' \subseteq V$ and $E' \subseteq E$; G' is a *spanning subgraph* of G if $V' = V$, i. e. a spanning subgraph contains all the points of G.

Figure 1.10 illustrates a cubic graph G_{10} (called the Petersen graph), a subgraph G'_{10} of G_{10}, and a spanning subgraph G''_{10} of G_{10}.

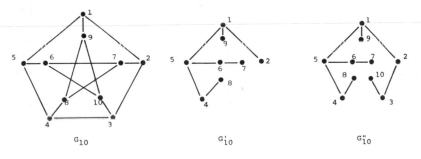

Figure 1.10

Given a subset $W \subseteq V$ of the points of a graph $G = (V, E)$, we denote by $\langle W \rangle$ the subgraph of G *induced by* W, where $V(\langle W \rangle) = W$ and where two points u and v of W are adjacent in $\langle W \rangle$ if and only if they are adjacent in G.

Similarly, given a subset $F \subseteq E$ of the lines of G, we denote by $\langle F \rangle$ the subgraph *induced by* F, where $E(\langle F \rangle) = F$ and where u is a point of $V(\langle F \rangle)$ if and only if it is incident with a line of F.

The graph G_{11} in Figure 1.11 is the subgraph of G_{10} in Figure 1.10 which is induced by the set of points $W = \{1, 2, 3, 4, 5, 6, 7, 8, 9\}$; the graph G'_{11} is the subgraph of G_{10} induced by the set of lines $F = \{15, 12, 67\}$.

The graph G_{11} in Figure 1.11 can also be described as the subgraph of G_{10} (in Figure 1.10) which is obtained by *deleting* point 10, i. e. $G_{11} =$

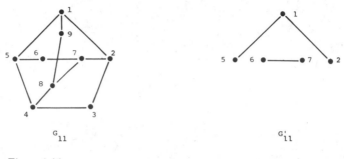

Figure 1.11

G_{10} – 10; in deleting a point v from a graph G, one deletes not only the point v but all lines of G incident with v. In like manner, G – uv denotes the graph obtained from G by deleting the line uv but not the points u and v. We also use the notation G + uv to denote the graph obtained from G by adding a new line uv between two non-adjacent points u and v.

1.5 Isomorphism

Two graphs G and G′ are *isomorphic* if there exists a one-to-one correspondence between the points of G and G′ such that two points u and v are adjacent in G if and only if their corresponding points are adjacent in G′. Stated more formally, G = (V, E) is *isomorphic* to G′ = (V′, E′), written G ≅ G′, if there exists a one-to-one function h from V onto V′ which satisfies the property that uv ∈ E if and only if h(u) h(v) ∈ E′.

The problem of determining whether or not two graphs are isomorphic is a deceptively difficult one, even though for small graphs the problem may seem trivial. We will treat this topic in greater detail in Chapter 3; for the moment we will simply illustrate the idea with several examples. The two graphs in Figure 1.12 are isomorphic, even though they are drawn differently.

The three graphs in Figure 1.13 are all isomorphic.

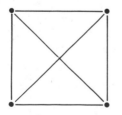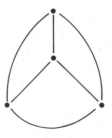

Figure 1.12

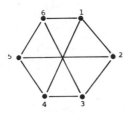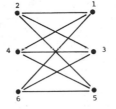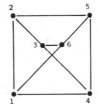

Figure 1.13

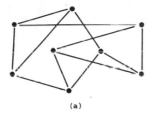

(a)

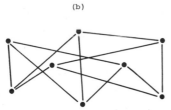

(b)

(c)

Figure 1.14

The reader is challenged to determine which of the 8-point graphs in Figure 1.14, if any, are isomorphic.

1.6 Walks and connectedness

A large number of applications of graph theory involve optimal routes or paths through networks. We shall discuss the nature of these applications in some detail in section 4. For now we present the basic definitions.

A *walk* in a graph $G = (V, E)$ from a point u_1 to a point u_n is a (finite) sequence of points $W = u_1, u_2, \ldots, u_n$ with the property that for every $1 \leqslant i \leqslant n - 1$, $u_i u_{i+1} \in E(G)$. The *length* of such a walk, denoted by $|W|$, is one less than the number of points in the sequence, i. e. $|W| = n - 1$. We say that W is *closed* if $u_1 = u_n$, otherwise it is *open*.

Given a walk $W = u_1, u_2, \ldots, u_n$, we refer to the lines $u_i u_{i+1}$ as the lines of W. A walk W is called a *trail* if no line appears more than once in W. A walk is a *path* if no point (and therefore no line) appears more than once in W; we often refer to W as a $u_1 - u_n$ path. A *cycle* is a closed path of length three or greater, that is, a sequence $u_1, u_2, \ldots, u_n, u_1$ of points for which $u_i \neq u_j$ if $i \neq j$. The following examples illustrate the above ideas using the graph G in Figure 1.15.

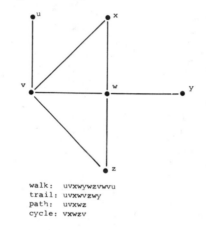

```
walk:   uvxwywzvwvu
trail:  uvxwvzwy
path:   uvxwz
cycle:  vxwzv
```

Figure 1.15

The *distance* $d(x, y)$ between any two points x and y in a graph is the length of a shortest path between these points. If no such path exists, we define $d(x, y) = \infty$. This concept can be extended in an obvious way to graphs whose lines are weighted with a nonnegative real number.

A graph G is *connected* if and only if for any two points u and v of G there exists a $u - v$ path, otherwise G is said to be *disconnected.* In a disconnected graph G we refer to the maximal connected subgraphs as the *connected components* of G. The graph G_{16} in Figure 1.16 has three connected components.

Theorem 1.3 For any graph G, either G or its complement $\overline{G}$ is connected. The reader should try to construct a proof for this theorem.

If G is a connected graph which contains a point v such that the graph $G - v$ is disconnected, then G is said to have a *cutpoint* v. The points v and

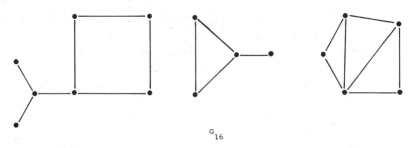

Figure 1.16

w in Figure 1.15 are both cutpoints. The following result provides two other ways of characterizing cutpoints.

Theorem 1.4 Let v be a point of a connected graph G. The following statements are equivalent:

(i) v is a cutpoint;

(ii) there exists two points u and w not equal to v such that v lies on every u-w path; and

(iii) the points in V – {v} can be partitioned into two subsets say V_1 and V_2, such that v lies on every path joining a point in V_1 with a point in V_2.

If a connected graph has no cutpoint then we say that G is a *block*. Any graph can be expressed as a sum of its blocks. In Figure 1.17(a) we present a graph G_{17}; in Figure 1.17(b) we decompose G_{17} into its blocks.

Figure 1.17

There are quite a number of different ways of defining or characterizing a block. In the next result we present several of these.

Theorem 1.5 Let G be a connected graph having at least three points. The following statements are equivalent:

(i)   G is a block;

(ii) any two points of G lie on a common cycle;

(iii) any two points of G are joined by two, point-disjoint paths;

(iv) any point and any line of G lie on a common cycle;

(v)   any two lines of G lie on a common cycle;

(vi) given any two points and any line of G, there is a path joining the points which contains the line;

(vii) given any three points of G, there is a path joining any two of the points which contains the third point; and

(viii) given any three points of G, there is a path joining any two of the points which does not contain the third point.

The counterpart for lines to the concept of a cutpoint is a bridge. A bridge is a line of a connected graph whose removal disconnects G. The graph G_{17} in Figure 1.17 has four bridges, i. e. lines 12, 23, 24, and 78.

A result similar to Theorem 1.5 can also be established for bridges.

Theorem 1.6 Let uw be a line of a connected graph G. The following statements are equivalent:

(i) uw is a bridge;

(ii) uw does not lie on any cycle of G; and

(iii) there exists a partition of V into two subsets U and W such that $u \in U$, $w \in W$ and uw is the only line joining a point of U with a point of W.

For directed graphs the concept of connectedness breaks down into three main types. We say that a sequence of points $u_1, u_2, \ldots, u_n$ in a directed graph $G = (V, E)$ is a *directed walk* from u_1 to $u_{n'}$ if for every i, $1 \leqslant i \leqslant n - 1$, $(u_i, u_{i+1}) \in E(G)$. In a digraph therefore, it is quite possible that there exists a directed walk from u to v but not from v to u.

Therefore, we say that a directed graph is

> . . . *strongly connected* if for any two points u and v of G there exists a directed walk from u to v and from v to u;

> . . . *unilateral* if for any two points u and v of G, there exists either a u – v directed path, or a v – u directed path, but not necessarily both; and

> . . . *weakly connected* if for any two points u and v there exists a u – v *semi-walk*, i. e. a sequence $u = u_1, u_2, \ldots, u_n = v$ such that for $1 \leqslant i \leqslant n - 1$, either $(u_i\ u_{i+1})$ or $(u_{i+1}, u_i) \in E(G)$.

2. Trees

2.1 Introduction

A *tree* is an undirected, connected graph which has no cycles. Any graph without cycles is a *forest*, and so the connected components of any such graph are trees. Figure 2.1 illustrates all the non-isomorphic trees with six points. The entire figure might be considered as a forest with 36 points and 6 components.

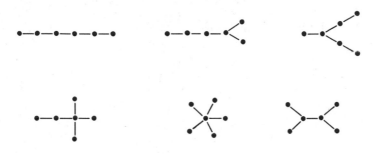

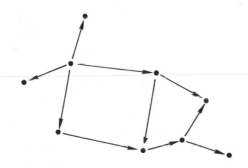

Figure 2.1

A digraph is a tree if and only if it is a tree with its arcs considered to be undirected lines. An *acyclic digraph* is a digraph with no directed cycles. The digraph in Figure 2.2 is acyclic but not a tree.

Figure 2.2

Trees are unquestionably the most widely used graph-theoretic structures. They are indispensable aids in the study of computer-data structures (Knuth 1969), integer programming (Garfinkel and Nemhauser 1972), game theory (Trakhtenbrot 1963), discrete probabilistic processes (Raiffa 1970), and sorting (Knuth 1973). In addition, they are useful in the study of various problems in physics (Fetter and Walecka 1971), chemistry (Balaban 1974), electrical engineering (Chen 1971), psychology (Lewin 1936), sociology (Harary-Cartwright-Norman 1965) and various other mathematical disciplines (Riordan 1958).

Example 2.1 It is planned to construct a communications network of some kind between a set of N cities. The cost of constructing a network link between any two cities i and j is given by a cost function $c(i, j) > 0$. Economics is a controlling factor and the basic policy is to build a minimum cost network that permits any city to communicate with any other city.

This problem can be modelled mathematically by a complete graph K_N whose lines are weighted so that line (i, j) has weight $c(i, j)$. The objective is to choose a spanning, connected subgraph such that the sum of the line weights is minimum. The required subgraph will be a tree. To see this, we note that if S were an optimal subgraph solution with at least one cycle, then a cheaper solution could be found by removing the most costly line on any cycle in S. We thus contradict the assumption that a graph with a cycle could solve this problem. An algorithm for finding a minimum weighted spanning tree, i. e. an algorithm for solving this problem, will be presented in section 2.3.

Example 2.2 Six matches are on a table. The first player picks up 1 or 2 of the matches. The second player then picks up 1 or 2 of the remaining matches. Then it is the first player's turn to pick up 1 or 2 of those that remain. The players continue to alternate turns until the player who is forced to pick up the last match is declared the loser. Can one of the players adopt a strategy that can guarantee himself a win regardless of how his opponent moves?

This game is a somewhat "stunted" version of a large class of games that can be effectively modeled and solved using trees. Such games can be characterized by the following four properties.

1) The game is played by two players who alternately take turns.

2) A limit is placed on the maximum number of moves in the game.

3) Each move consists of a choice by the player of one of a set of admissible moves, i. e. the player, not chance, controls his own actions.

4) At each stage of the game, both players have full information as to what moves have already been made and what moves are admissible.

Note that this class includes quite a large number of games, and can effectively be made to include chess. In section 2.4 we describe how such games can be handled with the aid of trees.

2.2 Properties of trees

There exists a variety of useful characterizations of trees.

Theorem 2.1 Let T be a graph with $n \geqslant 2$ points. Then all of the following statements are equivalent:

(i) T is a tree, i. e. T is connected and has no cycles;

(ii) T has $n - 1$ lines and no cycles;

(iii) T has $n - 1$ lines and is connected;

(iv) T is connected and every line is a bridge;

(v) Any two points of T are joined by a unique path;

(vi) T has no cycles, but the addition of any new line creates exactly one cycle.

Proof: (i) implies (ii). Since T contains no cycles the removal of any line disconnects T into two trees. This follows from the fact that a line is a bridge if and only if it is not contained in any cycle (Theorem 1.6). By induction on n it is easy to show that the number of lines in each of these two trees is one fewer than the number of points and (ii) follows.

(ii) implies (iii). If T is not connected, then each component of T is connected and has no cycles. Thus, by (ii), the number of points in each component exceeds the number of lines by one. It then follows that the total number of points in T is at least two greater than the total number of lines, thereby contradicting the hypothesis (ii).

(iii) implies (iv). We first prove the following lemma.

Lemma: If G has n points, m lines, and k components then $n - k \leqslant m$.

Proof: We induct on the number of lines. The result is immediate for $m = 1$. Let G contain as few lines as possible, say m_0, then the removal of any line of G must increase k by one, leaving a graph with n points, $k + 1$ components, and $m_0 - 1$ lines. It follows from the induction hypothesis that $m_0 - 1 \geqslant n - (k + 1)$, i. e. $m_0 \geqslant n - k$. This proves the lemma.

Statement (iv) then follows by contradiction from statement (iii) and the lemma, since $k = 1$ and the removal of any line leaves $n - 2$ lines and n points.

(iv) implies (v). Each pair of points is joined by at least one path since T is connected. If every pair of points is joined by two or more distinct paths, then any two such paths form a cycle and we have a contradiction, since no line on such a cycle can be a bridge by Theorem 1.6.

(v) implies (vi). If T contained a cycle then any two points in the cycle would be connected by at least two paths. If line 1 is added to T, then two paths (line 1, and the unique path given by (v)) will exist in $T + 1$ between the end points of 1. This is the only cycle in $T + 1$ because any other cycle would also have to contain line 1 and this would imply the existence of two points in T between which there exists at least two distinct paths, a contradiction to (v).

(vi) implies (i). Assume T is not connected. If we add a line to T that joins points in two components, then no cycle can be created, contradicting (vi). Thus, T must be connected, and Theorem 2.1 is proved.

Corollary 2.1 Every tree with $n \geqslant 2$ points has at least two endpoints.

Proof: The corollary follows directly from Theorems 1.1 and 2.1.

Note that Theorem 2.1 also applies to tree digraphs. Such a digraph is said to have *root* v_0 if the unique (undirected) path from v_0 to every point w (see Theorem 2.1 (v)) is also a directed path from v_0 to w.

The *eccentricity* e(v) of a point v in a connected graph is the maximum value of the distance d(u, v) over all points $u \in G$. The *radius* r(G) is the minimum eccentricity over all points in G. A point v is a *central point* of G if $e(v) = r(G)$. The *center* of a connected graph G is defined to be the set of all central points. The point labels in Figure 2.3 are the eccentricities of the points in the given tree, and point u is the only central point.

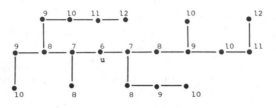

Figure 2.3

Note that the center of the tree in Figure 2.3 can be found by iteratively stripping off all the current endpoints of the tree. This procedure can be used to prove

Theorem 2.2 Every tree has a center consisting of either one point or two adjacent points.

The iterative process just described gives a canonical rooting to any un-rooted (and possibly undirected) tree and is central to at least one tree-naming scheme (Busacker-Saaty 1965).

The interested reader can find a much more extensive treatment of the basic mathematical properties of trees in section 2.3.4 of Knuth (1969).

2.3 Spanning trees

A *spanning tree* of a graph G is a subgraph that is a tree and contains all of the points of G. It is easy to demonstrate that

Theorem 2.3 A graph is connected if and only if it contains a spanning tree.

If G has m lines and n points then, by Theorem 2.1, every spanning tree T has n – 1 lines, and each of the m – n + 1 remaining lines gives rise to a unique cycle in G. This set of cycles is called a *fundamental cycle set* of G (relative to T). The number $c(G) = m - n + 1$ is called the *cycle rank* or *cyclomatic number* of G.

A *(minimal) cut-set* of a graph is a set of lines the removal of which will increase the number of connected components in the remaining subgraph, but the removal of any proper subset will not. Figure 2.4 shows a graph (a), a spanning tree (b), and a minimal cut-set (c).

Theorem 2.4 Any cut-set and any spanning tree must have at least one line in common.

Proof: Assume there is a cut-set that does not share at least one line with every spanning tree. Then the removal of this cut-set will leave at least one

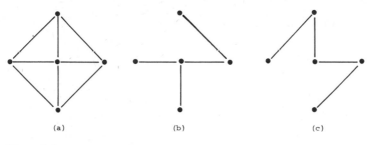

Figure 2.4

spanning tree intact and therefore not increase the number of components in the remaining graph. This contradicts the definition of a cut-set.

A serious study of cut-sets, spanning trees, and fundamental cycle sets requires considerably more space than we have available here. The interested reader is referred to Chapters 7 and 10 in Liu (1968).

We return now to the minimum connection problem of Example 2.1. For any connected graph G with n points, a spanning tree can be obtained by repeatedly finding a cycle C in G and removing any line of C. This process is repeated until only n – 1 lines remain. Theorem 2.1 guarantees that the remaining graph is a spanning tree. This procedure is not terribly efficient. It also does not guarantee a particularly good spanning tree in the case where the lines are weighted and a minimum weighted spanning tree is sought. An efficient algorithm for this problem (Prim 1957) is given below.

Algorithm 2.1 (To find a minimum weighted spanning tree)

Step 1: Choose an arbitrary point.

Step 2: Repeatedly make the least costly connection from an unchosen point to a chosen point, until all points have been chosen. Then stop.

In Algorithm 2.1 it is understood that cost $c(i, j) = \infty$ if line (i, j) does not exist. Algorithm 2.1 which makes the best "local" move at each iteration, seems likely to get a "good" spanning tree, but it is not clear that it gets an optimum spanning tree. Such "locally optimizing" algorithms (sometimes called "greedy algorithms") usually *do not* yield global optima in graph theory; however, this one does. A proof and a very efficient computer implementation of this algorithm can be found in Knuth (1969).

A related, but much more difficult, problem arises when the points to be connected are fixed in some two or three dimensional Euclidean space and cost $c(i, j)$ is the Euclidean distance between points i and j. Such a weighted graph is often called a *metric graph*. The problem can be further complicated by permitting the addition of new points which can help shorten the final solution. Figure 2.5(a) shows three points, the best spanning tree using only

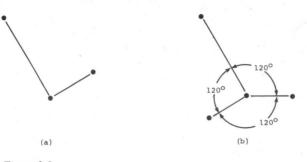

(a)   (b)

Figure 2.5

these points, and a better tree obtainable using a strategically placed fourth point (Figure 2.5(b)).

Further discussion of this problem, known as the minimum Steiner tree problem, can be found in Kaufmann (1967).

2.4 Trees as an aid in searching and enumeration

Perhaps the most important application of trees is as an aid in organizing and keeping track of sets of objects. The more mathematically developed sciences use tree structures not only to store and represent various sets, but also to dynamically produce and operate on information with some sort of ultimate problem-solving objective in mind.

In this section we present two simple examples which illustrate the difference between these two uses of trees as an aid in problem solving. Example 2.3 solves a problem by "beating it to death" and uses a tree structure to make sure that nothing is missed and everything is tried only once. Example 2.4 requires considerably more finesse to obtain a solution, and the tree plays a more active role in solving the problem.

Example 2.3 A combination lock for a safe consists of a set of N switches, each of which can be "on" or "off". Exactly one setting of all the switches, with 0 or more in the "on" state and the rest "off", will permit the safe to be opened. A burglar is prepared to try all combinations in the hope that he can open the safe (our burglar is a fool). He needs an algorithm to enable him to try all possible combinations without duplication.

Since there are 2^N possible combinations, our burglar might have a reasonable chance if $N \leqslant 7$. Most such safes put the matter totally beyond hope by using large N or having more than two states on each switch. Without more information about the safe, all we can do is come up with a method for systematically generating all 2^N possible states. We model each possible state with a sequence of N 0's and 1's. Switch i is "on" if the i-th digit is 1 and "off" if that digit is 0. We use a *binary tree representation* where each

point branches downward with at most two branches. Each branching downward corresponds to the two possible choices of the next digit in the sequence.
The tree will have N levels and 2^N nodes representing all possible states at
the N-th level. Figure 2.6 (for N = 3) should make the general procedure clear.

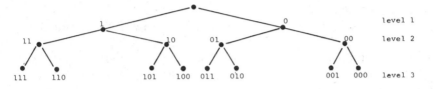

Figure 2.6

Before we go on to Example 2.4 we note that the straightforward procedure
just described can be modified so as to provide a good deal of information
about the class of games described in Example 2.2.

The game of 6 matches (and any other game in the class) can be modelled
using a game tree as illustrated in Figure 2.7. We denote the first player by A
and the second player by B. Each level in the tree denotes a move by the
appropriate player and all possible moves are shown. The bottom points label
final states (wins) with a $\oplus$ denoting an A win and a $\ominus$ a B win. The numbers
along each line of the tree give the total number of matches removed after that
particular turn. For convenience, a 2-match choice is given by a left branch
and a 1-match choice by a right branch. A play of the game consists of a path
from the root v_0 to one of the terminal ($\oplus$, $\ominus$) points. For example, the
hatched path in Figure 2.7 is the sequence: A takes 2, B takes 1, A takes 2,

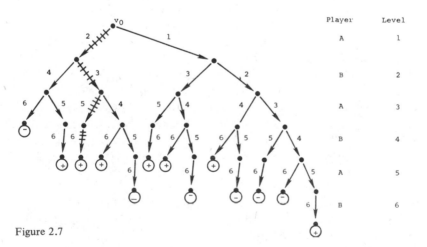

Figure 2.7

B takes 1 and loses. The observant reader will note that A can always guarantee a win by first removing two matches.

The game tree just described provides the basis for the following, slightly surprising result.

Theorem 2.5 In any game satisfying the properties given in Example 2.2, there is a guaranteed winning strategy for one of the players.

The theorem can be proved inductively and is given in Trakhtenbrot (1963).

In view of Theorem 2.5 one might ask: why is chess a difficult game? If we put an upper bound of M on the total number of moves (M = 100,000 is a lifetime game of chess) we can, in principle, construct a game tree for chess that is M levels deep. If there are at most N possible moves at any turn, then each point in the tree might have as many as N downward branchings. Thus, we may have as many as N^M points at the M-th level of our game tree.

Let us very conservatively (relative to chess) take N = 10 and M = 15. Then the number of branches in our game tree would be

$$\sum_{j=1}^{15} 10^j = \frac{10(1 - 10^{15})}{1 - 10} > 10^{15}$$

using the finite sum formula for the geometric series. Assume we have a very powerful computer and a very efficient program that enables us to enumerate a million (10^6) branches per second. At this rate it would take our super computer about a century (working every second of the time) to construct the appropriate game tree. Although it has been conjectured (conjectures are cheap) that white has a guaranteed winning strategy in chess, these numbers suggest that we are not likely to find it in the near future.

Example 2.4 Smith, Brown and Jones (hereafter denoted S, B and J) agree to fight a 3-way duel under the following rules:

1) they draw lots to see who fires first, second and third;
2) they stand at the corners of an equilateral triangle;
3) they successively fire shots in the drawn order until two are dead; and
4) at each turn, the man who is firing can shoot at either of the others.

It is a fact that S is a dead shot and never misses at this range. At the given range B hits his target about 80% of the time, and J about 50% of the time.

What is the best strategy for each player and what are their survival probabilities if they play these strategies?

If S shoots first, he can do no better than to kill B. For if he kills J, then B (with probability .8) will then have the next shot and must aim at S (since J is dead). Clearly, S would rather have J do the shooting.

Similarly, if B shoots first he will try to kill S, for if he does not S will shoot at him at his first opportunity and S is a dead shot.

J has something of a dilemma. He does not really want to kill anyone if he goes first. For if he does, the survivor (who is a good shot) is guaranteed to try to kill him on the very next turn, regardless of the draw order. So J decides to miss on purpose until one of the other duelists is dead. Then it will be J's turn and he can make the most of his relatively poor shooting ability. This strategy dominates the duel in the sense that, if J adopts it, it will maximize J's survival probability. If either S or B choose to deviate from their previously given strategy (without calling off the whole duel) his corresponding survival probability will decrease.

We model the progress of the duel using a tree that initially has only two branches since J does not effectively enter the picture until either S or B is dead. In this way the tree is kept binary and fairly small.

Each point on the tree denotes an event (e. g. J kills B), and the lines are weighted with the probability that the event at the end of the line (the point furthest from root START) will occur given the event at the beginning of the line (the point closest to the root). The tree for the duel is given in Figure 2.8.

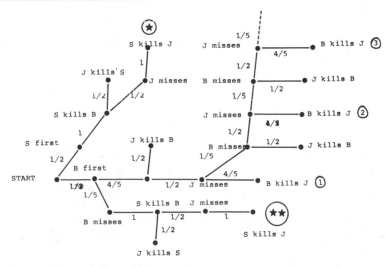

Figure 2.8

The dotted branch on the upper right side in Figure 2.8 denotes an infinite repetition of the basic pattern shown just before in which B and J keep shooting at each other (and possibly missing *ad infinitum*).

We now compute the various survival probabilities. Consider S first. There are two paths in our tree that denote a win by S, and they are labelled ★ and ★★. The two paths represent mutually exclusive events, so their probabilities are additive. Consider the event ★ first. We have (from the definition of conditioning)

$P(\star)$ = P(S first) · P(S kills B | S first) ·
        P(J misses S | S first, S kills B) ·
        P(S kills J | S first, S kills B, J misses S)
    = 1/2 · 1 · 1/2 · 1 = 1/4.
Similarly,
$P(\star\star)$ = 1 · 1/2 · 1 · 1/5 · 1/2 = 1/20.

Note how the tree structure (and Theorem 2.1) guarantee a one-to-one relationship between winning events and the unique paths from the root to the terminal points. The tree has been designed so that computation of the various complicated conditioning probabilities amounts to nothing more than multiplying together all the numbers on the lines of the path. We are effectively computing compound probabilites as we "grow" the tree. We then have

$$P(S \text{ survives}) \triangleq P_S = 1/4 + 1/20 = 3/10.$$

We go to B next. We have

$$P(B \text{ survives}) \triangleq P_B = P(B \text{ kills } S) \cdot P(B \text{ kills } J \mid B \text{ kills } S)$$
$$= P(B \text{ first}) \cdot P(B \text{ kills } S \mid B \text{ first}) \cdot P(B \text{ kills } J \mid B \text{ kills } S)$$
$$= 1/2 \cdot 4/5 \cdot \sum_{n=1}^{\infty} 4/10^n = 2/5 \cdot 4/9 = 8/45,$$

where we have used the fact that all of B's winning events occur on the upper right branch of the tree in Figure 2.8 (all such events are denoted by circled numbers). The reader should check the sum term.

J's survival probability P_J can be obtained from the normalization $P_S + P_B + P_J = 1$. We find that $P_J = 47/90$. So, with a little thought, J can guarantee himself the best chance of survival in what might, at first, appear to be a situation that is badly stacked against him.

Further discussion of the 3-way duel can be found in Gardner (1961).

Before we complete this section we mention a number of important applications of trees which could not be included here since any one of them would at least double the size of this section. These include the use of trees as grammatic markers and dictionaries, Chapter 5 of Berztiss (1971), trees in automatic textual emendation, in section 8 of Kaufmann (1967), the analysis of strings in natural language, in chapter 6 of Busacker-Saaty (1965), and just about everything on earth in sorting and searching in Knuth (1973).

Each of these references in turn contains a multitude of other references
for the interested reader.

2.5 The concept of a good computational algorithm

In section 2.4 we saw that it is possible for graph-theoretic algorithms to
become combinatorially explosive. Unfortunately, this sort of thing happens
more frequently than we would like, and the problem is by no means limited
to graph-theoretic algorithms. It would seem appropriate at this time to present
a quantitative measure by which we could distinguish a "good" computational
algorithm from a "bad" one. In particular, we will try to see why Algorithm
2.1 is quantitatively superior to the algorithm in section 2.4.

Let A denote an algorithm for solving a particular class of problems. Let
n denote a measure of the size of a particular problem in this class. In most
of the problems in this chapter, n is just a scalar representing the number of
points in a graph. In general however, n might be an array or a tensor. Define
$f_A(n)$ as a *work function* that gives an upper bound on the maximum number
of basic operations (additions, comparisons, etc.) that algorithm A might have
to perform to solve any problem of size n. We use the following criterion
(Edmonds 1965a) to judge the quality of algorithm A. Algorithm A is said
to be *good* if $f_A(n)$ grows no more rapidly than a polynomial in n, and *exponential* otherwise. This criterion is based on worst-case run time, but similar
criteria could also be specified for expected run time and storage. The "experimental" basis for this measure of quality is that sequential or parallel machines
seem to be more or less capable of digesting polynomial algorithms for large
problems, but they "choke" rather quickly on exponential algorithms.

A function f(n) is defined to be $O(g(n))$ if

$$\lim_{n \to \infty} \frac{f(n)}{g(n)} = \text{const} \neq 0$$

An algorithm is good therefore if $f_A(n) = O(P(n))$ where P(n) is any polynomial
function of n.

By this standard, Algorithm 2.1 is $O(n^2)$ and our safecracking algorithm is
$O(2^n)$. So the former is quite good (particularly when one considers that there
could be $O(n^2)$ costs to consider) and the latter is "mildly" exponential (2^n
is mild compared to n!, for example).

For a given algorithm, the derivation of a function like a worst case upper
bound falls under the heading of an "analysis of the algorithm". It is also of
interest to investigate all possible algorithms that work on the same kind of
problem and to choose which of these is best relative to a given criterion.

This activity goes under the heading of "computational complexity" and is very difficult. Algorithm 2.1 is one of the few that is known to be best in its class with respect to the worst case run time gauge.

Advanced treatments of general topics in algorithm complexity are given in Karp (1972) and Aho-Hopcroft-Ullman (1974).

3. Representations of graphs

3.1 Introduction

A graph $G = (V, E)$ can be completely specified by simply listing its set of points V and its set of lines E. For most purposes, however, this method of representing a graph provides relatively little insight into various properties that it may or may not have.

By far the most common method of describing a graph is to draw a (somewhat arbitrary) picture of it, as we have done frequently in chapters 1 and 2. The cliche, "a picture is worth a thousand words", is certainly appropriate in this regard. On the other hand, pictures of graphs have certain limitations.

In the first place, one seldom draws a picture of a graph that has as many as twenty points, for example, especially if the graph has a large number of lines. In the second place, a picture is seldom a good means of verbally conveying information about a graph. Consider the problem of talking to someone on the phone and trying to describe to him a particular graph, a picture of which you are viewing. In the third place, a picture is not always suitable for computing various parameters of a graph.

The advent of computers has changed our thinking about means of representing graphs, particularly for purposes of carrying out mathematical computations on them. Computers have greatly improved our ability to check conjectures and gather data on thousands of graphs having relatively large numbers of points.

This has led researchers to consider a variety of ways of representing a graph in a computer. In this chapter we will present several of the more widely used techniques that have been developed for this purpose.

In general, no one technique is really better than any other for representing a graph; it all depends on the problem one wishes to solve. One should exercise caution in this regard, for the particular representation one uses can noticeably effect the speed and efficiency of a graph theoretic algorithm. Unfortunately, it seems that experience is the best guide to choosing which representation to use.

3.2 The adjacency matrix

Any graph $G = (V, E)$ having p points can be represented by a $p \times p$ matrix, provided the points of G are given some (arbitrary) labelling. If the points of G are labelled $v_1, v_2, \ldots, v_p$, then the *adjacency matrix* A(G) is defined as follows:

$$A(G) = [a_{ij}], \quad \text{where} \quad a_{ij} = 1 \text{ if } v_i \text{ adj } v_j,$$
$$a_{ij} = 0 \text{ otherwise.}$$

Figure 3.1 illustrates a graph and its adjacency matrix.

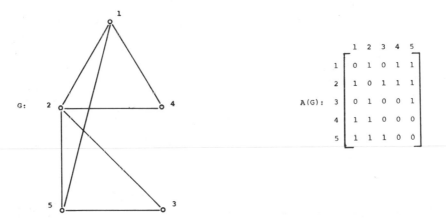

Figure 3.1

Note that for an undirected graph G, A(G) will always be a symmetric, (0, 1)-matrix, with zeroes on the diagonal. Note also that the degree of point v_i equals the number of 1's in either the i-th row or i-th column of A(G).

For a number of reasons it is worthwhile to consider the meaning of powers of the adjacency matrix $A^n(G)$. The general statement here is that the a_{ij} entry in $A^n(G)$ equals the number of distinct walks of length n from point v_i to point v_j in G. Furthermore, the a_{ii} entry in $A^2(G)$ equals the degree d_i of v_i in G, and the a_{ii} entry in $A^3(G)$ equals twice the number of triangles in G which contain point v_i. It can also be seen that if G is connected and has p points, then the distance from v_i to v_j in G equals the least integer n for which the a_{ij} entry in $A^n(G)$ is non-zero.

3.3 The incidence matrix

Next to the adjacency matrix, the most common matrix representation of a graph is the incidence matrix I(G). If the points of G are labelled (arbitrarily)

$v_1, v_2, \ldots, v_p$, and the lines are labelled $e_1, e_2, \ldots, e_q$, then the $p \times q$ *incidence matrix* is defined as follows:

$$I(G) = [b_{ij}], \quad \text{where} \quad b_{ij} = 1 \text{ if } v_i \text{ is incident to } e_j,$$
$$b_{ij} = 0 \text{ otherwise.}$$

Figure 3.2 contains the incidence matrix $I(G)$ of the graph G in Figure 3.1.

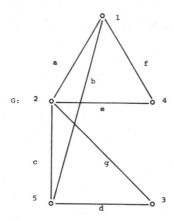

$$I(G): \quad \begin{array}{c c} & \begin{array}{c c c c c c c} a & b & c & d & e & f & g \end{array} \\ \begin{array}{c} 1 \\ 2 \\ 3 \\ 4 \\ 5 \end{array} & \left[\begin{array}{c c c c c c c} 1 & 1 & 0 & 0 & 0 & 1 & 0 \\ 1 & 0 & 1 & 0 & 1 & 0 & 1 \\ 0 & 0 & 0 & 1 & 0 & 0 & 1 \\ 0 & 0 & 0 & 0 & 1 & 1 & 0 \\ 0 & 1 & 1 & 1 & 0 & 0 & 0 \end{array} \right] \end{array}$$

Figure 3.2

Note that every column in $I(G)$ contains exactly two 1's and that no two columns are identical. Note also that the number of 1's in the i-th row equals the degree d_i of v_i in G. The incidence matrix is useful for solving a variety of problems in graph theory, for example, problems involving cycles in graphs or the minimum number of lines in a graph which cover all the points of G. On the other hand, the incidence matrix requires more memory ($p \times q$, i. e. on the order of p^3 words) and uses it more inefficiently, insofar as $(p-2) \times q$ of these words of memory have a zero stored in them.

3.4 Adjacency vectors

Instead of representing graphs by (0, 1)-matrices, one can use a matrix in which the entries correspond directly to the labels $v_1, v_2, \ldots, v_p$ given the points of G. In such a matrix the i-th row contains a vector of all points adjacent to point v_i. The order of the elements in such a vector is usually determined by the order in which the lines of G are presented, for example, as input to a computer program. In Figure 3.3 we present a graph G, a random listing of the lines of G, and an adjacency-vector representation of G.

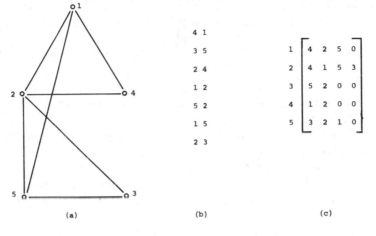

Figure 3.3

The size of a matrix containing adjacency vectors need only by p × D, where D is the maximum degree of a point in G.

Adjacency vectors are a particularly good means for representing a graph when the problem can be solved by making a small number of passes over every line of G.

The following is a segment of FORTRAN code which can be used (subject to minor modifications in the READ and IF(EOF) statements) to create the adjacency vector representation of the graph in Figure 3.3(a), given the lines in the order indicated in Figure 3.3(b).

```
C
C   WE ASSUME THAT ARRAYS GRAPH (I, J) AND
C   DEGREE(I) ARE INITIALIZED TO ZERO
C
C   READ IN THE NUMBER P OF POINTS
C
    READ P
C
C   READ IN THE LINES MN OF G
C
1   READ M, N
    IF(EOF) 3, 2
2   GRAPH(M,DEGREE(M)+1) = N
    DEGREE(M) = DEGREE(M) + 1
    GRAPH(N,DEGREE(N)+1) = M
    DEGREE(N) = DEGREE(N) + 1
    GO TO 1
3   . . .
```

3.5 Intersection graphs

The adjacency vector representation is strikingly similar to a standard graph theoretic method for representing a graph using subsets. Let $P = \{p_1, p_2, \ldots, p_k\}$ be a finite set and let $S = \{S_1, S_2, \ldots, S_n\}$ be a family of distinct, non-empty subsets of P. By the *intersection graph on S* we mean the graph $\cap S = (S, E)$, whose points correspond one-to-one with the subsets of S, and in which two points are adjacent if and only if the corresponding subsets have a non-empty intersection.

Theorem 3.1 Any graph $G = (V, E)$ can be represented as an intersection graph on some family S of subsets of a finite set P.

Proof: Consider the set $P = V \cup E$. Let each point v_i in V correspond to the subset of P which consists of v_i together with all lines incident to v_i. It is easy to see that two points v_i and v_j of V are adjacent if and only if their corresponding subsets of P have a non-empty intersection.

In Figure 3.4 we provide an intersection graph representation of the graph G in Figure 3.3(a), where we label the lines with the integers 6 through 12. Notice that the subsets corresponding to the points of G are constructed according to Theorem 3.1. Notice also that this representation of G is in terms of a family of subsets of a set P which has twelve elements.

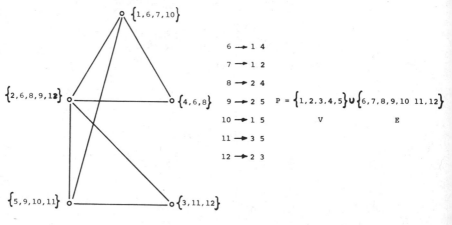

Figure 3.4

In Figure 3.5(a) we represent the same graph as an intersection graph on a set $P' = \{1, 2, 3, 4\}$ having only four elements. We could therefore represent the graph by means of an even smaller matrix (Figure 3.5(b)) than in Figure 3.3(c).

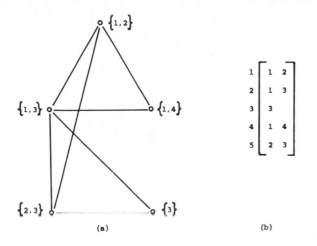

$$
\begin{array}{c|cc}
1 & 1 & 2 \\
2 & 1 & 3 \\
3 & 3 &   \\
4 & 1 & 4 \\
5 & 2 & 3
\end{array}
$$

(a)   (b)

Figure 3.5

Smaller representations such as these have prompted graph theorists to define the *intersection number* $\omega(G)$ of a graph G to be the smallest order of a set P on which G has an intersection graph representation. The most notable result about $\omega(G)$ is the following (Harary 1969: 19).

Theorem 3.2 Let G be a connected graph having $p \geqslant 3$ points and q lines. Then $\omega(G) = q$ if and only if G has no triangles.

3.6 Adjacency lists
Perhaps the most efficient means of representing a graph in use today involves linked lists of adjacencies. This representation strongly resembles adjacency vectors, except that it is generally more conservative in its use of memory. Figure 3.6 provides a linked list representation of the same graph which we have used throughout this chapter. Such a representation also depends on the labelling given the points $v_1, v_2, \ldots, v_p$, and on the order in which the lines of G are given. We use the same ordering given in Figure 3.3(b).

In order to determine which points are adjacent to a given point in a linked list representation, one must follow the pointers given in the column marked "NEXT". For example, to find the points adjacent to point 3, we find that NEXT(3) = 19. Looking in the nineteenth row, we see that HEAD(19) = 2, i. e. 3 is adjacent to 2. We also see that NEXT(19) = 8. Since HEAD(8) = 5, we know that 3 is also adjacent to 5. Finally, since NEXT(8) = 0, we know that 3 is not adjacent to any other points.

Notice that this representation requires $(p + 2q) \times 2$ words of memory, $2 \times p$ of which will have a zero stored in them. On the other hand, the first

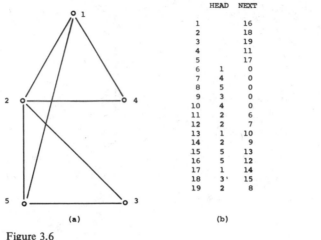

	HEAD	NEXT	
1		16	
2		18	
3		19	4 1
4		11	
5		17	3 5
6	1	0	
7	4	0	2 4
8	5	0	
9	3	0	1 2
10	4	0	
11	2	6	5 2
12	2	7	
13	1	10	1 5
14	2	9	
15	5	13	2 3
16	5	12	
17	1	14	
18	3'	15	
19	2	8	

(a)   (b)   (c)

Figure 3.6

p words of the array NEXT could be used to store useful information about the points $v_1, v_2, \ldots, v_p$, in particular, they could be used to store the values of the degree d_i of v_i.

The following is a segment of FORTRAN code which can be used (subject to minor modifications in the READ and IF(EOF) statements) to create the adjacency lists in Figure 3.6(b), given the lines in the order indicated in Figure 3.6(c).

```
      C
      C  WE ASSUME THAT ALL ENTRIES IN HEAD AND NEXT
      C  ARE INITIALIZED TO ZERO
      C
      C  READ IN THE NUMBER OF POINTS P
      C
         READ P
         I = P + 1
      C
      C  READ IN THE LINES MN OF G
      C
      1  READ M, N
         IF(EOF) 3, 2
      2  NEXT(I) = NEXT(M)
         HEAD(I) = N
         NEXT(M) = I
         I = I + 1
         NEXT(I) = NEXT(N)
         HEAD(I) = M
         NEXT(N) = I
         I = I + 1
         GO TO 1
      3  . . .
```

3.7 Binary trees

Since trees occur frequently in applications, it is worthwhile to consider at least one class of representations of trees. The one we will present is designed for representing binary trees and uses linked lists with two pointers. We illustrate this using sort trees, which are perhaps best defined by example.

Suppose we wanted to write a computer program which would read-in a given sentence or text, one word at a time, and sort the words alphabetically. Figure 3.7(a) presents a part of the binary tree which would be constructed, given the first sentence of this section.

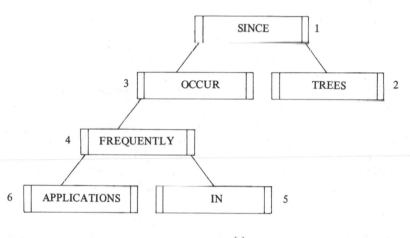

(a)

	L	WORD	R	COUNT
1	3	SINCE	2	1
2	0	TREES	0	1
3	4	OCCUR	0	1
4	6	FREQUENTLY	5	1
5	0	IN	0	1
6	0	APPLICATIONS	0	1

(b)

Figure 3.7

Figure 3.7(b) illustrates a data structure which represents the tree in Figure 3.7(a); this structure contains arrays L and R, which indicate the location (row) of the words which appear below and to the left and right, respectively, of a given word. The array WORD contains the complete list of words as they were read-in.

If one wanted to count the number of times each word appears in a particular text, an array COUNT could be added to the above representation.

When the above program has completed reading a text, it would be desirable to be able to print out the words in the text in alphabetical order. Relatively simple programs for doing this can be constructed (Knuth 1969: 334).

3.8 Graph isomorphism

Sooner or later a particular application may give rise to a variety of graph structures and it will become important to identify them as to their type. In such situations it would be valuable to have an efficient procedure for determining of two given graphs, whether or not they are isomorphic.

Unfortunately, such procedures do not exist. The graph isomorphism problem is perhaps the most celebrated, difficult, computational problem in all of graph theory.

Recall from section 1.5 the definition of graph isomorphism: two graphs $G = (V, E)$ and $G' = (V', E')$ are *isomorphic* if and only if there exists a one-to-one function h: $V \leftrightarrow V'$, such that uv is a line of E if and only if h(u) h(v) is a line of E'.

It follows from the definition that if graphs G and G' are isomorphic and an isomorphism h is found, then any point v_i having degree d_i in G must map onto a point $v_{i'}$ in G' having the same degree, i. e. degree v_i must equal degree $h(v_i)$.

Consider, therefore, two cubic graphs G and G' having ten points each. Any possible one-to-one function h from V onto V' will satisfy the above-mentioned degree condition; there are 10^{10} such functions. Thus, in order to decide if G and G' are isomorphic, one might have to try each of 10^{10} possible functions to see if one exists which satisfies the isomorphism condition.

In the face of this possible combinatorial explosion, researchers have tended to forego the search for an efficient graph isomorphism algorithm in favor of simple, heuristic procedures which seem to perform well in most cases, or isomorphism algorithms which perform well on the special classes of graphs which appear in a particular application.

One example of a relatively simple, heuristic procedure for deciding if two graphs G_1 and G_2 are isomorphic involves the adjacency matrix A(G).

One first computes $A^2(G_i)$, $A^3(G_i)$, ..., $A^k(G_i)$, for i = 1, 2, and some appropriate power k. One then reorders the rows and columns of $A^2(G_i)$ so that the elements of the diagonal appear in ascending order. One continues such a reordering process for all of the powers $A^k(G_i)$ of G_1 and G_2.

If G_1 and G_2 are isomorphic, then all of these reorderings must produce identical matrices. If at any time the respective matrices cannot be reordered so as to produce identical matrices, then the graphs are not isomorphic.

If, on the other hand, all the powers of the adjacency matrices can be made to be identical, then the evidence is strong (but not necessarily con-clusive) that the graphs are isomorphic.

For most graphs which are not isomorphic, this heuristic procedure will terminate quickly, for example, by the time $A^3(G_i)$ is considered.

One of the best papers that has been written on graph isomorphism is Corneil-Gottlieb (1970). The interested reader should consult this paper for a detailed discussion of this problem.

4. Traversals in graphs

4.1 Introduction
A large number of graph theoretic applications, and a good deal of graph theory itself, is concerned with traversing all or part of a graph. One might be interested in finding a path or a cycle which satisfies certain properties, or establishing that no such structure exists. Many of the oldest and most seriously studied problems in graph theory fall into this category; we shall look at a number of these problems in this chapter.

4.2 Eulerian walks
The oldest problem in graph theory (and in topology) is the Königsberg Bridge Problem, which was solved in 1736 by the great mathematician-physicist, Leonhard Euler. The usual statement of the problem (Euler 1953) is:

"In the town of Königsberg (recently renamed Kaliningrad) there were in the 18th century seven bridges which crossed the river Pregel. They connected two islands in the river with each other and with the opposite banks. The townsfolk had long amused themselves with this problem: is it possible to cross the seven bridges in a continuous walk and return to the starting point without recrossing any of them?"

Figure 4.1(a) shows the bridge layout, and Figure 4.1(b) the correspond-ing graph.

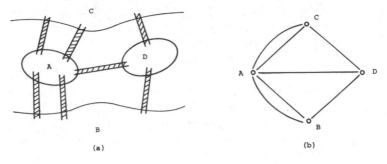

Figure 4.1

A more modern, and more general, statement of the problem is as follows. For a given connected graph G, does there exist a closed walk which traverses each line exactly once? If such a closed walk exists, G is called *Eulerian*. Euler solved the problem with the following characterization:

Theorem 4.1   A connected graph G is Eulerian if and only if every point has even degree.

Proof: 1) To show that if G is Eulerian, then every point has even degree:

Let W be a closed walk in G which traverses each line exactly once. Let v be an arbitrary point which is not the initial (and therefore not the final) point of W. Each time we enter v (along a line that is being traversed for the first time) we must be able to leave it along an unused line. If any such point v had odd degree, there would come a time when we could enter v but not leave it; this contradicts the assumption that G is Eulerian. A similar argument can be used to show that the initial point must also have even degree. Actually, since the walk is closed it is not possible to distinguish an "initial" point.

2) To show that if every point has even degree, then G is Eulerian:

We exhibit an explicit construction of a closed walk W that traverses each line exactly once. Start at an arbitrary point and traverse any incident line. Once a line has been traversed, call it used. Having arrived at a point v, continue the walk W by traversing any unused line incident with v. Since all points have even degree, this walk must end by returning to the initial point. Furthermore, all the lines incident with the initial point must be used. Note that as we walk through the graph an odd number of lines incident with the initial point will have been used.

At this stage, either we have used all the lines, in which case we are finished, or we have not. If not, then since G is connected there is a point on our current walk W which has at least two unused incident lines. Call this point v, and repeat the procedure just described starting at point v. Ultimately, we must stop at v after completing a walk W'.

We now take our current walk W and, upon our first arrival at v, we traverse W', returning to v, and complete the walk W. If we have traversed all the lines, we are finished. If not, we continue as above until we have traversed all the lines.

Corollary 4.1a If G is an Eulerian graph, then the lines of G can be partitioned into line-disjoint cycles.

Corollary 4.1b If G is a connected graph having exactly two points u and v of odd degree then G has an open walk which begins at u, traverses every line of G exactly once, and ends at v.

Corollary 4.1c If G is a connected graph having 2n points of odd degree, then the lines of G can be partitioned into n line-disjoint open walks.

All three of these corollaries can be proved using arguments similar to those used in Theorem 4.1.

The algorithm described in the proof of Theorem 4.1, for constructing a walk in an Eulerian graph, can be implemented on a computer. Using linked-list techniques the algorithm in $O(N^2)$ for a graph with N points, which is best possible in its complexity class. In the worst case, just describing a "divinely offered" solution would involve listing $O(N^2)$ pieces of data. Even a very rudimentary implementation, using an adjacency matrix representation (cf. section 3.2) is $O(N^3)$.

In the case of arbitrary graphs, we might ask for the minimum length closed walk that traverses each line at least once; such a walk is called an *Eulerian walk*. The problem of constructing an Eulerian walk was first stated by Kwan (1962) and is often called the Chinese postman's problem. Kwan's problem appeared in *Chinese mathematics* and was stated as follows:

"A mailman has to cover his assigned segment before returning to the post office. The problem is to find the shortest walking distance for the mailman."

Let G be a connected graph having q lines and 2n points of odd degree. Denote the set of odd points of G by $O(G) = \{u_1, u_2, \ldots, u_{2n}\}$. Define a *pair-partition of the odd points of G* to be a partition π of $O(G)$ into n pairs, say $\pi = \{(u_{11}, u_{12}), (u_{21}, u_{22}), \ldots, (u_{n1}, u_{n2})\}$. Given a pair-partition π, we define

$$d(\pi) = \sum_{i=1}^{n} d(u_{i1}, u_{i2})$$

i. e. $d(\pi)$ is the sum of distances in G between the pairs of points listed in π. Let $\pi(G)$ denote the set of all pair-partitions of G and define

$$m(G) = \min_{\pi \in \pi(G)} d(\pi),$$

$m(G)$ is clearly a finite integer for any graph G.

Let $\bar{\pi}$ be any pair-partition such that $d(\bar{\pi}) = m(G)$. For each pair (u_{i1}, u_{i2}) in π, let P_i be any path in G from u_{i1} to u_{i2} of minimum length $d(u_{i1}, u_{i2})$. Such a set of n paths $\{P_i\}$ will be called an *m-set* of G.

Theorem 4.2 Let G be a connected graph and let W be a closed walk in G. Then the following statements are equivalent:

1) W is an Eulerian walk.

2) W contains all the lines of G and the set of lines appearing more than once in W forms an m-set of G.

3) W contains all the lines of G and

    i) no line of G appears more than twice in W,

    ii) for any cycle C of G, the number of lines of C which appear twice in W does not exceed half the length of C.

A proof of Theorem 4.2 is quite long; the interested reader should consult Goodman-Hedetniemi (1973).

Statement 3)ii) of Theorem 4.2 contains the germ of a simple iterative algorithm for finding Eulerian walks in small graphs. A much more complicated algorithm for large graphs can be found in Edmonds-Johnson (1973).

When an m-set is found, the lines of the m-set are added to G to form a multigraph G'. The thoughtful reader will observe that every point in the multigraph G' will have even degree. An application of the algorithm given as part of the proof of Theorem 4.1 will find an Eulerian walk in the multigraph. The corresponding walk in G (where traversal of multilines corresponds to the multiple traversal of the appropriate line in G) is also an Eulerian walk.

This situation is depicted in Figure 4.2. A graph G is shown in Figure 4.2(a) with its odd points circled. Figure 4.2(b) illustrates an m-set of G, while Figure 4.2(c) is the multigraph G'. Figure 4.2(d) shows an Eulerian walk in G' found by using the algorithm given as part of the proof of Theorem 4.2. The direction of traversal of each line is shown by an arrow, and the sequence is given by the line number. The final Eulerian walk for the original graph G is shown in Figure 4.2(e). Note that three lines are traversed twice. Another Eulerian walk is shown in Figure 4.2(f), which shows that a line may be traversed twice in the same direction.

Most of the ideas presented here are readily extended to digraphs.

4.3 Hamiltonian traversals

A *Hamiltonian cycle* in a graph G is a cycle that passes through each point of G. The problem of deciding whether or not a given graph contains a Hamiltonian cycle is superficially similar to the Eulerian walk problem, but is in fact much more difficult. The problem was fathered by the great mathematical physicist Sir William Rowan Hamilton in 1859. Today the problem is still

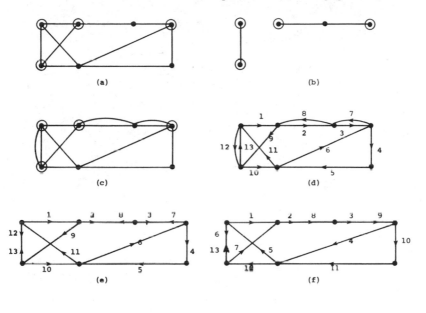

Figure 4.2

unsolved: we cannot effectively characterize those graphs with Hamiltonian cycles.

Note that there seems to be no significant relationship between the class of Eulerian graphs and the class of Hamiltonian graphs. In Figure 4.3, G_1 is non-Hamiltonian and Eulerian; G_2 is non-Eulerian and Hamiltonian; G_3 is neither; and G_4 is both.

Although no effective conditions have been found which are both necessary and sufficient for a graph to be Hamiltonian (i. e. contain a Hamiltonian cycle), a number of conditions which are either necessary or sufficient are known. Unfortunately, the known necessary conditions are not very impressive. The graph G_3 in Figure 4.3 is known as the *theta-graph*. The following result can be found in Harary (1969: 66).

Theorem 4.3 All Hamiltonian graphs are blocks. Every non-Hamiltonian block contains the theta-graph as a subgraph.

The situation is rather different when it comes to sufficiency conditions. Most of the research in this area has been modelled after Theorem 4.1, i. e. sufficiency conditions in terms of the degrees of the points. The basic idea is that if a graph has "enough" lines, then it must be Hamiltonian. Theorem 4.4 (Berge 1973) is one of the strongest and most complicated of such results.

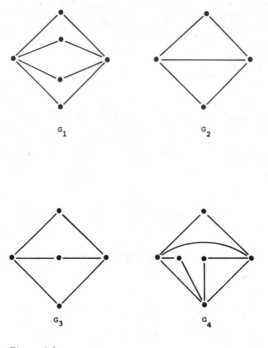

Figure 4.3

Theorem 4.4 Let G = (V, E) be a block with p points and degree sequence $d_1 \leqslant d_2 \leqslant \ldots \leqslant d_p$. Let q be an integer, $0 \leqslant q \leqslant p - 3$. If, for every k with $q < k < 1/2 (p + q)$, the following condition holds:

$$d_{k-q} \leqslant k \text{ implies } d_{p-k} \geqslant p - k + q \, ,$$

then for each subset F with q lines such that the connected components of (V, F) are paths, there exists a Hamiltonian cycle of G that contains F.

Corollary 4.4a (Chvátal 1972): Let G = (V, E) be a block with $p \geqslant 3$ points and degree sequence $d_1 \leqslant d_2 \leqslant \ldots \leqslant d_p$. If $d_k \leqslant k < p/2$ implies $d_{p-k} \geqslant p - k$, then G is Hamiltonian.

Corollary 4.4b (Dirac 1952): Let G be a block with $p \geqslant 3$ points. Then G is Hamiltonian of every point in G is adjacent to at least half of the other points.

Corollary 4.4b is one of the earliest of the "general" sufficiency conditions. Many other degree sequence conditions also exist, but most can be expressed as corollaries of Theorem 4.4 (cf. Berge 1973). Other sufficiency conditions based on subgraph structure rather than degree sequences also exist (Goodman-Hedetniemi 1974a).

A number of generalizations and variations of the basic Hamiltonian problem exist. We will mention a few of them here.

The Hamiltonian walk problem (Goodman-Hedetniemi 1974b) seeks the shortest closed walk through a graph G which visits each point at least once. This problem contains the Hamiltonian cycle problem as a special case.

The best known variation of the Hamiltonian cycle problem is the traveling salesman problem. A salesman starts at an arbitrary city and seeks to visit every city in his region and then return to his initial city. Each city is directly reachable from every other city, there being a cost function (time, money, distance) $c(i, j)$ giving the cost of travel from city i to city j. The objective is to plan a tour that visits each city exactly once and has minimum cost. In graph theoretic terms we seek a minimum cost Hamiltonian cycle on a complete graph K_n with lines weighted by the costs $c(i, j)$. The weight of a Hamiltonian cycle is the sum of the line weights of the cycle, and n is the number of cities. The problem has been widely studied and some very sophisticated (but exponential) algorithms exist (Bellmore-Nemhauser 1968; Held-Karp 1971). The problem is important because it is a prototype for general deterministic scheduling problems. A polynomial average performance algorithm is contained in Bellmore-Malone (1970).

4.4 Shortest path problems

It is often of interest to know the shortest path between two specified points in a graph or digraph. In addition to the obvious minimum trip application, this problem is important because other problems (cf. Lawler 1975) can be reformulated as shortest path problems and because shortest path algorithms are often useful subalgorithms in larger problems (e. g., algorithms for finding Eulerian walks). The standard shortest path problem is stated as follows:

Given a set of N points (arbitrarily numbered from 1 to N), and the *distance matrix* D, defined such that d_{ij} equals the length (> 0) associated with the arc (or line) from point i to point j, find a path of shortest distance from point 1 to point N. We let $d_{ij} = \infty$, initially, if there is no arc from point i to point j in the graph or digraph.

One of the best algorithms for solving this shortest path problem is by Dijkstra (1959); it procedes by iteratively "flowing" from point 1 to point N. We start by labelling point 1 with the permanent label of 0 and give all the other points an initial label of infinity. We proceed by updating these labels in such a way that point N will ultimately be labelled with the shortest distance from point 1. For each point i compare the label currently on i with the sum of the label on point 1 and the direct single arc distance d_{1i}. The new label for point i will be the smaller of these two numbers.

Now find the smallest of the N - 1 tentative labels and make it permanent. Let point j be the one that we permanently label. Then compare each of the N - 2 remaining tentative labels with the sum of the label just assigned to point j and the direct arc distance from j to the node under consideration. The smaller of these two numbers, the current tentative point label or this new sum, becomes the new tentative point label. After doing this for each non-permanently labelled point, find the minimum of all the tentative labels and declare it permanent. Continue iterating as described; at each iteration the point most recently permanently labelled forms the base point for the next iteration. The algorithm stops as soon as point N is given a permanent label. This gives us an upper bound of N - 1 iterations. Shortest distances from point 1 to every other point can be obtained by letting the algorithm run through N - 1 iterations.

An explicit shortest path can be found at the end of the labelling procedure by tracing back from point N to point 1. We start at point N and see which "predecessor" point caused point N to be permanently labelled. This will be the point whose permanent label differs from that of point N by exactly the value of the arc connecting the two points.

Before we prove the algorithm, we will illustrate it with an example. Note that a point is given a permanent label if and only if a shortest path to it from point 1 has been found. The reader familiar with dynamic programming will recognize that the algorithm uses the basic Principle of Optimality. Figure 4.4(a) illustrates the weighted, labelled graph under consideration. Successive iterations are given in Figures 4.4(b), (c), (d), and (e). Note from Figure 4.4(b) that in case of ties, more than one iteration can be simultaneously completed. Figure 4.4(e) traces back an explicit shortest path to point N. Labels are shown in parentheses next to the point number. Permanent labels are italicized.

We establish the correctness of Dijkstra's algorithm inductively following Dreyfus (1969). The basic inductive step is as follows. After any iteration, the points can be partitioned into two sets S_1 and S_2. The first set S_1 contains those points which have been permanently labelled; the second set S_2 contains the tentatively labelled points. Assume that the labels in S_1 are correct minimum distances from point 1 (this is clearly true after the first iteration). The tentative point labels in S_2 are the shortest distances from point 1 that can be attained by a path in which all except the terminal point belong to S_1. Then the point in S_2 with minimum label, say point k, can be moved to S_1, because if a shorter path to point k existed, it would have to contain a first point that is currently in S_2. However, such a point would have to be further

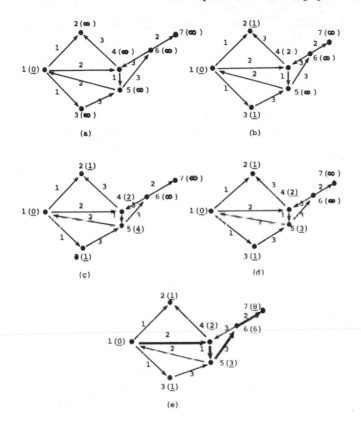

Figure 4.4

away from point 1 than point k, since its label exceeds that of point k, be-cause the continuation path from this point to point k has positive length.

Dijkstra's algorithm requires $O(N^2)$ basic steps. Since a graph may have $O(N^2)$ lines which have to be examined, this is a very good algorithm.

As mentioned earlier, much effort has gone into the study of shortest path algorithms. Other algorithms, and algorithms for assorted variants of the problem, can be found in survey articles (Dreyfus 1969; Hu 1967).

4.5 Network flows

In this section we introduce a class of problems, known as network flow problems, which have a wide variety of applications in areas such as opera-tions research. We content ourselves with a brief description of the proto-type network flow problem as is given by Fulkerson (1966). The subject is both vast and difficult and we refer the more serious reader to Ford-Fulker-son (1962), Hu (1969) and Lawler (1975).

Consider a digraph G. Let each arc (i, j) of G have associated with it a number $c_{ij} > 0$, called the *capacity* of arc (i, j). The capacity is typically used to represent the maximal amount of some commodity that can travel through arc (i, j).

We now ask for the maximum amount of commodity flow from one given point to another through the entire network. More explicitly label the "source" point as 1, and the "sink" as N. The other points are labelled arbitrarily. We define a *flow of amount v* from point 1 to point N as a function x_{ij} from the arc set of G to the real numbers that satisfies the following constraints:

$$\sum_j x_{ij} - \sum_j x_{ji} = \begin{cases} v, & i = 1 \\ -v, & i = N \\ 0, & \text{otherwise} \end{cases} \qquad \text{(Equation 4.1)}$$

$$0 \leqslant x_{ij} \leqslant c_{ij} \qquad \text{(Equation 4.2)}$$

We interpret variable x_{ij} as the amount of commodity in arc (i, j) in the flow. Equation 4.1 says that a flow of v "gushes" out of point 1 and "goes down" point N. Since the commodity cannot accumulate at any other point, the flow balance at all other points must be 0, i. e. there is a conservation of mass flux at every other point. Equations (4.2) guarantee that the capacities of all the arcs are not exceeded. The objective is to find a flow that maximizes v.

Figure 4.5 illustrates a flow in a network. Each arc is labelled with a pair (c_{ij}, x_{ij}) for the flow shown. Notice that the net flow in and out of points 2, 3, 4 and 5 is zero, and that the flow out of point 1 and into point 6 is $v = 7$.

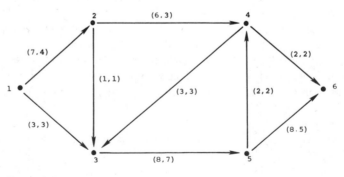

Figure 4.5

A very rudimentary algorithm for computing a flow is as follows. Find a directed path from point 1 to point N. Find the smallest arc capacity along this path and ship that amount of commodity from point 1 to point N. Add this new flow to the current value of v (which may initially be taken as 0). Now reduce all the arc capacities along the path by the amount of commodity just shipped over this path. Note that this will reduce the capacity of at least one arc to zero and thereby effectively eliminate it from further consideration. Remove all 0-capacity arcs from the network. Repeat this process until point 1 is disconnected from point N.

While this rudimentary procedure usually gets us a respectably high value of v, it does not guarantee an optimal flow. In Figure 4.5, the removal of the "saturated" arcs $(1, 3)$, $(2, 3)$, $(4, 3)$, $(5, 4)$, and $(4, 6)$ disconnects points 1 and 6, so that it is not possible to find an unsaturated 1–6 directed path that could be used to increase the flow. But this is not a maximum flow. An improved flow, with $v = 9 > 7$, is shown in Figure 4.6.

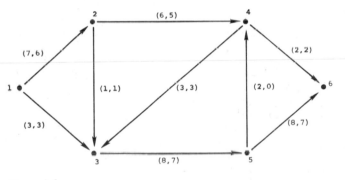

Figure 4.6

Nevertheless, we are quite close to the fundamental characterization of a maximal flow. We define a *cut* which separates points 1 and N as a partition of the points into two sets, S_1 and S_2, such that point 1 is in S_1 and point N is in S_2. The *capacity of the cut* is then defined to be

$$\sum_{\substack{i \in S_1 \\ j \in S_2}} c_{ij} .$$

In Figure 4.6 one possible cut would be $S_1 = \{1, 2, 3, 4\}$ and $S_2 = \{5, 6\}$. The capacity of this cut would be $c_{35} + c_{46} = 9$. All cuts of minimum capacity are called *min-cuts*. Note that for any given flow and any given cut, the net flow across the cut is always equal to the flow value v.

We need one more definition, that of a flow-augmenting path, before we can fully characterize maximal flows in a graph or network. Any path from one point to another is essentially a sequence of adjacent arcs. Arcs traversed in the sense of their direction are called *forward arcs* of the path, while those traversed against their direction are called *reverse arcs* of the path. A path from point 1 to point N is called *flow-augmenting with respect to the flow x* provided that the current flow in all forward arcs in smaller than the arc capacities and that the flows in the reverse arcs are positive.

In Figure 4.5 the sequence of arcs (1, 2), (2, 4), (4, 5), (5, 6) is an augmenting path with only (5, 4) as a reverse arc. In Figure 4.7 we show how we can use this flow-augmenting path to increase the value of v by an amount e. In this case, the most we can do is set e = 2, and this gives us the flow in Figure 4.7. Any value of e > 2 renders the path as non-augmenting.

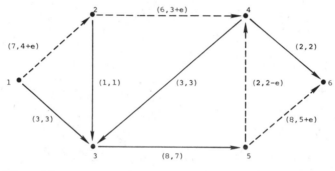

Figure 4.7

We are now ready for two fundamental theorems.

Theorem 4.5 For any graph, the maximum flow from a given source u to a given sink v is equal to the minimum cut capacity of any cut which separates u and v.

Theorem 4.6 A flow x from a source u to a sink v is maximum if and only if there is no flow-augmenting path with respect to x.

Both of these theorems can be proved constructively using a forward-backward labelling scheme that is similar to, but more sophisticated than, the procedure used in our shortest path algorithm. This algorithm has recently been thoroughly analyzed (Edmonds-Karp 1972) and found to be very efficient. We refer the interested reader to the cited reference.

The maximum flow problem just described is the simplest prototype of a wide variety of practical network problems which have extensive applications in operations research. The study of these problems draws heavily from both graph theory and mathematical programming.

5. Orderings and matchings

5.1 Relations and orders

In this section we will consider some of the ways that graph theory can be used to represent relations between members of sets. As we shall see, graph theoretic models not only provide convenient and useful "static" representations of relations, but they also enable us to carry out analysis and optimization.

Definition 5.1: The *Cartesian product*, A × B, of sets A and B is the set of ordered pairs whose first coordinates are members of A and whose second coordinates are members of B. In standard set notation:

$$A \times B = \{(a, b) | a \in A, b \in B\}.$$

Definition 5.2: A *binary relation* R from set A to set B is a subset of A × B. If $a \in A$ and $b \in B$ are related under R, we denote this by aRb.

Example 5.1 One of the most commonly considered binary relations is that of parentage. Let A be the set of all people, past and present. Let R be a relation on A × A such that for $a \in A$, aRb if and only if a is a parent of b.

Example 5.2 Mathematical functions provide a wealth of examples of binary relations. Let R' be the set of real numbers, and let Z' be the set of complex numbers. Let f(x) be the square root function, where if $x \in R'$, then $f(x) \in Z'$. We define a binary relation S on R' × Z' such that for $x \in R'$ and $f(x) \in Z'$, xSf(x) if and only if $f^2(x) = x$.

Definition 5.3: Let R be a relation on S × S. Then R is:
1) *reflexive* if xRx for all $x \in S$;
2) *irreflexive* if xRx for no $x \in S$;
3) *transitive* if xRy and yRz imply that xRz for all x, y $z \in S$;
4) *symmetric* if xRy implies yRx for all $x, y \in S$;
5) *antisymmetric* if xRy and yRx imply x = y for all $x, y \in S$.

The parentage relation in Example 5.1 is clearly irreflexive, since nobody is his/her/its own parent. It is not transitive since x the father of y and y the father of z do not imply that x is the father of z, although x is a grandfather, but that does not count under R. For our parentage relation it is not possible for xRy and yRx to hold simultaneously under any circumstances. Therefore parentage is an antisymmetric relation.

Definition 5.4: A relation R on S × S is an *equivalence relation* if it is reflexive, symmetric and transitive.

Example 5.3: Equality on the set of real numbers is an equivalence relation i. e. xRy if and only if x = y.

Definition 5.5: An irreflexive, transitive, antisymmetric relation on S × S is called a *partial order*.

Some definitions of a partial order permit the relation to be reflexive.
Definition 5.6: If < is a partial order on S × S, and a < b for some a, b ∈ S, then we say a *precedes* b, or b *follows* a.

We now take up the matter of graphical representations of binary relations on a set N (really N × N). Assume that N is a finite set, and denote the elements of N by $\{n_1, n_2, \ldots, n_m\}$. Let R be a binary relation on N. A digraph D represents the relation R on N if the nodes of D are the elements of N and an arc (n_i, n_j) exists in D if and only if $n_i R n_j$. We denote the digraph representation of a relation R on a set N by D = (N, R). There is a one-to-one correspondence between such a relation and its digraph representation.

If R is symmetric, then the graph representation of R is an undirected graph. Reflexive relations are often represented by loops at each node. The counterparts of transitivity are directed paths. If R is a partial order on N, then D = (N, R) is an acyclic loopless digraph. We see this last statement from the fact that our definition of a partial order does not permit $n_i R n_i$ for any $n_i \in N$, either directly or through transitivity.

5.2 Critical path scheduling

Partial orders and their digraph representations arise in a number of useful applications. One of these is scheduling. Consider a large project in which a number of groups are working on a variety of subprojects which have to be synthesized. The large project is much too big for one group to handle by itself. The various subprojects are not independent, for example, subprojects 8 and 11 must be completed before subproject 15 can be started. Some of the subprojects can be completed very early and the groups working on them can be freed to do other subprojects. A limited amount of resources is available which can be used to shorten the completion times for certain subprojects (for example, by buying equipment or hiring additional help). The basic problem is to model such an activity and analyze the model to determine a best schedule and which subprojects are the bottlenecks in the schedule.

To illustrate some of these ideas, we will consider a simple example from Berztiss (1971). A more advanced treatment is given by Whitehouse (1973).

Example 5.4 The S. family is going to write a letter. Actually Mrs. S. is going to write the letter, but she has Mr. S. and Junior around to help out.

The basic activities, their duration times, and the people assigned to each activity are as follows:

activity	duration	labor
A. Get paper and envelope.	2 min.	Mrs. S.
B. Get pen.	.5 min.	Mr. S.
C. Write letter.	30 min.	Mrs. S.
D. Address envelope.	5 min.	Mr. S.
E. Put letter in envelope and seal.	1 min.	Mrs. S.
F. Get stamp.	20 min.	Jr.
	(trip to P. O.)	
G. Affix stamp.	.5 min.	Jr.
H. Mail letter.	5 min.	Jr.

Since the family has only one pen, activities C and D cannot be done concurrently. We assume D precedes C. In our digraph model, each arc will correspond to an activity, and each node will correspond to an event (i. e. the completion of an activity).

We start by noting that activities A, B, and F can be done concurrently. This is permitted by the nature of these activities and our division of labor. Now we send Mr. S. to get the pen and address the envelope. Mrs. S. gets started on the letter as soon as Mr. S. is finished. Note that when Mr. S. is addressing the envelope, Junior is still out after the stamp but Mrs. S. is idle. Unfortunately some idle time is unavoidable in most schedules. Note that D cannot start unless both A and B are complete. We denote this fact by using a dotted arc with an associated duration of zero minutes from the end of arc A to the end of arc B. No event is considered to occur until all the activities leading into the event have been completed. We also should not do G until D is complete (we might waste a stamp if we botch the envelope). To denote this, we use another 0-time dummy activity. Activity G can be done while Mrs. S. is still writing, but E must wait for C (by which time G is done, although G could also be done after E). Activity H must await the completion of E. Figure 5.1 is the digraph of our partial order. We will complete the analysis of this example later in this section.

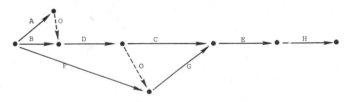

Figure 5.1

Let us now consider the problem of trying to "linearize" a partial order, i. e. draw the corresponding digraph in such a way that all the nodes lie on a straight line and all the arcs are directed from left to right. One procedure for doing this is called *topological sorting* (cf. Knuth 1969: 258–268) and is equivalent to finding a numbering of the nodes such that if arc (i, j) is in D = (N, R), where R denotes the partial order on N, then i < j i. e. the integer label at the head of an arc is greater than the label at the tail. For a given acyclic digraph, there may be more than one valid topological sort.

Algorithm 5.1 (Topological Sort)

Step 1: Consider any node in the acyclic digraph with in-degree 0. Such a node must always exist and represents an element in the partial order that is not preceded by any other. Clearly such a node may be placed first in the output order. Remove this node and all adjacent arcs from the digraph.

Step 2: Place this node at the end of the list of ordered nodes (initially empty).

Step 3: Repeat Steps 1 and 2 until the digraph is empty.

The proof of the correctness of this algorithm is very simple and should be attempted by the reader. Note that the removal of a node in Step 1 leaves a digraph that still represents a partial order. Topological Sort can be implemented efficiently on a computer using adjacency lists (cf. 3.6).

Figure 5.2(a) shows a digraph whose nodes are initially numbered arbitrarily. Figure 5.2(b) shows the same graph, before the nodes are renumbered,

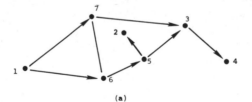

(a)

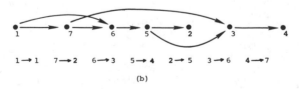

1 → 1   7 → 2   6 → 3   5 → 4   2 → 5   3 → 6   4 → 7

(b)

Figure 5.2

after the topological sort. The renumbering is shown below Figure 5.2(b). Figure 5.3 shows our scheduling problem of Example 5.4 with its nodes numbered by a topological sort; the activity arcs have been weighted by their duration times.

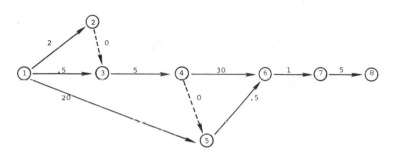

Figure 5.3

It is now time to see how we can analyze a scheduling problem like the one we considered in Example 5.4. We first collect the properties that we will use to define a scheduling network.

Definition 5.7: A *scheduling network* is an acyclic connected digraph characterized by a 6-tuple (V, n_s, n_f, A, D, W) where:

V = a set of numbered nodes in a topological order;
n_s = a "start" node, the only node with 0 in-degree;
n_f = a "finish" node, the only node with 0 out-degree;
A = a set of arcs;
D = a set of weights; and
W = a function $W: A \to D$ which assigns weights to arcs.

We interpret V as a set of events, A as a set of activities, and D as the duration times of the activities. Arcs with weight zero represent dummy activities.

For a given scheduling network we now wish to find the earliest completion time and isolate those activities that are holding things up. In practice, we might make some effort to lower the duration times of these bottleneck activities. The technique we will describe is known as the Critical Path Method (CPM). Other network-based scheduling procedures also exist. These methods have been extensively developed since 1957 and there have been occasions when they have been impressively successful. The operations-research literature should be consulted for details (cf. indices for the journals *Operations Research* and *Management Science*).

Let $(V, 1, n, A, D, W)$ be a scheduling network. We define the *earliest event time* $t^-(i)$ and the *latest event time* $t^+(i)$ recursively as follows:

a) $t^-(1) = 0$;

b) $t^-(k) = \max_{i \in V, (i,k) \in A} [t^-(i) + W(i, k)], \qquad k \neq 1$

c) $t^+(n) = t^-(n)$;

d) $t^+(i) = \min_{k \in V, (i,k) \in A} [t^+(k) - W(i, k)], \qquad i \neq n$

Intuitively, we want $t^-(k)$ to tell us the earliest possible time that even k can take place. Clearly $t^-(1) = 0$. For $k \neq 1$, the earliest time that k can take place is the earliest time at which all arcs (activities) into node k have been completed. Criterion b) above tells us exactly that. Note that the topological sort guarantees that we need only consider nodes $i < k$ in order to determine $t^-(k)$.

Criterion c) says that once you find the earliest time for the project completion, you insist that it be a deadline. Criterion d) determines the latest times by which activities must be completed in order to meet the project deadline. Note that d) moves backward through the network by looking at nodes all of whose successors have latest times computed for them.

Table 5.1 gives the $\{t^-(i)\}$ and $\{t^+(i)\}$ for the network developed in Example 5.4 using Figure 5.3.

Table 5.1

Event (node) i	$t^-(i)$	$t^+(i)$
1	0	0
2	2	2
3	2	2
4	7	7
5	20	36.5
6	37	37
7	38	38
8	43	43

We now define

$$s(i, j) = t^+(j) - t^-(i) - W(i, j), (i, j) \in A.$$

The $s(i, j)$ can be viewed as a slack time for activity (i, j). It measures how long we can delay i and still not hold up j beyond $t^+(j)$. Table 5.2 gives the $\{s(i, j)\}$ for the problem in Example 5.4. An activity with $s(i, j) = 0$ is called a *critical*

Table 5.2

Arc (i, j)	s (i, j)					
(1, 2)	2	– 0 –	2	=	0	
(1, 3)	2	– 0 –	.5	=	1.5	
(1, 5)	36.5 –	0 –	20	=	16.5	
(2, 3)	2	– 2 –	0	=	0	
(3, 4)	7	– 2 –	5	=	0	
(4, 5)	36.5 –	7 –	0	=	29.5	
(4, 6)	37	– 7 –	30	=	0	
(5, 6)	37	– 20 –	.5	=	16.5	
(6, 7)	38	– 37 –	5	=	0	
(7, 8)	43	– 38 –	5	=	0	

activity. It is necessary to start these activities as soon as possible or the project cannot be completed by the deadline $t^-(n)$.

Note that the earliest possible time we can complete the project in our example in is 43 minutes. We also observe that the set of critical activities forms a directed path from node 1 to node 8 (path 1234678) whose duration is exactly 43 minutes.

Let us now show that at least one *critical path* always exists in any scheduling network. It is clear that the longest path (sum of arc weights) determines the earliest project completion time, and that every scheduling network must have at least one start to finish path.

Theorem 5.1 Every longest path in a scheduling network is a critical path.

Proof (by contradiction): Assume that the statement is not true. This implies the existence of a longest path which is not a critical path, i. e. there is at least one activity (i, j) along this path for which $s(i, j) = t^+(j) - t^-(i) - W(i, j) > 0$. Note that we always have that $s(i, j) \geqslant 0$. So, for this arc, we have

$$t^+(j) > t^-(i) + W(i, j) .$$

Now recall that the length of any longest path equals the earliest completion time, i. e. $t^-(n) = \Sigma W(k, l)$, where (k, l) is an arc in the longest path in question. However, if $s(i, j) > 0$ for some activity (i, j) on a longest path, this means we can delay the start of this activity for a time $s(i, j)$ and still complete the project by $t^-(n)$. This contradicts the assumption of a longest path.

The activities along a critical path are, of course, the bottleneck activities we were seeking.

5.3 Matchings and coverings

In this section we will study the basic theory of an important class of problems known as matching and covering problems. Such problems are often concerned with finding a subset of a binary relation that is optimal in some sense. More advanced treatments can be found in Garfinkel and Nemhauser (1972) and Berge (1973). Our treatment will be similar to that given by Garfinkel and Nemhauser. We will consider only connected graphs $G = (V, E)$.

Definition 5.8: Let $S \subseteq E$ be a set of lines of a graph $G = (V, E)$. We define the *degree of point i with respect to S* as $d_S(i)$ = number of lines of S incident to i.

Definition 5.9: A subset $M \subseteq E$ is called a *1-matching* of G if $d_M(i) \leqslant 1$ for all $i \in V$. More generally, for an arbitrary p-tuple of positive integers $b = (b_1, b_2, \ldots, b_p)$, $M \subseteq E$ is called a *b-matching* if $d_M(i) \leqslant b_i$ for all $i \in V$. A b-matching M^* is a *maximum b-matching* if

$$|M^*| = \max |M|, \quad M \text{ a b-matching.}$$

We will not treat the generalization to the case where the lines of G have weights associated with them (cf. Edmonds 1965b; Lawler 1975).

The problem of finding a maximum b-matching is easily stated algebraically as an integer linear program. Let x be a binary $|E|$-vector defined as

$$x_j = \begin{cases} 1 & \text{if line j is included in the b-matching} \\ 0 & \text{otherwise} \end{cases}$$

The problem of finding a maximum b-matching M^* consists of finding a vector x such that

$$z = \max_{j} \Sigma \, x_j \, ,$$

subject to

$$Ax \leqslant b; \\ x \text{ binary};$$

where A is the incidence matrix $I(G)$ of G (cf. section 3.3).

In what follows, we only consider 1-matchings.

Example 5.5 Let V_1 = {a set of employees} and V_2 = {a set of jobs}. If an employee i can be assigned to job j then there is a line joining $i \in V_1$ with $j \in V_2$. A maximum 1-matching on this bipartite graph represents the maximum number of jobs that can be worked on at any one time.

Definition 5.10: A subset of lines $C \subseteq E$ is called a *cover* of $G = (V, E)$ if $d_C(i) \geqslant 1$ for all $i \in V$. A cover C^* is a *minimum cover* if

$$|C^*| = \min |C|, \quad C \text{ a cover.}$$

Coverings and 1-matchings are closely related.

Theorem 5.2 Let C^* be a minimum cover of a graph G. For every point i having $d_{C^*}(i) > 1$, remove $d_{C^*}(i) - 1$ of the lines incident with it. The resulting set of lines M^* is a maximum 1-matching.

Theorem 5.3 Let M^* be a maximum 1-matching. Add one line incident to each point for which $d_{M^*}(i) = 0$. The resulting set of lines is a minimum cover.

It follows therefore that if we can solve either the minimum covering problem or the maximum 1-matching problem, then the other problem is easily solved using Theorem 5.2 or Theorem 5.3. Figure 5.4 illustrates these ideas.

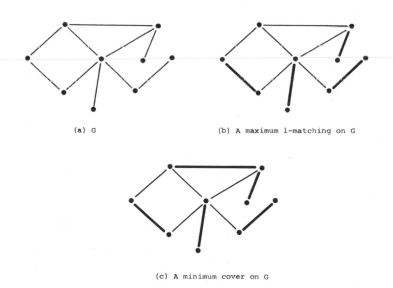

(a) G   (b) A maximum 1-matching on G

(c) A minimum cover on G

Figure 5.4

The superficially similar problem of trying to find a minimum set of points S such that each line in G has at least one of its points in S (the point covering problem) is actually much more difficult than the line covering problem.

Definition 5.11: Consider a matching $M \subseteq E$ on a graph $G = (V, E)$. An *alternating path relative to M on G* is a path whose lines alternate between lines in M and lines not in M.

Definition 5.12: A point $i \in V$ is said to be *exposed* relative to a 1-matching M on G if $d_M(i) = 0$.

Definition 5.13: An alternating path relative to a 1-matching M on G is called *augmenting* if its initial and final points are exposed.

Note that if P is an augmenting path relative to a matching M, then it is possible to obtain a matching M′ with more lines by putting those lines of P not in M into the matching and removing those lines currently in M from P. Figure 5.5 illustrates this. In Figure 5.5(a) the heavy lines denote lines that are in M and the dotted lines denote an augmenting path P. In Figure 5.5(b) the roles of the lines in P relative to M have been reversed. The new matching M′ has $|M'| = |M| + 1$.

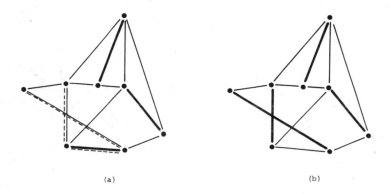

(a)   (b)

Figure 5.5

Augmenting paths play a central role in the theory of matching.

Theorem 5.4 A 1-matching M is maximum if and only if there is no augmenting path in G relative to M.

Proof: Clearly, if G has an augmenting path relative to M, then a new matching M′ with $|M'| = |M| + 1$ can be obtained as above and M could not be maximum.

Conversely, assume that there is no augmenting path relative to M and there is a matching M′ such that $|M'| = |M| + 1$. Let S be the set of lines defined by the ring-sum

$$S = (M \cup M') - (M \cap M').$$

We first note that $|S|$ is odd, since $|S| = |M| + |M'| - 2|M \cap M'| = 2|M| + 1 - 2|M \cap M'|$.

Consider the subgraph $G^* = (V^*, S)$ defined by S and the points incident with lines in S. Let $G_1 = (V', D')$ be any component of G^*; G_1 is either a simple path or a cycle, since all the lines in D' are either in M or M' and no point of V' can be incident to more than two lines in D'. The lines of D', therefore, must alternate between M and M' and if D' is a cycle it must contain an equal number of lines from M and M'. Thus, if $|D'|$ is odd, D' must be a simple path and augmenting with respect to either M or M'. Since $|M'| = |M| + 1$, there must be at least one component of G^* that is an augmenting path with respect to M'.

Theorem 5.4 suggests a procedure for finding a maximum 1-matching on an arbitrary connected, undirected graph G. Start with an arbitrary 1-matching (the null matching is always available) and choose an exposed point. See if there exists an augmenting path with this point as initial point. If such a path is found, we increase the current matching as described earlier and continue looking for exposed points and augmenting paths. Once we run through all the exposed points, which exist at a given stage, without finding an augmenting path, we can stop the algorithm and the current matching must be maximum by Theorem 5.4.

The obvious trouble spot in this algorithm is the matter of trying to find an augmenting path from a given exposed point. Can this be done efficiently without an exponential search? Fortunately, it can. Unfortunately, the various algorithms that have been developed for this problem for arbitrary graphs (cf. Edmonds 1965a; Garfinkel-Nemhauser 1972; Balinski 1969; Dixon 1974; Lawler 1975) are too long and detailed for inclusion here. Most of these algorithms involve point-labelling schemes and can be very efficiently implemented on a computer. For example, 2-matching can be shown to be worst case $O(N^4)$ (Dixon 1974) for any graph with N points. Computational experience, which reflects average performance, is roughly $O(N^{2.5})$.

6. An overview of graph theory

It would be neither possible nor appropriate for us to attempt to cover all the major areas of graph theory in this short introduction to the subject. Yet to the reader seeing this material for the first time or the reader who is not well versed in the subject, an overview might be of some value. In this section we provide a *brief* discussion of most of the areas of graph theory in which a reasonable amount of research has been done. A certain amount of arbitrariness is a necessity in this regard; we make no claims therefore that this overview is either definitive or comprehensive.

This discussion will typically consist of a brief statement of either the basic concepts in the area, the type of question typically asked, or one or more of the most often cited results.

We will now sketch the major areas within each heading.

6.1 Topological

On trees, traversals and matchings see sections 2, 4 and 5 respectively.

6.1.1 Connectivity

The *point connectivity* $\kappa(G)$ of a graph G equals the minimum number of points whose removal results in either a disconnected graph or a graph with one point. By definition therefore, if a graph G is disconnected then $\kappa(G) = 0$. Furthermore, $\kappa(G) = 1$ if and only if either G has a cutpoint or $G = K_2$.

The *line connectivity* $\lambda(G)$ of a graph G equals the minimum number of lines whose removal from G results in a disconnected graph. It follows from the definition therefore that $\lambda(G) = 1$ if and only if G is connected and has a bridge.

If we let $\delta(G)$ denote the minimum degree of any point in G then it is relatively easy to see that for any connected graph G,

$$\kappa(G) \leqslant \lambda(G) \leqslant \delta(G).$$

In Figure 6.1 we provide an example of a graph having $\kappa(G) = 1$, $\lambda(G) = 2$, and $\delta(G) = 3$; notice that G – {u} and G – {a, b} are disconnected graphs.

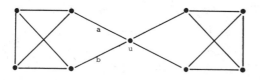

Figure 6.1

The following result is a typical and classical result in connectivity theory.

Theorem 6.1 (Ford-Fulkerson 1962): The maximum number of line-disjoint paths joining any two points u, v in a graph G equals the minimum number of lines whose removal from G separates u and v.

Generally, in connectivity theory one is interested in finding a maximum number of either point-disjoint or line-disjoint paths between various pairs of points. One application of this theory is to the study of what are called invulnerable graphs, i. e. graphs having a relatively high degree of connectivity with relatively few lines (cf. Boesch and Felzer 1972). A second application of connectivity theory is to the study of network flows (cf. section 4.5). The most comprehensive study of connectivity is by Tutte (1966).

6.1.2 Planarity

A graph G is called *planar* if it can be drawn (embedded) in the plane in such a way that no two lines intersect, except possibly at a point of G; once G has been drawn in this way, it is referred to as a *planar map*. In planarity theory one considers such questions as (i) whether or not a given graph can be embedded in a particular topological surface, for example, a plane, a torus (a ball with one handle), or in general, a surface of *genus* n (a ball with n handles);

(ii) the minimum number of planar subgraphs into which an arbitrary graph can be decomposed (i. e. its *thickness*); or

(iii) the minimum number of lines which must cross in any embedding of G in the plane (i. e. its *crossing number*).

Perhaps the best known result in all of planarity theory (and topology and the theory of polytopes) was discovered by Euler in 1752; it is elegant, yet simple, and is one of the most frequently cited results in the entire theory.

If a planar graph has been drawn in the plane, then the plane will be divided into a number of regions, or faces, i. e. areas of the plane bounded by simple closed curves or cycles. The graph G in Figure 6.2 has five interior faces, numbered 1–5, and a sixth face, numbered 6, called the exterior face.

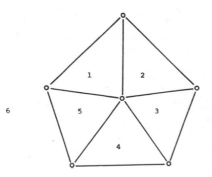

Figure 6.2

Theorem 6.2 (Euler 1752): For any planar map G having V points, E lines and F faces,

$$V + F - E = 2 .$$

Notice that for the planar map in Figure 6.2, V = 6, F = 6, and E = 10.

A second notable result in planarity theory answers the question: which graphs are planar? Kuratowski's result is based on the notion of homeomorphic equivalence, which in turn is based on the simple process of *subdividing* a line uv, i. e. deleting a line uv and adding two new lines ux and xv, where x is a new point. Two graphs G and G' are *homeomorphic* if they can be made isomorphic by a sequence of operations which subdivide lines of G and G'.

In Figure 6.3 the graphs G_1 and G_2 are homeomorphic; G_1 is reduced to the graph H by subdividing line $u_1 w_1$ and then line $u_1 v_1$; G_2 is reduced to H by subdividing line $v_2 w_2$ twice.

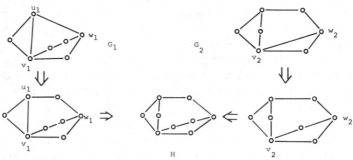

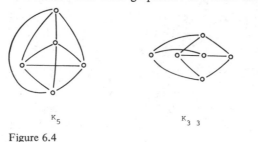

Figure 6.3

Theorem 6.3 (Kuratowski 1930): A graph G is planar if and only if it does not contain a subgraph which is homeomorphic to either K_5 or $K_{3,3}$.

Figure 6.4 contains the two "forbidden" subgraphs of Theorem 6.3; they are drawn in the plane in such a way that there is only one line-crossing, in order to illustrate that these graphs are in a sense minimally non-planar.

$$K_5 \qquad K_{3\ 3}$$

Figure 6.4

An important application of planarity considerations is the problem of decomposing a complicated electronic network into planar components for circuit-board manufacturing purposes.

6.1.3 Colorings

A *coloring* of a graph $G = (V, E)$ is an assignment of colors to the points of G in which adjacent points are assigned different colors. The *chromatic number* $\chi(G)$ of G is the minimum number of colors needed in any coloring of G. The entire subject of graph colorings, and indeed much of graph theory itself, exists because of the most famous problem in all of graph theory, the Four Color Conjecture (4CC), which originated in 1859 (cf. Ball-Coxeter 1947). The Four Color Conjecture simply states: any planar graph can be colored with 4 colors. Over 100 years of mathematical effort has failed to produce either a planar graph which requires 5 colors or a proof that only 4 colors are necessary. One of the most notable results on this conjecture was obtained in 1890.

Theorem 6.4 (Heawood 1890): Any planar graph can be colored with five colors.

The amount of research that has been conducted on the 4CC is fairly extensive, so much in fact that an entire book has been written on the problem (Ore 1967). Even though the subject of colorings arose out of the 4CC, applications of the notion of coloring arise in such areas as timetable and examination scheduling (cf. Welsh-Powell 1967).

6.1.4 Coverings

A point or line is said to *cover* any adjacent point or line. The theory of coverings is generally concerned with finding a minimum number of elements of a given kind (point or line) which cover all of the points or lines of a graph.

Let $\alpha_0(G)$ denote the minimum number of points in a set S which cover all the lines of G, and let $\beta_0(G)$ denote the maximum number of points in a set S such that no two points in S are adjacent.

Theorem 6.5 (Gallai 1959): For any graph G having p points, $\alpha_0(G) + \beta_0(G) = p$.

Notice in Figure 6.5 that $\alpha_0(G) = 3$ (points u, x and w together cover all the lines of G), and $\beta_0(G) = 2$ (points v and y form a maximum independent set of points).

Another covering parameter of a graph G is $\alpha_\infty(G)$, the minimum number of points in a set S which cover all the points of G; this parameter has been called the *domination number* of G. One application of the notion of domination is the problem of placing a minimum number of queens on a chessboard

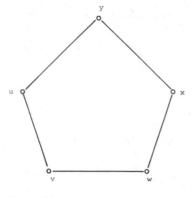

Figure 6.5

so that any other piece placed on the board can be captured by one of the queens in one move. The interested reader can verify by inspection that five queens can be appropriately placed so that every other square of the chessboard is covered by at least one queen.

A second application of the notion of domination occurs in communication networks. If we let the points of a graph G represent cities, and the lines of G represent communication links, then $\alpha_\infty(G)$ is the minimum number of cities which, acting as transmitting stations, can communicate with every city in the network.

6.1.5 Intersection graphs

In Section 3.5 we introduced the concept of an intersection graph as a means of representing a graph. The subject of intersection graphs, however, is considerably broader in scope. A relatively large number of classes of intersection graphs have been studied in the literature, a sampling of which we include in this section.

Let $G = (V, E)$ be a graph; by the *line graph* $L(G)$ of G we mean the graph $L(G) = (V', E')$, the points V' of which correspond one-to-one with the lines E of G; two points u, v are adjacent in $L(G)$ if and only if the lines corresponding to u and v in G have a point in common. In Figure 6.6 we provide a graph G and its line graph $L(G)$.

The most notable theorem about line graphs is the following:

Theorem 6.6 (Whitney 1932): For any graphs $G, G', L(G) \cong L(G')$ if and only if either $G \cong G'$ or $G = K_{1,3}$ and $G' = K_3$.

This theorem states that only two non-isomorphic graphs, $K_{1,3}$ and K_3 have isomorphic line-graphs; thus except for these two graphs a line graph $L(G)$ uniquely determines the graph G from which it is derived. Notice that

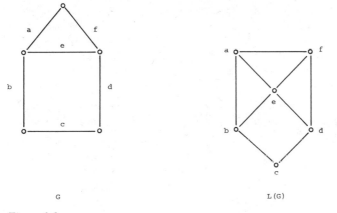

Figure 6.6

the line graph L(G) can be viewed as the intersection graph on the family of all lines of G.

A *clique* in a graph G is a maximal complete subgraph of G, i. e. a complete subgraph C of G which is not a proper subgraph of an even larger complete subgraph of G. Let $C_1, C_2, \ldots, C_k$ be the family of all distinct cliques in a graph G. Then the intersection graph on this family of subsets is called the *clique graph* K(G) of G. In Figure 6.7 we provide a graph G, a list of all the cliques of G, and the clique graph K(G).

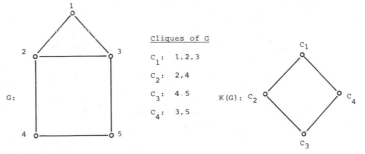

Figure 6.7

Three other examples of intersection graphs are:

(i) interval graphs; the intersection graphs of families of closed intervals (a, b) on the real line (cf. Lekkerkerker-Boland 1962; Gilmore-Hoffman 1964);

(ii) independence graphs; the intersection graphs of the family of all independent sets of points in a graph (cf. Cockayne-Hedetniemi 1974); and

(iii) chordal graphs; the intersection graphs of families of subtrees of a tree (cf. Gavril 1974).

6.2 Combinatorial

6.2.1 Algebraic
In section 1.4 we introduced the concept of an isomorphism of a graph G. A more general concept is that of a homomorphism. A *homomorphism* from a graph $G = (V, E)$ onto a graph $G' = (V', E')$ is a function h from $V(G)$ onto $V(G')$ which satisfies the condition $uv \in E$ if and only if $h(u) h(v) \in E'$. An *endomorphism* of a graph G is a homomorphism of G onto a subgraph G' of G; an *automorphism* of G is a homomorphism of G onto itself.

The idea of a homomorphism or an endomorphism of a graph can be illustrated by considering a carpenter's wooden ruler, which has several hinges by which it can be folded into various positions.

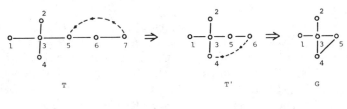

Figure 6.8

If we fold point 7 of the tree T, in Figure 6.8, onto point 5, we essentially define an endomorphism of T onto the subtree T'. If, furthermore, we fold point 6 of T' onto point 4, then the two foldings essentially define a composite homomorphism of T onto the graph G.

An automorphism of a graph G can be illustrated by considering any "symmetry" of G. For example, consider the graph C_5 in Figure 6.9.

If we flip the 5-cycle C_5 about the vertical line, Figure 6.9(a), or rotate it, as indicated in Figure 6.9(b), then we essentially define two distinct automorphisms of C_5, where the functions h_1 and h_2 which map V onto V are indicated below the figures.

Algebraic graph theory essentially consists of the study of either the collection of endomorphisms (the *semigroup*) of a graph, or the collection of automorphisms (the *group*) of a graph.

This study in turn can be divided into two branches. The first is concerned with purely algebraic questions, for example

(i) given an abstract group Γ characterize the class of graphs having Γ as their automorphism group.

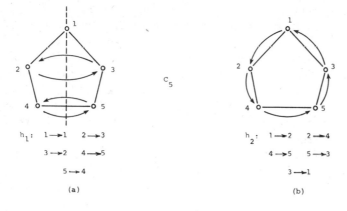

Figure 6.9

(ii) if a graph G has an automorphism group Γ, determine the automorphism group of the graph G – v or G – uv;

(iii) characterize the class of graphs having either no non-trivial endomorphisms (rigid graphs) or no non-trivial automorphisms (identity or asymmetric graphs); or

(iv) characterize the (point-)symmetric graphs, i. e. those for which for any two points u and v, there is an automorphism mapping u onto v.

The second branch of algebraic graph theory is concerned with using the automorphism groups of graphs to attempt to determine how many distinct graphs there are which have a given property, e. g. how many cubic planar graphs are there which have fewer than 40 points (cf. 6.2.2).

6.2.2 Enumeration

Sooner or later it seems that just about everyone who deals with special classes of graphs finds himself in a position where he wants an answer to the question: how many are there? It is not surprising therefore that an entire theory has emerged for handling this question, cf. the recent book on the subject (Harary-Palmer 1973).

The theory appears to have two distinct levels of complexity. On the low complexity level, the question, "how many are there?" can be answered using permutations, combinations and relatively simple counting techniques, e. g. how many regular graphs are there having 10 points?

On the high complexity level more sophisticated techniques are required. The most outstanding result on this level is due to Polya in 1937, who provided an algebraic method for counting an impressively large variety of classes of graphs. Unfortunately a detailed explanation of this result is beyond the scope of this book; the interested reader can consult Harary (1969: 180–184) for a relatively simple explanation of Polya's Enumeration Theorem.

Results in enumeration on the high level of complexity can be placed into two main categories: in the first category are results from which it is relatively easy to answer the question, "how many graphs are there having N points?"; in the second category are counting theorems which are called closed-form solutions, yet they are so involved that it is extremely difficult to determine the exact number of graphs on a given number of points which have the property in question.

Examples of the first category include results which enable us to determine the number of undirected graphs having p points or the number of undirected trees having p points, cf. Figure 6.10 and the excellent appendices in Harary (1969).

Points	Number of Graphs	Number of Trees
1	1	1
2	2	1
3	4	1
4	11	2
5	34	3
6	156	6
7	1044	11
8	12346	23
9	274668	47

Figure 6.10

6.2.3 Generalized Ramsey theory

An impressive body of results has grown out of the following very innocent-looking theorem.

Theorem 6.7 (Ramsey 1930): If G is a graph having 6 points, then either G or the complement $\overline{G}$ of G contains a triangle.

Proof: Either G or $\overline{G}$ must contain at least one point of degree $\geqslant 3$. Let v be a point having degree $\geqslant 3$ in G, let v be adjacent to points u_1, u_2 and u_3 in G. Consider the three lines $u_1 u_2$, $u_2 u_3$, and $u_3 u_1$. If any one of these, say $u_1 u_2$, is a line of G then G will contain a triangle v, u_1, u_2. On the other hand, if none of these is a line of G, then together these lines form a triangle in $\overline{G}$.

The question Ramsey was really considering concerned a generalization of Theorem 6.7, which for graphs can be stated as follows: for fixed values of integers m and n, determine the smallest integer p such that for every graph G having p points, either G contains K_m as a subgraph or G contains K_n as a subgraph. Ramsey's main contribution to this problem was to prove that such numbers p, for arbitrary integers m and n, do indeed exist!

These numbers p for fixed values m and n have become known as the Ramsey numbers r(m, n). Theorem 6.7 can therefore be interpreted as asserting that $r(3, 3) \leqslant 6$. Since the 5-cycle C_5 provides an example of a graph G having 5 points for which neither G nor G contains a triangle, we can conclude that in fact $r(3, 3) = 6$. The determination of values r(m, n) for even small values of m and n has proved to be extremely difficult. A comprehensive survey of known Ramsey numbers is given by Graver and Yackel (1968).

An alternate statement of the Ramsey problem is: determine the smallest integer p such that for every coloring of the lines of K_p with two colors, say red and blue, there exists either a (monochromatic) red K_m or a blue K_n.

This restatement suggests two generalizations, for each of which a large number of additional results exist. The first of these is the following: given graphs G_1 and G_2, determine the smallest integer $p = r(G_1, G_2)$ such that every coloring of the lines of K_p with colors red and blue contains either a red G_1 or a blue G_2. For a variety of small graphs G_1 and G_2 the numbers $r(G_1, G_2)$ have been determined (Chvátal-Harary 1972).

A second line of generalization concerns the original Ramsey theorem, alluded to earlier, and a seemingly related theorem due to Schur.

Theorem 6.8 (Ramsey 1930): For any positive integers k, l and r, there exists an integer n such that any partition $\pi = \{S_1, S_2, \ldots, S_r\}$ of a set S having $\geqslant n$ elements into r subsets (i. e. an r-coloring of S) has the property that there exists a subset T of S, having l elements, such that all k element subsets of T are in one subset of π (i. e. have one color).

Theorem 6.9 (Schur 1916): For any integer r, there exists an integer n such that for any r-coloring of the positive integers from 1 through n, there will exist integers x, y and $z \leqslant n$, which all have the same color and satisfy the equation $x + y = z$.

A good discussion of results of this variety is given by Graham and Rothschild (1971).

6.2.4 Extremal problems
The vast majority of work in extremal graph theory, much of which has been influenced in one way or another by P. Erdös (cf. Erdös 1959, 1964, 1967a, 1967b), has been based on a 1941 result due to Turán.

Let $f(n; K_r)$ denote the minimum number of lines such that every graph with n points and at least $f(n; K_r)$ lines contains K_r as a subgraph.

Theorem 6.10 (Turán 1941):

$$f(n; K_r) = (1 + O(1)) \frac{n^2}{2} (1 - \frac{1}{r-1})$$

Corollary 6.10a Every graph having n points and $1 + [n^2/4]$ lines contains a triangle.

A straightforward generalization of the type of problem mentioned by Turán is to consider a set of graphs $G_1, G_2, \ldots, G_k$ and to let $f(n; G_1, G_2, \ldots, G_k)$ equal the smallest number of lines such that every graph with n points and this number of lines contains at least one of the graphs $G_1, G_2, \ldots, G_k$ as a subgraph.

While problems of this type become very much more difficult, certain special cases have interesting solutions. For example, Gallai-Erdös (1959) and Andrasfai (1962) nearly completely answered the question: what is the smallest number of lines $e(n, k)$ such that every graph having n points and at least $e(n, k)$ lines contains a path of length k?

6.3 Computing

In recent years computer scientists have been carrying on extensive research into the complexity of a variety of algorithms in different areas of mathematics. This has given rise, in particular, to the development of a rather large number of algorithms for determining various properties of graphs. In this section we simply list those properties of graphs for which algorithms have been written, and cite the source of the best algorithm known to us. It should be pointed out, however, that these algorithms are presented in the original literature in varying degrees of completeness, ranging from quick sketches to detailed computer programs.

On general complexity theory see section 2.5 and the references given there.

6.3.1 Isomorphism

It is difficult to decide which of many graph isomorphism algorithms is best. Ideally such an algorithm should be polynomial for any two arbitrarily given graphs; however, no known algorithm meets this requirement. Alternately, an isomorphism algorithm should be fast for "most" graphs, should be easy to use, and should work for all graphs. An abundance of algorithms exist which can relatively quickly decide that two, random, non-isomorphic graphs are, in fact, non-isomorphic, including an algorithm which can be constructed from the heuristic procedure given in section 3.8.

One of the better-known isomorphism algorithms (Corneil-Gottlieb 1970) has been shown to be, in fact, incorrect, i. e. it is possible to construct two very special, non-isomorphic, regular graphs which this algorithm will decide are isomorphic. However, for "most" graphs this algorithm is correct and works in polynomial time $(O(n^5))$. This algorithm also suffers in that it does not appear to be particularly easy to use.

A second algorithm, which is correct, easier to use, but not quite as fast as the Corneil-Gottlieb algorithm, in general, is that of Berztiss (1973); the interested reader is referred to this reference for a general discussion of the isomorphism problem and a good list of additional references on the subject.

As suggested in 3.8, it is possible to construct polynomial isomorphism algorithms for special classes of graphs. For example, using a method suggested by Read (1972) one can construct an $O(n\log n)$ algorithm for isomorphism of trees. An $O(n\log n)$ algorithm has also been constructed for isomorphism of 3-connected planar graphs (Hopcroft-Tarjan 1973a).

6.3.2 Matchings and traversals

Most of the references in section 5.2 give and analyze explicit matching algorithms. The most comprehensive reference is to Lawler (1975).

Most of the references in section 4 present explicit traversal algorithms.

6.3.3 Connectivity

$O(\max(V, E))$ algorithms have been constructed by Tarjan (1972) for deciding if a graph is connected and for finding the strong components of a directed graph; by Hopcroft and Tarjan (1973b) for finding the blocks and connected components of an undirected graph (and for decomposing a graph into paths); and also by Hopcroft and Tarjan (1973c) for dividing a graph into 3-connected components.

In related papers, Paton (1971) has also constructed an algorithm for finding the blocks and cutpoints of a graph; Pecault (1974) has an algorithm for finding the weak components of a directed graph; and Moyles and Thompson (1969) have an algorithm which finds the maximum number of lines which can be removed from a directed graph G such that in the resulting graph G' there exists a path from point u to point v if and only if there exists a path from u to v in G.

6.3.4 Shortest paths

An abundance of algorithms have been written for finding shortest paths in graphs, either from one given point to another, from one given point to every other point, or between all pairs of points. For an excellent survey of various shortest path algorithms the reader should consult either Dreyfus (1969) or Hu (1967). One of the best shortest path algorithms is by Dijkstra (1959) (cf. 4.4). Most of the known all-pair shortest path algorithms require $O(n^3)$ operations; a recent algorithm of Spira (1973) computes shortest paths in average time $O(n^2 \log^2 n)$.

6.3.5 Spanning trees

An algorithm which enumerates all of the spanning trees of an undirected graph has been constructed by McIlroy (1969); this algorithm, written in ALGOL, has the attractive feature not only of being fast, but of listing each spanning tree once and only once. It should be mentioned here that an arbitrary graph can have exponentially many spanning trees, for example, Harary mentions (1969: 154) that the number of labelled spanning trees in K_p is p^{p-2}. In the face of this combinatorial explosion one cannot expect, in general, to enumerate all spanning trees, rather to enumerate what one can by spending as little time as possible enumerating each tree.

6.3.6 Cycles

Approximately a dozen different algorithms have been written either to find one cycle in a graph or to enumerate all cycles in a graph. Holt and Reingold (1970) have written a paper on the time required to detect cycles and connectivity in directed graphs.

An algorithm for enumerating all cycles in a graph with polynomial upper bound per cycle is due to Tarjan (1973). For graphs with relatively few lines, an algorithm of Dixon (1974) appears to be faster than Tarjan's. Another good algorithm for enumerating all cycles in a graph is due to Syslo (1973).

6.3.7 Cliques and maximal independent sets

Since a clique in a graph G corresponds to a maximal independent set in the complement $\bar{G}$ of G, any algorithm for finding cliques can also be used to find maximal independent sets. A good algorithm for finding cliques in a graph is due to Bron and Kerbosch (1973). Another algorithm is due to Akkoyunlu (1973). Two older algorithms, written expressly to find independent sets of points, are those of Maghout (1963) and Bednarek and Taulbee (1966).

6.3.8 Chromatic number

The problem of determining the chromatic number $\chi(G)$ of a graph G appears to be exponentially difficult (Karp 1972). Two of the best algorithms for computing the value of $\chi(G)$ are those of Corneil and Graham (1974) and Wilkov and Kim (1970). A paper by Matula, Marble and Isaacson (1972) presents heuristic procedures for obtaining reasonably good colorings of arbitrary graphs and 5-colorings of arbitrary planar graphs.

6.3.9 Planarity
Approximately a dozen different algorithms have been written for deciding if an arbitrary graph is planar. The best of these, and one of the best of all algorithms involving graphs, is the impressive linear $(O(p))$ algorithm of Hopcroft and Tarjan (1974). Two additional algorithms which consider other aspects of planarity are: an algorithm for connecting N points with a minimum number of crossings (Lerda-Majorani 1964), and an algorithm for straight-line representations of simple planar graphs (Woo 1969).

6.3.10 Line graphs
Two algorithms have been written to determine whether an arbitrary graph H is a line graph, i. e. to determine if there exists a graph G such that L(G) = H; the first is due to Kuhn (1974); the second, by Lehot (1974) is shown to require $O(p^2)$ operations. A fast algorithm was also constructed by Goodman and Hedetniemi (1974a) for determining if a graph is the line graph of an Eulerian graph.

6.3.11 Ordering the points of a graph
Several algorithms have been written for obtaining special orderings of the points of a graph. The best known of these is the topological sort algorithm for ordering the points V of an acyclic directed graph G in such a way that if uv is a line of G then u comes before v in the ordering of V (cf. Knuth 1969: 258–268; and Algorithm 5.1).

A second algorithm (Sekanina 1971) orders the points of a graph in such a way that for any two consecutive points in the ordering say u_i, u_{i+1}, $d(u_i, u_{i+1}) \leqslant 3$.

A third algorithm (Earnest-Balke-Anderson 1972) constructs what is called a straight order of a single-entry directed graph, i. e. a directed graph having one point of in-degree zero (called the entry point) from which there is a directed path to every other point in the graph. A straight ordering of such a graph is used to reveal information about the strong components and cycles in graphs of computer programs.

An algorithm related to straight orders (Tarjan 1974) has been written to find the dominators in directed graphs, where a point u is a dominator of a point v if it lies on every path to v.

6.3.12 Partitioning the points of a graph
Let the points of a graph G = (V, E) be numbered 1, 2, . . ., n and let each point i have associated with it a weight w_i such that $0 < w_i \leqslant p$ for some

fixed positive number p. Let each line ij of G have associated with it a non-negative cost $c(i, j)$. In Kernighan (1971) an $O(E)$ algorithm is presented which partitions the points of G into subsets in such a way that the sum of the costs on the lines joining points in different subsets is minimum, subject to two constraints:

(i) the points in each subset must be numbered consecutively, say $j, j + 1$, $j + 2, \ldots, m - 1, m$, and

(ii) the sum of the weights w_i of the points in any subset must be less than or equal to p.

6.4 Generalizations

Several mathematical structures or disciplines exist which treat graphs or problems on graphs as special cases of a more general situation. We mention three such areas here.

6.4.1 Matroids

A matroid is a structure defined on a finite set E. Let $\mathbb{C}$ be a family of non-empty subsets of E. We say that the members of $\mathbb{C}$ are the *circuits* of a *matroid* M on E if the following two axioms hold:

Axiom 1: No member of $\mathbb{C}$ is a proper subset of another.

We note that a family of subsets of a set which satisfies Axiom 1 is also called a *clutter* (Edmonds-Fulkerson 1970).

Axiom 2: Let x and y be members of E and let C_1 and C_2 be circuits of $\mathbb{C}$ such that $x \in C_1 \cap C_2$ and $y \in C_1 - C_2$. Then there exists a circuit $C_3 \in \mathbb{C}$ such that $y \in C_3 \subseteq C_1 \cup C_2 - \{x\}$.

A variety of matroids can be associated with a given graph G, perhaps the most natural is what is called the cycle matroid of G, i. e. let E represent the set of lines of G and let $\mathbb{C}$ consist of the set of all cycles in G. It is easy to see that Axioms 1 and 2 are satisfied.

A second axiom system for a matroid can be given as follows. Let $E = \{e_1, e_2, \ldots, e_m\}$. A family $\mathbb{F}$ of subsets of E is a matroid on E if the following axioms are satisfied:

Axiom 1': $\{e_i\} \in \mathbb{F}$ $(i = 1, 2, \ldots, m)$.

Axiom 2': $\emptyset \neq F' \subseteq F \in \mathbb{F}$ implies $F' \in \mathbb{F}$.

Axiom 3': For each subset $E' \subset E$, the subsets of $\mathbb{F}$ that are maximal in E' have the same cardinality.

A second matroid (using the second axiom system) can be associated with a graph G (without isolated points) by letting $\mathbb{F}$ consist of the family of sets of points which are saturated (i. e., incident with a line) in some matching of G (Edmonds-Fulkerson 1965).

Matroids were first introduced by Whitney (1935) as a means of studying the concept of linear independence. Today, matroids are being used to obtain a significant number of generalizations of standard results in graph theory on such subjects as connectivity, minimum weight spanning trees, chromatic number, matchings and independent sets (cf. Berge 1973: Chapter 21). A fairly complete treatment of matroids is given by Lawler (1975).

6.4.2 Hypergraphs

Let $V = \{v_1, v_2, \ldots, v_p\}$ be a finite set and let $E = (E_i | i \in I)$ be a family of non-empty subsets of V. Then $H = (V, E)$ is said to be a *hypergraph* (or *set system*) on V if $\underset{i \in I}{\cup} E_i = V$.

As with graphs, the elements of V are called the *points* and the subsets of E are called the *lines* of H. Hypergraphs differ from graphs in that a line needn't consist of just two points; a line can have an arbitrary number of points.

The standard notions of a path and a cycle in a graph generalize in a straightforward manner to hypergraphs. A *path* in a hypergraph $H = (V, E)$ is defined to be a sequence $(v_1, E_1, v_2, E_2, \ldots, E_k, v_{k+1})$ such that

(i) $v_1, v_2, \ldots, v_{k+1}$ are distinct points of V,

(ii) $E_1, E_2, \ldots, E_k$ are distinct lines of E, and

(iii) $v_i, v_{i+1} \in E_i$, for $i = 1, 2, \ldots, k$.

If $v_{k+1} = v_1$ and $k > 1$ then we have a cycle in the hypergraph H.

A number of other graph theory definitions can be generalized to hypergraphs in a similar manner. With such definitions in mind, it is not surprising that a large number of graph theoretic results have been generalized to results about hypergraphs. It is surprising, however, that some problems which had been unsolved for graphs were solved using hypergraphs (Lovasz 1968). A fairly complete treatment of hypergraphs can be found in Berge (1973).

6.4.3 Integer linear programming (ILP)

As we have seen in sections 4 and 5, integer programming provides a very general format for analytically stating a variety of graph theoretic optimization problems. Unfortunately, formulation of a problem as an ILP does not guarantee an efficient solution procedure. Only a few integer programming problems are known to have good algorithms which solve them. Most of these are discussed by Lawler (1975), and include basic network flow problems and the Chinese postman's problem. On the other hand, many other ILP's, including the Hamiltonian cycle problem and the traveling salesman problem, are only known to have exponential worst case performance algorithms, and it is strongly suspected that there never will be polynomial worst case performance algorithms for these problems. The interested reader is referred to Garfinkel-Nemhauser (1973). Nevertheless, integer programming does provide a unifying framework for graph theoretic optimization problems and a great deal of progress has been made because of this.

References

Aho, Alfred V. – John E. Hopcroft – Jeffrey D. Ullman
    1974   *The design and analysis of computer algorithms* (Reading, Mass.: Addison-Wesley).
Akkoyunlu, E.
    1973   "The enumeration of maximal cliques of large graphs", *Society for Industrial and Applied Mathematics Journal of Computing* 2: 1–6.
Andrasfai, B.
    1962   "On the paths, circuits and loops of graphs", [in Hungarian] *Mathematik Lapok* 13: 65–107.
Balaban, A. T. (ed.)
    1974   *Chemical applications of graph theory* (London: Academic).
Balinski, M. L.
    1969   "Labelling to obtain a maximum matching", in: *Combinatorial mathematics and its applications*, edited by R. C. Bose and T. A. Dowling (University of North Carolina Press), 585–602.
Ball, W. W. R. – H. S. M. Coxeter
    1947   *Mathematical recreations and essays* (New York: Macmillan).
Bednarek, A. – C. Taulbee
    1966   "On maximal chains", *Revue Roumaine de Mathematique Pure et Appliquée* 11: 23.
Bellmore, M. – J. C. Malone
    1971   "Pathology of traveling-salesman subtour elimination algorithms", *Operations Research* 19: 278–307.
Bellmore, M. – G. L. Nemhauser
    1968   "The traveling salesman problem: A survey", *Operations Research* 16: 538–558.
Berge, Claude
    1973   *Graphs and hypergraphs* (New York: American Elsevier).
Berztiss, A. T.
    1971   *Data structures: Theory and practice* (New York: Academic).
    1973   "A backtrack procedure for isomorphism of directed graphs", *Journal of the Association for Computing Machinery* 20: 365–377.
Boesch, F. T. – A. P. Felzer
    1972   "A general class of invulnerable graphs", *Networks* 2: 261–283.
Boland, J. – C. Lekkerkerker
    1962   "Representation of a finite graph by a set of intervals on the real line", *Fundamental Mathematics* 51: 45–64.
Bron, D. – J. Kerbosch
    1973   "Algorithm 457 finding all cliques of an undirected graph", *Communications of the Association for Computing Machinery* 16: 575–577.
Busacker, R. G. – T. L. Saaty
    1965   *Finite graphs and networks: An introduction with applications* (New York: McGraw-Hill).

Chen, W.
1971   *Applied graph theory* (New York: American Elsevier).
Chvátal, V.
1972   "On Hamilton's ideals", *Journal of Combinatorial Theory, Series B* 12:
            163–168.
Chvátal, V. – F. Harary
1972   "Generalized Ramsey theory for graphs, III: Small off-diagonal numbers",
            Pacific Journal of Mathematics 41: 335–345.
Cockayne, E. J. – S. T. Hedetniemi
1974   "Independence graphs", *Proceedings of the Fifth Southeastern Conference
            on Combinatorics, Graph Theory and Computing* (Boca Raton, Fla.).
Corneil, D. G. – C. C. Gottlieb
1970   "An efficient algorithm for graph isomorphism", *Journal of the Associa-
            tion for Computing Machinery* 17: 51–64.
Corneil, D. – B. Graham
1974   "An algorithm for determining the chromatic number of a graph", *Society
            for Industrial and Applied Mathematics Journal of Computing* 3: 311–
            318.
Dijkstra, E. W.
1959   "A note on two problems in connexion with graphs", *Numerische Mathe-
            matik* 1: 269–271.
Dirac, G. A.
1952   "Some theorems on abstract graphs", *Proceedings of the London Mathe-
            matical Society* 2: 69–81.
Dixon, E. T.
1974   "Some combinatorial cycle problems in graph theory", Ph. D. Thesis,
            University of Virginia.
Dreyfus, S. E.
1969   "An appraisal of some shortest-path algorithms", *Operations Research*
            17: 395–412.
Earnest, C. P. – K. G. Balke – J. Anderson
1972   "Analysis of graphs by ordering of nodes", *Journal of the Association for
            Computing Machinery* 19: 23–42.
Edmonds, J.
1965a   "Paths, trees and flowers", *Canadian Journal of Mathematics* 17: 449–467.
1965b   "Maximum matching and a polyhedron with 0,1-vertices", *Journal of
            Research National Bureau of Standards Section B* 69: 125–130.
Edmonds, J. – D. R. Fulkerson
1965   "Transversals and matroid partitions", *Journal of Research National Bureau
            of Standards Section B* 69: 147–153.
1970   "Bottleneck extrema", *Journal of Combinatorial Theory* 8: 299–306.
Edmonds, J. – E. L. Johnson
1973   "Matching, Euler tours and the Chinese postman", *Mathematica Programm-
            ing* 5: 88–124.
Edmonds, J. – R. M. Karp
1972   "Theoretical improvements in algorithmic efficiency for network flow
            problems", *Journal of the Association for Computing Machinery* 19:
            248–264.
Erdös, P.
1964   "Extremal problems in graph theory", in: *Theory of graphs and its applica-
            tions, Proceedings of Symposium Smolenice*, edited by M. Fiedler (Prague:
            Czechoslovak Academy of Sciences), 29–36.
1967a   "Extremal problems in graph theory", in: *A seminar on graph theory*,
            edited by F. Harary (New York: Holt), 54–59.

1967b   "Some recent results on extremal problems in graph theory", in *Theory of graphs*, edited by P. Rosenstiehl (New York: Gordon and Breach), 117–123.

Erdös, P. – T. Gallai
1959   "On the maximal paths and circuits of a graph", *Acta mathematica Academiae scientiarum Hungaricae* 10: 337–356.

Euler, L.
1953   "The Königsberg bridges", *Scientific American* 189: 66–70. [Prepared by J. R. Newman.]

Fetter, A. L. – J. D. Walecka
1971   *Quantum theory of many-particle systems* (New York: McGraw-Hill).

Ford, L. R. – D. R. Fulkerson
1962   *Flows in networks* (Princeton University Press).

Fulkerson, D. R.
1966   "Flow networks and combinatorial operations research", *American Mathematical Monthly* 73: 115–138.

Gallai, T.
1959   „Über extreme Punkt- und Kantenmengen", *Annals University Science Budapest. Eötvös Section Mathematics* 2: 133–138.

Gardner, Martin
1961   *The second Scientific American book of mathematical puzzles and diversions* (New York: Simon and Schuster)

Garfinkel, R. S. – G. L. Nemhauser
1972   *Integer programming* (New York: Wiley)
1973   "A survey of integer programming emphasizing computation and relations among models", *Mathematical programming* (New York: Academic), 77–155.

Gavril, F.
1974   "The intersection graphs of subtrees of trees are exactly the chordal graphs", *Journal of Combinatorial Theory Series B* 16: 47–56.

Gilmore, P. – A. J. Hoffman
1964   "A characterization of comparability graphs and interval graphs", *Canadian Journal of Mathematics* 16: 539–548.

Goodman, S. E. – S. T. Hedetniemi
1973   "Eulerian walks in graphs", *Society for Industrial and Applied Mathematics Journal of Computing* 2: 16–27.
1974a   "Sufficient conditions for a graph to be Hamiltonian", *Journal of Combinatorial Theory Series B* 16: 175–180.
1974b   "Hamiltonian walks in graphs", *Society for Industrial and Applied Mathematics Journal of Computing* 3: 214–221.

Graham, R. L. – B. L. Rothschild
1971   "A survey of finite Ramsey theorems", *Proceedings of the Second Southeastern Conference on Combinatorics, Graph Theory and Computing* (Baton Rouge, La.), 21–40.

Graver, J. E. – J. Yackel
1968   "Some graph theoretic results associated with Ramsey's theorem", *Journal of Combinatorial Theory* 4: 125–175.

Harary, F.
1969   *Graph theory* (Reading, Mass.: Addison-Wesley).

Harary, F. – R. Z. Norman – D. Cartwright
1965   *Structural models: An introduction to the theory of directed graphs* (New York: Wiley).

Harary, F. – E. M. Palmer
1973   *Graphical enumeration* (New York: Academic).

Heawood, P. J.
  1890   "Map colour theorems", *Quarterly Journal of Mathematics Oxford Series*
           24: 332–338.
Held, M. – R. M. Karp
  1971   "The traveling-salesman problem and minimum spanning trees. Part II",
           Mathematical Programming 1: 6–25.
Holt, R. C. – E. M. Reingold
  1972   "On the time required to detect cycles and connectivity in directed graphs",
           Mathematical Systems Theory 6: 103–106.
Hopcroft, J. E. – R. E. Tarjan
  1973a   "A VlogV algorithm for isomorphism of triconnected planar graphs",
           Journal of Computer System Science 7: 323–331.
  1973b   "Efficient algorithms for graph manipulation", *Communications of the
           Association for Computing Machinery* 16: 372–378.
  1973c   "Dividing a graph into triconnected components", *Society for Industrial
           and Applied Mathematics Journal of Computing* 2: 135–158.
  1974   "Efficient planarity testing", *Journal of the Association for Computing
           Machinery* 21: 549–568.
Hu, T. C.
  1967   "Revised matrix algorithms for shortest paths", *Society for Industrial and
           Applied Mathematics Journal of Applied Mathematics* 15: 207–218.
  1969   *Integer programming and network flows* (Reading, Mass.: Addison-Wesley).
Karp, R. M.
  1972   "Reducibility among combinatorial problems", in: *Complexity of computer
           computations*, edited by R. E. Miller and J. W. Thatcher (New York: Ple-
           num), 85–104.

Kaufmann, A.
  1967   *Graphs, dynamic programming and finite games* (New York: Academic).
Kernighan, Brian W.
  1971   "Optimal sequential partitions of graphs", *Journal of the Association for
           Computing Machinery* 18: 34–40.
Knuth, D. E.
  1969   *Fundamental algorithms* (Reading, Mass.: Addison-Wesley).
  1973   *Sorting and searching* (Reading, Mass.: Addison Wesley).
Kuhn, W. W.
  1973   "Inverse line graphs and Hamiltonian circuits", in: *Proceedings of the
           Fourth Southeastern Conference on Combinatorics, Graph Theory and
           Computing* (Boca Raton, Fla.).
Kuratowski, K.
  1930   "Sur le problème des courbes gauches en topologie", *Fundamental
           Mathematics* 15: 271–283.
Kwan, Mei-ko
  1962   "Graphic programming using odd or even points", *Chinese Mathematics-
           Acta* 1: 273–277.
Lawler, E.
  1975   *Combinatorial optimization: Networks and matroids* (New York: Holt,
           Rinehart and Winston).
Lehot, P.
  1974   "An optimal algorithm to detect a line graph and output its root graph",
           Journal of the Association for Computing Machinery 21: 569–575.
Lerda, F. – E. Majorani
  1964   "An algorithm for connecting n points with a minimum number of
           crossings", *Calcolo* 1: 257–265.

Lewin, K.
1936   *Principles of topological psychology* (New York: McGraw-Hill).
Liu, C. L.
1968   *Introduction to combinatorial mathematics* (New York: McGraw-Hill).
Lovász, L.
1968   "On chromatic number of finite set-systems", *Acta mathematica Academiae scientiarum Hungaricae* 19: 59–67.
Maghout, K.
1963   "Applications de l'algèbre de Boole à la théorie des graphes et aux programmes linéaires et quadratiques", *Cahiers Centre Études Recherche Opér.* 5: 193.
Matula, D. W. – G. Marble – J. D. Isaacson
1972   "Graph coloring algorithms", in: *Graph theory and computing*, edited by R. C. Read (New York: Academic), 109–122.
McIlroy, M. D.
1969   "Algorithm 354 generator of spanning trees", *Communications of the Association for Computing Machinery* 12: 511–513.
Moon, J.
1968   *Topics on tournaments* (New York: Holt, Rinehart and Winston).
Moyles, D., and Thompson, G.
1969   "An algorithm for finding a minimum equivalent graph of a digraph", *Journal of the Association for Computing Machinery* 16: 455–460.
Ore, O.
1967   *The four color problem* (New York: Academic).
Paton, K.
1971   "An algorithm for the blocks and cutnodes of a graph", *Communications of the Association for Computing Machinery* 14: 468–475.
Pecault, J.
1974   "Computing the weak components of a directed graph", *Society for Industrial and Applied Mathematics Journal of Computing* 3: 62–89.
Prim, R. C.
1957   "Shortest connection networks and some generalizations", *Bell System Technical Journal* 36: 1389–1401.
Raiffa, Howard
1970   *Decision analysis: Introductory lectures on choices under uncertainty* (Reading, Mass.: Addison-Wesley).
Ramsey, F. P.
1930   "On a problem of formal logic", *Proceedings of the London Mathematical Society* 30: 264–286.
Read, R. C. (ed.)
1972   *Graph theory and computing* (New York: Academic).
Riordan, J.
1958   *An introduction to combinatorial analysis* (New York: Wiley).
Schur, I.
1916   "Über die Kongruenz $x^m + y^m = z^m$ (mod p)", *Jahresbericht der Deutschen Mathematikervereinigung* 25: 114.
Sekanina, M.
1971   "On an algorithm for ordering of graphs", *Canadian Mathematical Bulletin* 14: 221–224.
Spira, P.
1973   "A new algorithm for finding all shortest paths in a graph of positive arcs in average time $O(n^2 \log^2 n)$", *Society for Industrial and Applied Mathematics Journal of Computing* 2: 28–32.

Syslo, M.
1973   "Algorithm 459 the elementary circuits of a graph", *Communications of the Association for Computing Machinery* 16: 632–633.
Tarjan, R.
1972   "Depth-first search and linear graph algorithms", *Society for Industrial and Applied Mathematics Journal of Computing* 1: 146–159.
1973   "Enumeration of the elementary circuits of a directed graph", *Society for Industrial and Applied Mathematics Journal of Computing* 2: 211–216.
1974   "Finding dominators in directed graphs", *Society for Industrial and Applied Mathematics Journal of Computing* 3: 62–89.
Trakhtenbrot, B. A.
1963   *Algorithms and automatic computing machines* (Lexington, Mass.: D. C. Heath).
Turán, P.
1941   „Eine Extremalaufgabe aus der Graphentheorie", *Mat. Fiz. Lapok* 48: 436–452.
Tutte, W. T.
1966   *Connectivity in graphs* (University of Toronto Press).
Welsh, D. J. A. – M. B. Powell
1967   "An upper bound for the chromatic number of a graph and its application to timetabling problems", *Computer Journal* 10: 85–87.
Whitehouse, Gary E.
1973   *Systems analysis and design using network techniques* (Englewood Cliffs, N. J.: Prentice-Hall).
Whitney, H.
1932   "Congruent graphs and the connectivity of graphs", *American Journal of Mathematics* 54: 150–168.
1935   "On the abstract properties of linear dependence", *American Journal of Mathematics* 57: 509–533.
Wilkov, R. S. – W. H. Kim
1970   "A practical approach to the chromatic partition problem", *Journal Franklin Institute* 289: 333–349.
Woo, L.
1969   "An algorithm for straight-line representation of simple planar graphs", *Journal of the Franklin Institute* 287: 197–208.

DAVID B. BENSON

Formal languages vis-à-vis 'natural' languages

0. Introduction

Our object is to contrast knowledge of formal languages with that of 'natural'
language. 'Natural' languages are those used by computer programs which
accept some reasonable fragment of English or other natural language as the
command language of the program. This review thus gives an overview of
contributions from formal language theory to the design of 'natural' languages.

While the term *formal language* is well-understood, the term *'natural'*
language is not. A 'natural' language is a designed language which models
various features of the natural languages and is used as input to a computer
program. Since a computer program is the embodiment of a formal system,
the 'natural' languages are then instances of formal languages (Thompson
1966; Palme 1971). This does not imply that all formal language theory is
applicable to the particular problems which arise in constructing these computer programs. This survey concentrates on those areas in the theory of
formal language which have guided the development of 'natural' language
computer programs.

Not all computer program input languages qualify as 'natural' languages.
There must be some attempt to mimic or model the features of natural
language in a rather direct sense. While the compiled programming languages
such as ALGOL can be considered to model aspects of the language of
mathematics, this is too indirect for consideration here. In spite of the
many resemblances in design between compilers for programming languages
and 'natural' language processing systems, programming languages are
excluded from the class of 'natural' languages. This division is imprecise
but reasonably clear now. The prospects are that it will grow less clear as
continued work in both programming languages and 'natural' languages
cause the former to become more 'natural'. For prospects in this direction,
see Halpern (1966), Sammet (1966, 1972), Thompson-Dostert (1972)

and Guiliano (1972). Attempts are reported in Napper (1966) and Modesitt (1972). The opposite view, which suggests some of the problems to be overcome, is expressed by Hill (1972) and Montgomery (1972).

'Natural' languages, then, look natural, without any apparent specialized syntactic conventions to distinguish their sentences from those of the parent natural language. The programs embedding these languages serve a variety of purposes, but we consider only those programs which do some sort of syntactic and semantic analysis. We exclude work in statistical summaries, concordances, stylistics and the like, in part for their lack of relation to formal language theory and in part for lack of space. To further restrict the survey, the strictly syntactical programs such as the Harvard Syntactic Analyzer (Kuno-Oettinger 1963) and computer implementations of transformational grammars such as Klein-Kuppin (1970), Friedman (1969, 1971) are omitted. This leaves the 'natural' language understanding systems.

The 'natural' language understanding systems are characterized by their capabilities to respond meaningfully to their input. Many of these systems have a very narrow domain of discourse, but within these domains the program evidences an understanding of its 'natural' language input. The understanding can be evidenced in diverse fashions. Some systems solve mathematical problems stated in words (Bobrow 1968; Charniak 1969); others paraphrase (Schank 1973a, 1973b), possibly in a different language (Wilks 1973a, 1973b). Still others act as research assistants (Woods 1973b; Thompson 1969).

The common theme is semantical: the 'natural' language processing done by these programs is a device to get at the meaning the user intends to convey and is not a goal in itself. The programs, in the literature cited above and in the additional citations to follow, display a vigor which derives from their weak commitment to linguistic traditions. This is due in part to the non-linguistic or even anti-linguistic backgrounds of their authors, but in greater part to the stringent demands of the computer itself. Since the origins of formal language theory lie in linguistics, it is interesting to see the extent to which the practice of 'natural' language understanding programs has been influenced by the theory. Unfortunately, as we will demonstrate, formal language theory has been but little influenced by the specific problems encountered in designing 'natural' language processing programs. This is in large part due to the greater theoretical and practical tractability of problems arising from the design of programming language compilers. As the compiler problems become understood and solved at a theoretical level, one expects that additional attention will be turned to the 'natural' language processing programs. Because of the close relationships between formal language theory and programming language compiler design, and because many of the same design principles are used in compilers and 'natural' language processing programs, compilers are considered to a small extent. To reiterate, our interest is in contrasting formal language theory with the practice of 'natural' language understanding programs. The emphasis is on the syntactic portions of these systems, but this study requires review of some of the semantic parts of these systems as well.

This review is in two major sections. In the first, the main areas of formal language theory are mentioned, some quite briefly. At the same time, we mention the relevance of these subjects for the practice of 'natural' language processing. The second major section views the practice of 'natural' language parsers and understanding systems, and attempts to bring out those areas which seem worthy of attention by theorists, in the hope that appropriate theory will strengthen the practice.

1. Formal language theory

1.1 Introduction
Here, *theory* means axiomatic and mathematical theory. Thus, theory without a modifying prefix means such mathematical reasoning and results. Other forms of theory, such as linguistic theory, are specifically identified as such. This survey avoids mathematical notations whenever possible. Theoretical reasoning about formal languages is filled with detailed notation which can be largely avoided in a survey of its applications to 'natural' language understanding systems.

The purpose of theory is to provide a coherent framework unifying a body of practice. The abstractions so obtained often fail to do justice to the details required in practice, but the simplification of the subject matter often leads to deep and interesting theorems which would be impossible to state, let alone prove, in the concrete situation. The views in Gross et al. (1973) oppose those of Daly (1973) regarding the value of such abstractions.

Formal language theory has been surprisingly successful in three main areas: the classification of language classes by the complexity of their defining grammars and recognizing automata, the explication, simplification and specific construction of parsers, and in the theoretical study of syntactic structure and structural transformations. It has been somewhat less successful in treating the relationship of syntax to semantics in a realistic way, but recent work is beginning to suggest how this might profitably be accomplished (Knuth 1968, 1971; Benson 1970, 1974).

Formal language theory offers a variety of techniques suitable for use in 'natural' language processing, as well as a point of view. While formal language theory does not span the myriad of detail necessary to successfully approximate natural languages, to the extent that the axioms of the theory reflect practice, the theorems apply to the concrete situation. Choosing a design for a 'natural' language understanding system requires deciding upon a linguistic theory in which to evolve the specific formal mechanisms offered by formal language theory. Here linguistic reports such as those of Bach (1967), Nilsen (1972), Chafe (1970), Platt (1971), Klima (1964), and Weintraub (1968) offer some guidance in deciding how such a mechanisable linguistic theory and practice is to be chosen.

Formal languages are defined in terms of specific sets of symbols. Let Σ denote such a set. The symbols, from the standpoint of theory, are simply entities which are distinguishable from one another and possess no further structure. In practice, Σ may be an alphabet of letters and other symbols, or a dictionary of words, a system of syntactic categories, or a set of trees. The level of abstraction at which the theory is applied is up to the user. Strings of symbols over the set Σ are denoted by Greek letters, $\alpha, \beta, \gamma, \ldots$. The set of all strings over Σ is the free monoid Σ^*. Any subset of Σ^*, $L \subseteq \Sigma^*$, is a *formal language*. This definition encompasses far more than what many people are willing to call a formal language. It is usual to restrict attention to those formal languages which can be finitely specified in some way. A common method of giving a finite specification is by a rewriting system or by a formal grammar (cf. Salomaa 1973). An alternative finite specification is in terms of recognizing automata (Hopcroft-Ullmann 1969). Other formalisms are possible, and two are mentioned for their potential applications to 'natural' languages.

Formal language theory has been previously surveyed by Aho-Ullman (1968), Joshi (1973), and Book (1973). These have a rather different emphasis than this discussion and complement our remarks. There are several texts on formal languages, including Ginsburg (1966), Hopcroft-Ullman (1969), Gross-Lentin (1970), Hotz-Claus (1972), Aho-Ullman (1972), Salomaa (1973), and Ginsburg (1974). Other aspects of the mathematics of language are considered in Edmundson (1967) and Marcus (1967).

The survey of formal language theory in its relation to 'natural' languages in this section is organized approximately from the more abstract and theoretical to the more concrete and practical.

1.2 Definition and classification of formal languages via grammars

The formal grammars of interest here are the 'phrase-structure' grammars, which might better be called the 'immediate constituent phrase-structure grammars', since the classifications capable in these grammars are accomplished by rewritings which are local in a string, not distributed over several remote substrings. Other notions of formal grammar are possible. For earlier notions, see Bobrow (1963, 1967). Subsequently we will mention some variations on the theme of phrase-structure grammars. Since the vast majority of the theory is cast in terms of phrase-structure grammars, the unmodified term *grammar* will refer to these formal systems. We begin by defining a rewriting system as a particular form of directed graph. Rewriting systems underlie grammars.

Let $R = (V^*, P, s, t)$ be a directed graph in which the set of strings V^* is the set of nodes or vertices of the graph, P is the set of arcs, the source function, $s: P \to V^*$, assigns to each arc its source node, while the target function, $t: P \to V^*$, assigns to each arc its target node. For example, let $V = \{a, b\}$, $P = \{p_1, p_2, p_3, p_4, p_5\}$. The graphics

$$p_1$$
$$ab \qquad bab$$
$$p_2$$

$$a \xrightarrow{\quad p_3 \quad} aba$$

$$ba \xrightarrow{\quad p_4 \quad} \lambda \xrightarrow{\quad p_5 \quad} bb$$

denote such a directed graph, where λ is the null string of V^*. Formally, the directed graph is determined by the data

$s(p_1) = ab$	$t(p_1) = bab$
$s(p_2) = ab$	$t(p_2) = bab$
$s(p_3) = a$	$t(p_3) = aba$
$s(p_4) = ba$	$t(p_4) = \lambda$
$s(p_5) = \lambda$	$t(p_5) = bb$

Ordinarily in formal language work the arcs in P are written

p_1: $ab \to bab$
p_2: $ab \to bab$
p_3: $a \to aba$
p_4: $ba \to \lambda$
p_5: $\lambda \to bb$

Each arc in P is called a *production* or *rewrite rule* of the generalized phrase-structure rewriting system $R = (V^*, P, s, t)$. The generalization is two-fold: allowing the null string to be a source or a target of any production in P (Griffiths 1968), and allowing several productions to share the same source and the same target (Benson 1975a). The first generalization is of theoretical interest, to discover the limitations of rewriting systems. The second generalization has applications in considerations of functional semantics, but it is unlikely that a syntax designer would want several productions rewriting some α to some β in his syntax unless there were overwhelming linguistic reasons to do so.

String rewriting is defined as follows:

> α *rewrites in one step to* β if $\alpha = \mu\rho\nu$ for strings μ, ρ and ν, $\beta = \mu\sigma\nu$ for some other string σ and there is a production p of the rewrite system such that $s(p) = \rho$ and $t(p) = \sigma$.
>
> α *rewrites to* β if there is a sequence of strings $\alpha_0, \alpha_1, \ldots, \alpha_n$ such that $\alpha = \alpha_0$, $\beta = \alpha_n$ and each α_{i-1} rewrites in one step to α_i, for $1 \leqslant i \leqslant n$.

Due to the great success which formal language theory has enjoyed, there are a variety of more complex notions of rewriting. Each is designed to explicate some particular notion of "grammatical structure". (For examples, see Benson 1975; Maibaum 1974; Peters-Ritchie 1973b).

In another direction of generalization, rewriting may be carried out over algebraic structures other than sets of strings. A set of strings forms the algebraic structure known as a free monoid. Using other algebraic structures, such as groups or rings, as the nodes of the rewriting system leads to the ideas of languages over algebras. This idea has been but little explored (Shepard 1969).

Returning to the main theme, let ζ be some particular fixed string in Σ^*, called the *point, axiom, start string,* or *sentential string*. Then (R, ζ) is a pointed rewrite system. The idea here is to capture the notion of all rewritings which begin from the chosen point. Next, let E and I be disjoint subsets of V which span V, that is, $E \cap I = \emptyset$ and $E \cup I = V$. E is called the set of *external* or *terminal* symbols, while I is called the set of *internal, nonterminal* or *variable* symbols. The terminology of (external, internal) is suggestive for computer processing and possibly for psycholinguistics, but unfortunately (terminal, non-terminal) is the standard terminology in the formal language literature. The *language* generated by the *generalized phrase-structure grammar* G = (I, E, R, ζ) is the set of all strings $\omega \in E^*$ such that there is a rewrite from ζ to ω using the rewriting system R. This simple notion of language has resulted in an amazing amount of fruitful theory since its first exposition in the ungeneralized form (Chomsky 1956).

Chomsky (1959) first presented a complexity hierarchy of grammars, which is basically a hierarchy of the rewriting systems underlying the grammars. The *type 0* grammars are those whose underlying rewriting system is representable. In a representable rewriting system the source of each production is a non-null string, that is, a string of non-zero length. The *type 1* grammars, also called context-sensitive grammars, are those in which, for each production, the length of its source is no greater than the length of its target. The *type 2* grammars, also called context-free grammars, are those in which the source of each production is a single symbol in the internal symbol set.

A language is said to be of type i if there is a grammar of type i which generates it. If L is a context-free language, then L is simultaneously of types 2, 1, and 0. Most of the theory has dealt with the context-free languages (Ginsburg 1966; Hopcroft-Ullman 1969; Salomaa 1973) for both theoretical and practical reasons. The theoretical and practical reasons for interest in the context-free languages derive from the simplicity of structure compared to the more general language classes. This is amply illustrated in the subsequent discussions of syntactic structure and parsers.

1.3 The equivalence of generating and recognizing devices

A set of strings L, L a subset of Σ^* for some symbol set Σ, may be determined by its *characteristic function*, χ_L. χ_L has strings for arguments and results in either "yes" or "no". If ω is a string in L then $\chi_L(\omega)$ = yes, while if ω is a string not in L then $\chi_L(\omega)$ = no. Every subset of Σ^* possesses such a characteristic function. χ_L is a *recognizer* for L, in that presented with strings it determines whether or not they are in L; it recognizes L. Some χ_L can be implemented on computers; most cannot be implemented on any computer, no matter how powerful (see Brainerd-Landweber 1974). Those formal languages L for which there exists a computer program implementing χ_L are called *recursive* languages. It is well known that the type 0 languages are not in general recursive, while type 1 languages, and hence type 2 languages as well, are recursive languages. Since a recognizer for L is often the first step in constructing a parser for the language, it appears that type 0 languages are too general for any use. In fact, the situation is not quite that bad − parsers for type 0 languages have been constructed and are currently used − but this result suggests that great care be taken in practical situations.

The power of the computer can be restricted in a number of formal ways. Such a formalism is the nondeterministic linear bounded automata, ndlba. The class of ndlba, used as recognizers, are exactly those computers capable of recognizing the type 1 languages. This give an alternate characterization of the type 1 languages but does not appear to be of practical value, since actual parsers for context-sensitive languages use the full power of the computer without the ndlba restrictions. Another such restriction is to the nondeterministic pushdown automata, ndpda. These can be further restricted to the deterministic pushdown automata, dpda. It is well-known (cf. Hop-croft-Ullman 1969) that the ndpda recognize exactly the type 2 languages. This characterization of the context-free languages is extremely important, since it provides the basis for numerous context-free parsers. The dpda recognize only a subset of the context-free languages. One defines a context-free language to be a *deterministic* context-free language just in case it is recognized by some dpda. The dpda provide the basis for several fast parsing algorithms. These are of particular value for programming language compilers, and are used in some 'natural' language work. Many of these parsers are thoroughly treated in Aho-Ullman (1972, 1973). The dpda are conceptually simpler to describe than the ndpda.

A deterministic pushdown automaton consists of a finite control and a pushdown store. At each move of the automaton, it reads an input symbol and reads the top symbol from the pushdown store, thereby eliminating this symbol from the pushdown. Based on these two pieces of information and the state of the finite control, the dpda will emit "yes" or "no" and push zero or more symbols down onto the top of the pushdown store. When the entire input has been read, the last "yes" or "no" emitted determines whether the input string is accepted or rejected. There are additional details to a complete description of a dpda, but the flavor is here. The dpda needs only a pushdown organization of memory with access only at the top of the pushdown. This lends itself to quality implementations. As an example, suppose that the context-free grammar $G = (I, E, R, \zeta)$ is such that every production is of the form

$$p_i: A \rightarrow a\alpha$$

where A is an internal symbol, a is an external symbol, and α is a (possibly null) string of internal and external symbols in any order. Further suppose that in each production the righthand side begins with a unique external symbol so that reading one of these symbols determines the production in question. With these restrictions the automaton to recognize L(G) moves as follows: If an internal symbol A is on top of the pushdown store, the external symbol a is the input symbol read and there is a production $p_i: A \rightarrow a\alpha$, then α is pushed onto the top of the pushdown store. Recall that A has already been removed. If there is no production matching (A, a) the automaton emits "no" and halts. If an external symbol b is on the top of the pushdown and b is also the next input symbol read, then the automaton goes on. If b is not the next input symbol, the automaton emits "no" and halts, since the input does not match the prediction on the push-down. The pushdown initially contains the start string ζ and if the end of the input is reached at the same time that the pushdown empties, then the automaton emits "yes" and halts. Each successive pushdown configuration is a prediction of the form of the remaining input. Due to the restrictions placed on the example grammar, the prediction must be fulfilled if the input string is in L and will not be fulfilled if the input string is not in L. We have avoided many details here, but these ideas form the basis for the predictive, or top-down parsing algorithms.

Most context-free languages require a ndpda for recognition. An ndpda moves just like a dpda except that it can make copies of itself. It may be that the choice of new string to push on the top of the pushdown store is not uniquely determined by the current input, the current top of the pushdown, and the state of the finite control. If α, β, γ are all predictions which must be pushed, the ndpda makes three copies of itself. α is pushed on the first, β on the second and γ on the third. Then all three automata continue to move. Each of these may in turn spawn additional copies if subsequent multiple predictions are required. By the time the end of the input string is reached, there may be a considerable number of automata all running. If *any* of these emit "yes", the input string is accepted since at least one prediction was fulfilled. While the implementations of ndpda do not create copies in just this way, the formalization of these ideas leads directly to the general predictive parsers.

The notions of recognition by a particular style of automata give a classification of types of languages. The more complex the automata allowed, the more complex the languages so recognized. In this view, the ndlba are more complex than the ndpda which are in turn more complex than the dpda. This helps justify the intuition that the context-sensitive languages are more complex than the general context-free languages, although perhaps intuition says that the deterministic context-free languages are more complex than the general context-free languages. This latter intuition rests upon the ease of finding a grammar for the language. It is much easier to find a general context-free grammar than to find a deterministic context-free grammar for languages of interest. The theory shows that recognizing, and hence parsing, is much easier, faster and more comprehensible in the deterministic case. Since it is generally agreed that natural language surface structure is ambiguous, theory shows that any context-free formalizations of it cannot be deterministic. Therefore, the more linguistically ambitious 'natural' language understanding projects use non-deterministic devices, at the cost of additional complexity. Certain specialized 'natural' language understanding systems, working in a highly restricted setting, might well benefit from using deterministic context-free languages despite the admitted linguistic inadequacy. After all, human users are considerably more adaptable than computer programs.

This is an appropriate point to introduce the simplest recognizing device of all, the finite state automaton. In this case, the automaton has no auxiliary memory and can record only a finite and bounded amount of information — bounded by the number of states it possesses. The languages recognized by such devices are called the *regular sets*. These are important to the development of formal language theory, but play a secondary role in practice. They are used in compilers for finding word boundaries and as a pre-classification device before the parser begins its work. For a description, see Aho-Ullman (1972: 251–263) and Johnson et al. (1968). These same techniques are sometimes suitable for use in 'natural' language understanding systems in the lexical phase, although even here a more complex automaton does a more precise and detailed job (cf. Winograd 1972: 64).

1.4 Classification theory and decidability

Classes of languages may be specified by other means than by the type of grammar or automata. Of theoretical importance are the abstract families of languages, which determine classes of languages by their mathematical closure properties (Ginsburg 1969, 1974). For example, the closure properties can be used to characterize a class of languages in terms of a single simple language in the class. Another method of classifying languages is by various transformational schemes. Some of these methods are explicated in section 1.5. The classification methods, of themselves, are not particularly relevant to 'natural' language processing, although the operations on language used in a classificational scheme are often suggestive.

Standard classification methods include the use of normal form grammars. The idea is to show that each language of type x has a normal form grammar so that further theorems about type x languages need refer to only the normal form grammars. These results have been extended to the point that even type 0 grammars look almost like context-free grammars (Savitch 1973; Stanat 1972). One such normal form is the Greibach form for context-free grammars. A grammar is in Greibach form if each production of the grammar is in the form $A \to a\alpha$ where A is an internal symbol, a is an external symbol and α is a (possibly null) string of internal symbols. The previous discussion of pushdown automata shows why this normal form is useful. The specification of a ndpda to recognize the language of a Greibach form grammar is particularly easy: for each production, $A \to a\alpha$, set up the ndpda so that when it reads a from the input while taking A off the pushdown, it then pushes the prediction α onto the pushdown store. While valuable to the theory, in practice the normal form grammars are overly restrictive and 'natural' language understanding system designers have discovered no benefit to using them. The primary difficulty is that the normal form often spoils the intuitively correct syntactic structures assigned to the strings in the language. Some normal forms do not change the syntactic structures too much, but there are few published results (Gray-Harrison 1972; Benson 1975b).

Another collection of theoretical results are the questions of decidability. For example, is there an algorithm which, when presented with two context-free grammars, will determine whether or not $L(G_1) = L(G_2)$? In this case it has been proved that there is no such algorithm, and the equality problem for context-free languages is *undecidable*. For a recent compendium of decidable and undecidable problems for the Chomsky hierarchy of languages, see Salomaa (1973: 283). The lack of decidability for a particular problem is a warning to the practitioner not to try to solve the problem. For example, define two grammars to be *weakly equivalent* in case they both generate the same language. This definition is without practical value, since there is no way to decide if two grammars are weakly equivalent or not. Such results' only impact in practice is that the design of computer programs should not require a solution to undecidable problems. But even in cases like the weak equivalence of grammars, two particular grammars under consideration may be sufficiently related and understood that, in that particular case, the weak equivalence can be decided. The general undecidability simply says that there is no general algorithm which will work in all cases.

1.5 Syntactic structure

The syntactic structures generated by context-free grammars are well-known, being the trees describing the immediate constituent phrase structure analysis of each string in the language. These trees depend essentially upon the productions of the underlying rewriting system. A variety of theoretical questions arise in considering syntactic structures, many of them motivated by the applications to programming language compilers, 'natural' language understanding systems, Chomskian transformation grammar as well as the theoretical motivations of language classification and the relations between syntax and semantics for formal languages. Among these theoretical questions are: Can the notion of syntactic structure be generalized beyond context-free? What are suitable syntactic structure transformations and how may they be classified? Is there a suitable complexity theory for syntactic structure transformations? How does this relate to semantics? Many of these questions appear to be rather directly motivated by the practice of syntax-directed systems such as compilers and some 'natural' language understanding systems. We begin with the generalized rewriting systems introduced in section 1.1.

There is a natural notion of syntactic structure for generalized rewriting systems (Benson 1975a). That the notion is the correct one is reinforced by the fact that the same notion has been defined in three disparate ways. The

108   David B. Benson

first is the idea of interchanging the order of rewrite rule applications whenever the rewrite rule applications do not interact (Griffiths 1968). The second
is to adduce an equivalence relation on derivations, called similarity, such
that two derivations are similar if they are only "inessential" variations of
one another (Hotz 1966). These two notions are rigorously defined and
shown to be equivalent by Benson (1975a). The third notion is semantic
equivalence. Benson (1970a) has shown that with a general notion of
semantics two derivations are semantically equivalent if and only if they are
similar. There are certain technical restrictions on the rewrite system in this
case, but the point is nonetheless sufficiently well made. Finally, it can be
shown that in the case of context-free grammars, syntactic structures
defined by similarity are isomorphic to the usual notion of tree as syntactic
structure.

Griffiths (1968) has given general conditions under which these syntactic
structures possess canonical, or leftmost, representations. The lack of canonical
representations arises from the interaction of rewrite rules in the form $\alpha \rightarrow \lambda$
and those in the form $\lambda \rightarrow \beta$, where λ is the null string and α, β are arbitrary
strings. Since type 0 grammars exclude rewrite rules of the form $\lambda \rightarrow \beta$,
Griffiths' results show that every syntactic structure of practical interest can
be uniquely represented by either a leftmost derivation or a rightmost derivation. This general result justifies the use of leftmost and rightmost derivations
as syntactic structure representations in the design of parsers.

All of these ideas find their most elegant expression in terms of categorical
algebra. Hotz (1966), Schnorr (1969), Schnorr-Walter (1969), Walter (1970),
Benson (1970a, 1970b), Walter (1974), and Benson (1975a) all use this tool.
In this view, the collection of syntactic structures generated by a rewrite
system forms a category. This naturally leads to considering the homomorphisms
between categories, called functors, as a form of syntactic structure transformation. The functors have a simple structure which is sufficiently rich so
that some interesting theoretical results can be obtained. This transformational
work is done on more restrictive grammars and will be mentioned later. Additional results could be obtained in the general setting, although the practical
implications are not obvious. Results of this type, using graph-theoretic rather
than category theoretic results, are in Buttelmann (1975). Formal power
series approximations for type 0 languages appear in Stanat (1972). The
primary interest in generalized rewriting systems is the theoretical interest in
pushing each concept to its most general form to find the necessary conditions for its existence. Often, these generalizations suggest other results of
more practical interest, which is indeed the case with the explorations of
syntactic structures in generalized rewriting systems.

The representable rewriting systems underlie the type 0 grammars. Since there are no rewrite rules of the form $\lambda \to \beta$, some rather surprising and profound results can be obtained, beyond the existence of leftmost and rightmost representatives for syntactic structures. Fixing a syntactic structure, the set of all "prefixes" of that structure form a distributive lattice (Benson 1975a). As an illustration, consider the tree

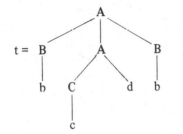

The trees

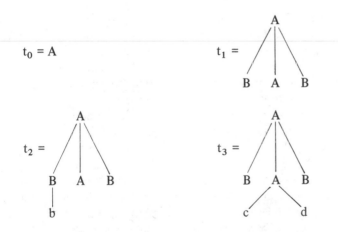

are all prefixes of t. Indeed, t_0 is a prefix of t_1, t_2, and t_3, t_1 is a prefix of t_2 and t_3, while neither of t_2 and t_3 are prefixes of the other. Fixing the tree t, the collection of all trees which are prefixes of t, including t itself, form a partially ordered set which in fact has the additional property of being a distributive lattice. One can go further. Call a rewriting system *semithue* if every rewrite rule is of the form $\alpha \to \beta$ with α, β non-null strings. As Walter (1974) has shown, the collection of all syntactic structures for a semithue rewriting system, ordered by "prefix", forms a meet semi-lattice. That is, every pair of syntactic structures which begin at a common string have a greatest lower bound prefix. These facts imply that this collection forms a topology (Walter 1974) and, therefore, the continuous functions from one grammar to another are syntactic structure transformations (Kuroda 1969, 1973a, 1973b). The interesting topologies on syntactic structures are T_0-topologies, which suggests interesting connections with the semantic topologies of Scott (1972). While of no immediate practical import, the continuous transformations and connections to semantics offer promise in the simplification and unification of structural transformations and semantics.

The context-sensitive grammars offer particularly difficult problems in both theory and practice. The practical problems are primarily in finding decent parsers for context-sensitive grammars. Woods (1970a), Kuno (1967), and Hays (1967: 148–151) all describe parsers, but they appear to be remarkably slow. There is a deeper difficulty, relating to the proper notion of syntactic structure for the context-sensitive systems. Benson (1970a) shows that, on semantic grounds, there are at least three different notions of syntactic structure for context-sensitive grammars.

The first is exactly the notion obtained when considering general rewriting systems. It is generally agreed that this is an inappropriate definition. It fails to capture the idea of a context-free rule restricted to a particular context. The other two notions both do relate to this idea of restricting a context-free rule. In both cases, the productions are written $A \to \beta/\gamma\_\delta$, to be thought of as the context-free production $A \to \beta$ restricted to the left context γ and the right context δ. The semantic difference between the two notions is in the allowed interpretations to functional semantics. In the most restrictive case, the functional semantics depends only on the context-free portion of the production $A \to \beta$. Benson (1970a) shows that in this case the syntactic structures are exactly the trees of the underlying context-free grammar. Naturally not every tree of the underlying context-free grammar is an allowable syntactic structure of the context-sensitive system, since not every such tree meets the context restrictions. In the less restrictive case, the functional semantics depends on the entire context-sensitive rule $A \to \beta/\gamma\_\delta$. Due to the inversions between syntax and semantics, this results in a more restrictive notion of syntactic structure. Benson (1970a) claims that these correspond to Kuno's (1967) trees augmented by quadruples of integers at each node. Equality of syntactic structure means in this case that the trees are equal and so are the quadruples of each tree node. Woods (1970a) claims his parser and Kuno's are structurally equivalent and further that such augmented trees constitute the correct notion of context-sensitive syntactic structure. The semantical analysis in Benson (1970a) substantiates this claim.

Reiterating, Benson's "type two context-sensitive" appears to be the proper notion of context-sensitive syntactic structure when the context is used in an essential way. Peters and Ritchie (1973b) offer an entirely different view of context-sensitive systems. In this interpretation the context-sensitive grammars are capable of no more than the context-free grammars. They claim that linguists have used context-sensitivity "purely to simplify grammars and to avoid the introduction of ad hoc grammatical categories, i. e., solely for reasons of strong generative capacity and never because of weak generative capacity". Perhaps, then, between the theoretical work of Benson (1970a) and Peters and Ritchie (1973b), the question of context-sensitive syntactic structure has been settled. A thorough discussion of other problems and results on context-sensitive languages may be found in Book (1973). As Woods' (1970a) parser and Kuno's (1967) parser show, using context-sensitive productions in an essential way results in a slow parser. The functional semantics possible in such systems appears to be more general than can currently be exploited in practical work. This suggests that context-sensitivity, while theoretically interesting, is not suitable for use in programming language compilers or 'natural' language understanding systems. The tree automata reviewed in section 1.6 provide a clearer and computationally better way to treat context restrictions.

The context-free syntactic structures are well-known: trees determined by the rewrite rules. These structures offer considerable visual appeal which greatly aids in understanding the actions of grammars and parsers. The fundamental reason for this is the fact that only one node of the tree is scanned at a time, for it is only single nodes which are rewritten. On the parsing side, only one node must be found to group together its immediate constituents. There are substantial semantic grounds for the appeal of trees. When computing a function, either by hand or by machine, one passes to the function computer the sequence of arguments at which the functional value is to be found. For example, the function $f(x, y) = x + y$ requires a sequence of two arguments while $g(x, y, z) = x \cdot y - 2z$ requires a sequence of three arguments. Furthermore, in each case one thinks of a single result as the value of the computation. This means the functional dependencies can be illustrated by trees such as

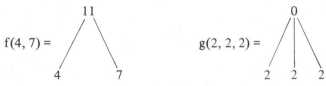

which show which arguments are combined to form values, or equivalently, which values depend upon which arguments. If the function results in a sequence of values, the situation is more complicated to describe. If one considers the pair $(f(x, y), g(x, y, z))$ as a single function, then the dependency diagrams would have to look like

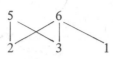

which is not as visually appealing — at least for pedagogy. It is just this kind of complexity that is found in the functional semantics for grammars more general than context-free. With context-free productions, a single-valued function may be associated with each production in a natural way. This functional semantics then gives a function for each syntax tree, which can be used to compute a semantic value for the tree. These ideas, frequently used in 'natural' language understanding systems, are more fully developed in section 1.6 on tree automata. At this point we just point out that these relationships to ordinary mathematics strongly suggest the vitality and naturalness of context-free syntactic structures.

It is these systems that are the setting for the topological ideas of Kuroda (1969, 1973). Scott's (1972) work on continuous lattices appears closely related to the semantics of context-free languages. These topological ideas may well bear their greatest fruit in the essentially context-free setting.

There is a variety of notions of grammatical systems resulting in language classes intermediate between the context-free and context-sensitive languages. Many of these are discussed in Book (1973), and additional results are in Salomaa (1973: 143–193, 252–260). A primary reason for introducing these intermediate grammatical devices is to formalize certain features of programming languages which cannot be specified by the use of context-free grammars. For example, in programming languages such as ALGOL, the variable identifiers must be declared before they are used in computational expressions. The declaration specifies the type of the identifiers, so that the computational expressions are then unambiguous.

Similar restrictions exist in some 'natural' language understanding programs, for example, the REL system of Thompson (1969), and the SHRDLU robot of Winograd (1972). In the REL system, new words and phrases can be introduced at any time, but they must be given in terms of the existing knowledge of the system at the time the word or phrase is introduced. This is a useful and important feature of a 'research assistant' program such as REL, but it is necessary to define such new words and phrases, using a special definition statement format, before the new material is otherwise encountered in textual input. Without a prior definition, REL is unable to parse an input using the new material. Winograd's program is slightly more flexible. Upon encountering a new word for the first time, it immediately asks for a definition. Once supplied, SHRDLU incorporates the new word and uses it accordingly. In both systems then, the requirement of prior definition exists. It is well known that such requirements are beyond the capability of a context-free grammar. Furthermore, this relatively simple requirement does not use the full power of context-sensitivity.

The indexed grammars (Aho 1968, 1969) and the macro grammars (Fischer 1968) extend the notions of context-free grammars just enough to take care of "definition before use". This is accomplished by fairly complicated rewrite rules which give the effect of duplicating subtrees during the generation of a sentence. The duplicated subtrees can then be used to generate all occurrences of identifiers and ensure that the first occurrence is in a definition or declaration. From a theoretic point-of-view, the indexed and macro grammars are a natural first extension from context-free to more general notions of rewriting (Greibach 1970).

Another solution, considerably more practical, provides a theoretical model of existing practice, in compilers and 'natural' language understanding systems, of just these non-context-free features in designed languages. In compiler practice each variable identifier is entered into a *symbol table*. Along with each symbol in the table are kept such attributes as: whether the symbol is defined or not, if defined, its type (semantic category), and other data depending on the compiler. Similar mechanisms are used by REL and SHRDLU. A theoretical model which combines a contextfree grammar with the symbol table manipulations is the property grammar scheme of Stearns-Lewis (1969). A few theoretical results have been obtained. For a recent compendium, see Aho-Ullman (1973: 811–843). In particular, it is shown that the speed of the symbol table portion of a property grammar is essentially linearly proportional to the length of the input. The property grammar processing can be viewed as a two-stage process: first the input is parsed to form a syntax tree, and then a tree automaton is run on the syntax tree to do the necessary symbol table computations. We return to this idea in section 1.6 on tree automata.

A large variety of generating devices reported in the literature are not immediate constituent phrase structure grammars. Strictly speaking, the indexed grammars and macro grammars mentioned just previously are not immediate constituent, since they have the capability of duplication at remote locations in the string undergoing rewriting. While many of these devices have been devised to explicate linguistic features or programming language features, most of them do not currently appear to have a practical orientation. There is one such scheme which has been put to use in a 'natural' language project of long standing. These are the string adjunct grammars, which are treated formally in Joshi et al. (1972). Roughly speaking, the process of generation in a string adjunct grammar begins with a string in the language, such as NtV or NtVN, where N is the lexical class *noun*, t is the class *tense*, and V is the lexical class *verb*. The adjunction rules specify how to insert additional substrings into the host string to form new strings in the language. Letting P denote *prepositions* and A denote *adjectives*, the proper adjunction rules would derive, for example, NPNtVN from NtVN and ANtV from NtV. The theory is rather completely worked out, although some open problems remain. The proponents of string adjunct grammars claim that it offers significant advantages for expressing certain of the regularities of language, and that a mixed system of rules, combining phrase structure and string adjunct, gives an advantageously condensed descriptive tool for "characterizing different aspects of natural language structure in a natural way". (Joshi et al. 1972: 94).

1.6 Tree automata

The theoretical work on tree automata has been recently surveyed by Thatcher (1973). Therefore, we concentrate to a greater extent on the applications of tree automata ideas to the comprehension of compilers and 'natural' language understanding programs. To begin, we show how to associate a function with each context-free syntax tree in a natural way and eventually proceed to a description of the tree automata which compute these functions.

Let $G = (I, E, R, \zeta)$ be a context-free grammar such that ζ is an internal string of length one, i. e., $\zeta \in I$. This is the usual formulation of context-free grammar. We only require that the start string ζ be a string of length one so that the trees have but a single root. This simplifies the discussion. With each symbol in $V = I \cup E$, associate a non-empty set, to be thought of as the set of semantic values of the symbol. For example, if 'boy' is a symbol of E, the associated set might be the set of all boys. If $\langle AREX \rangle$ is a symbol of I, for 'arithmetic expression', the associated set is the set of all real numbers. This association amounts to giving a function from the symbol set V to an appropriate class of sets, $\mathcal{S}$. Denote this function by F, $F: V \to \mathcal{S}$. A string of symbols α receives an interpretation as a product of sets. $F(\alpha) = A_1 \times A_2 \times \ldots \times A_n$ if $\alpha = a_1 a_2 \ldots a_n$ and $F(a_1) = A_1, F(a_2) = A_2, \ldots, F(a_n) = A_n$. $A_1 \times A_2 \times \ldots \times A_n$ is the set of all sequences of length n, $(x_1, x_2, \ldots, x_n)$, such that x_1 is a member of A_1, x_2 is a member of $A_2, \ldots, x_n$ is a member of A_n. Next, to each context-free rewrite rule $p_i : A \to \alpha$ is associated a function from $F(\alpha)$ to $F(A)$, denoted by $F(p_i): F(\alpha) \to F(A)$. To be concrete, consider the rewrite rule p_0 : $\langle AREX \rangle \to \langle AREX \rangle + \langle AREX \rangle$ where $F(\langle AREX \rangle) = \mathfrak{R}$, the set of real numbers and $F(+)$ is a set with one member. Then $F(p_0)$ is a function from $\mathfrak{R} \times F(+) \times \mathfrak{R}$ to $\mathfrak{R}$. That is, $F(p_0)$ takes two real numbers as arguments and produces a real number as a result, in particular, $F(p_0)$ sums its arguments, where $F(+)$ is a dummy argument thrown in for technical reasons we won't go into here. Writing f for $F(p_0)$, $f(x, y) = x + y$, leaving out the dummy argument.

The context-free syntax trees then specify a function by the composition of the individual functions associated with each rewrite rule. Continuing the $\langle AREX \rangle$ example, the sentence $7 + 4 + 3$ has an analysis:

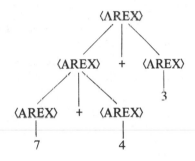

Slightly imprecisely, the associated function is $f(f(7, 4), 3) = (7 + 4) + 3$, giving the value 14 at the root of the tree. We have used a numerical example simply because it is shorter than a symbolic example. The functions associated with context-free rules are completely arbitrary, and may be thought of as computing numbers, truth values, answers to questions, etc., whatever the semantics of interest may be.

These ideas of functional semantics were first expressed, as far as I know, by Thompson (1966). That paper considered problems of semantics for 'natural' languages with essentially these formalisms, which provide a highly advantageous method of viewing semantics in the abstract. It is these abstract ideas which find expression in syntax-directed compilers (Feldman-Gries 1968; Aho-Ullman 1972, 1973), and in the syntax-directed 'natural' language understanding programs such as Coles (1972), Thompson (1969), Woods (1973b), Winograd (1972), and others.

Tree automata explicate the step-by-step process of computing a function defined on a tree. Continuing the $\langle AREX \rangle$ example, we describe how a tree automaton computes the value 14 from the tree for $7 + 4 + 3$ before considering how tree automata are defined in general. Writing the semantic values computed in parentheses, the tree is initialized to

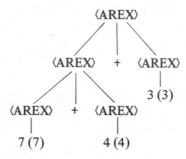

where the '7' in front of the parenthesis is an external symbol, while the '7' inside the parenthesis denotes the real number 7. The tree automaton begins at all the leaves of the tree in parallel, and moves up whenever it can. In this case, the only computation possible is to move the values up from the terminal nodes to the ⟨AREX⟩ nodes immediately dominating them. The tree at this state is

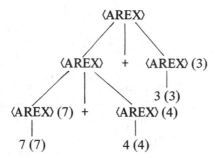

At this point the '+' node to the left is a sufficient clue to add. The tree automaton computes the result as the semantic value of the ⟨AREX⟩ node dominating ⟨AREX⟩ (7), +, and ⟨AREX⟩ (4). The resulting tree is

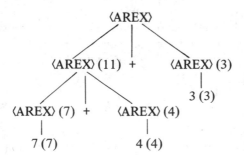

All the arguments to compute the semantic value at the top node are now present. The value 14 is computed and the automaton stops, since there are no nodes higher in the tree. We see that tree automata are nothing more than function value computers, but the explicit description of these processes gives a surprising amount of insight into a variety of problems in a syntax-directed language computation.

The *frontier-to-root tree automata*, fra, process from the leaves of an input tree toward the root. The term *frontier* refers to the sequence of leaves in left-to-right order. The moves, or calculations, of an fra at each unit of a tree are determined by the symbol heading the unit and the states immediately below the head. Thus,

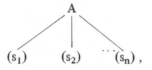

where A is the symbol at the head and $s_1, s_2, \ldots, s_n$ are the states at the descendent nodes, provides sufficient information to determine the state at the head node, A. The fra are either deterministic or non-deterministic. If the fra is deterministic, the state at the head node is uniquely determined in each case. If the fra is non-deterministic, each move determines a set of states, yielding multiple copies of the fra just as in the case of the ndpda. The fra can be used as recognizers for sets of trees, just as pda recognize sets of strings. Each state of the fra is either an "accept" state or a "reject" state. After the fra has computed on a tree t, the state at the root of the tree t determines whether the tree is accepted or rejected. A theoretical result which can be obtained using this notion of tree recognition is the following: For each context-free grammar G there is a tree recognizer which accepts all and only the syntax trees of G. There are a variety of results relating context-free languages and syntactic structures (see Thatcher 1967, 1973).

The fra model a number of processes used in 'natural' language understanding programs. The most abstract of these is the model for any syntax-directed process. The states of an fra may be arbitrarily complex entities, which include configurations of semantic data and output strings. One may abstractly model any syntax-directed process, such as a compiler or some 'natural' language understanding programs, in two stages. The first stage is the parser which produces the syntax trees for the input string. The second stage consists of a very complex fra which runs on the syntax tree. The state at the root of the syntax tree is to be the output string, the object program in the case of a compiler or an answer or response in the case of a 'natural' language understanding system. This abstraction provides a conceptual unification of syntax-directed processes, but fails to do justice to the complexities of the second (semantic) stage.

The fra provide quite a nice model for one portion of the semantic stage used in many compilers and 'natural' language understanding systems. This is the 'semantic rejection' method, also called semantic checking, semantic acceptance, or similar terms. The basic idea is that the syntactic rules are stated in greater generality than the understanding component will support. The semantic restrictions are used to remove partial or complete parses which fail to satisfy the semantic constraints (Simmons 1970).

The resulting system is conceptually simpler than one in which the selection criteria are placed directly in the grammar, which seems to result in a grammar overloaded with features, context-dependent rules and other complex devices. In the semantic rejection method, the parser does the first stage of rejecting strings which are syntactically ill-formed by the criteria of the grammar and the semantic rejection processor eliminates some of these in a second processing stage. In practice these two stages are often intertwined, but conceptually they may be viewed as distinct, serially connected processes, first the parser to find trees, and then the semantic rejection process to eliminate semantically unreasonable structures.

We illustrate how semantic rejection might be accomplished by an fra. Suppose the grammar contains the rules NP → Adj NP, NP → Noun. The input *colorless green ideas* parses to

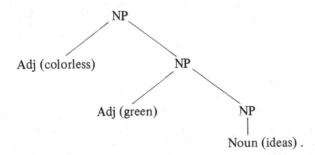

The lexical entities, *colorless*, *green*, and *ideas*, are treated as the initial states of the fra implementing the semantic rejection. More accurately, the semantic correspondents of the lexical entities constitute the initial states. After the fra moves *ideas* to the immediately ascendent NP, resulting in NP (ideas), the semantic acceptability of *green ideas* is then checked. If the fra is designed to reject this slang phrase, then the state at the dominating NP is *reject*, which the fra then passes to all higher nodes. Otherwise, the fra accepts *green ideas*

and its semantic correspondent, paraphrasable as 'new, unformed ideas', becomes the state at the dominating NP. Continuing in this way, the fra either accepts or rejects the entire phrase, depending upon the designer's intentions for the semantic rejection fra, typically the amount and type of understanding evidenced by subsequent stages of the system.

To illustrate the theorems applicable to semantic rejection techniques, let U be a set of trees and define $fr(U)$ to be the set of strings obtained by finding the frontier of every tree in U. If U is the set of syntax trees of a context-free grammar G, then clearly $fr(U) = L(G)$. It can be shown that if U is the set of trees recognized by an fra, then $fr(U)$ is a context-free language. Now let G be a context-free grammar and let U be the set of trees accepted by a 'semantic rejection' fra. Then the set of input strings accepted both by the parser for G and by the semantic rejection fra is the set $L(G) \cap fr(U)$. In general, the intersection of two context-free languages is not context-free, and this demonstrates that semantic rejection techniques are more powerful than context-free grammars. However, no additional computing power beyond type 0 grammars is created by this division into grammar and fra, but the two stage process is much clearer than a corresponding type 0 grammar.

Another use of fra is the explication of semantic type processing and define-before-use restrictions. In this case the abstract states of the fra are symbol tables. As the automaton moves up the tree, it combines the attributes of symbols in the various argument symbol tables. If, when the root of the tree is reached, all symbols are properly defined and no semantic type restrictions are violated, the input is accepted. Otherwise, the input is rejected and in a compiler application an error message is printed. For further details, see Aho-Ullman (1973: 811 843). This technique seems to offer considerable explanatory power for the introduction of new words in the style of SHRDLU (Winograd 1972). It does not explain the processes used in an extensible grammar system such as REL (Thompson 1969) or ENT (Benson 1973).

The other form of tree automaton is the root-to-frontier automaton, rfa. The deterministic rfa are not very powerful devices by themselves. The non-deterministic rfa recognize the same sets as the non-deterministic fra, however. The most interesting use of the rfa is in combination with the fra to construct a multi-pass device. The deterministic version of these multi-pass tree automata have been considered by Knuth (1968, 1971) in connection with defining functional semantics for programming language compilers. We sketch the idea. After a tree has been formed by the parser, the tree automaton is to pass 'semantic' attributes up and down the tree, repeating this process until every node has all the information required to generate code. Since there is a path from every node to every other node in the tree, it is clear that, after a sufficient number of passes up and down the tree, all nonlocal information can be routed from any node to any other node, processed locally, routed back and so on. The first pass is usually from frontier-to-root, since the original data appears on the frontier. The *synthesized* attributes, in the form of fra states, are passed to nodes in the interior of the tree and eventually to the root. The next automaton, an rfa, takes over passing *inherited* attributes into the interior of the tree, collecting information placed there by the previous fra pass, and eventually passing appropriate information to the frontier. Another fra now uses this data to start another synthesizing pass.

Typically three passes suffice, a synthesizing pass to collect the initial attributes, an inheriting pass to distribute the information, and a final synthesizing pass to compute the desired set of attributes. Frequently, the automata need not go all the way to the root or back to the frontier, but the principle of combining fra and rfa remains an appropriate description of Knuth's work. As Knuth points out, this multi-pass approach computes nothing which could not in principle be computed in a single pass of an fra. However, such a tree automaton would have a much more complex description in general, while each tree automaton in a multi-pass device is simpler, clearer and more natural. The time and storage trade-offs between the two approaches are unknown. Interestingly, a scheme much like these automata-theoretic devices is used by Winograd (1972) in the grammar for SHRDLU to collect non-local information.

Tree automata are also used to explicate structural transformations on trees. Abstractly, a tree transformation is a function from trees to trees, which acts on the structure of an input tree to produce the output. There are a variety of ways to describe such transformations. We proceed from the simplest to the more general.

The simplest tree transformation does not change the structure of the tree. It simply replaces the label at each node by a new label. Such transformations carry a set of trees into structurally, or strongly, equivalent sets of trees. Extending this notion slightly, it is clear that each unit subtree of the input can be mapped into a complex subtree of the output, provided the root and frontier of the result are compatible with the rest of the transformation. Stated another way, new interior nodes may be freely introduced. For example, suppose the transformation rules

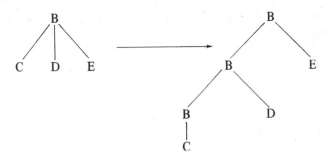

are given. Then the tree transformation carries

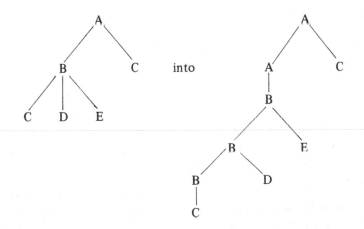

into

These simple ideas give a transformational classification of context-free grammars (Schnorr 1969) and an elegant and potentially useful decomposition theory for context-free grammars (Schnorr-Walter 1969; Walter 1970) which divides grammars into subgrammars in a manner which generalizes the algebraic decomposition theory for sequential machines (Hartmanis-Stearns 1966). The grammar decomposition theory seems worthy of further exploration for its implications to parser design. However, these functorial transformations are too limited to explicate the tree transformations used in programming language compiling and translation. The basic problem is that no reordering, duplication or elimination of subtrees is allowed.

A more general class of tree transformations are the so-called syntax-directed translations (Lewis-Stearns 1968; Aho-Ullman 1972: 215–223). This method has been widely advocated for use in computer programming language compilers and to some extent for 'natural' language understanding systems. The syntax-directed translations are tree-reordering systems in the following sense. Each context-free rewrite rule of the input grammar,

$$A \to x_0 B_1 x_1 \ldots B_n x_n$$

where $A, B_1, \ldots, B_n$ are internal symbols and $x_0, x_1, \ldots, x_n$ are strings of external symbols, is paired with a rewrite rule of the output grammar,

$$A \to w_0 C_1 \ldots C_n w_n$$

where the internal symbols $C_1, \ldots, C_n$ are the internal symbols appearing in the input rule, but possibly reordered, and $w_0, w_1, \ldots, w_n$ are strings of external symbols of the output grammar. For example,

$$A \to aBbcCD \quad \text{paired with} \quad A \to xzCDzBy ,$$

where A, B, C, D are internal symbols; a, b, c are external symbols on the input side and x, y, z are external symbols on the output side. As a tree is generated on the input side, a corresponding tree is generated on the output side. Specifically, an sdts, syntax-directed translation scheme, S, is the collection of data $S = (I, E_i, E_0, R, \sigma)$ where I is the set of internal symbols common to both the input grammar G_i and the output grammar G_0, E_i is the set of external symbols for the input grammar, E_0 is the set of external symbols for the output grammar, σ is the common start symbol and R is the collection of rules in the form

$$A \to (\alpha, \beta) (\pi)$$

where A is an internal symbol, α is a string of internal symbols and input-side external symbols, $\alpha \in (I \cup E_i)^*$, β is a string of internal symbols and output-side external symbols, $\beta \in (I \cup E_0)^*$, and π is a permutation relating the internal symbols in α and β. That is, the internal symbols in β are the internal symbols in α, permuted according to π. This permutation gives the subtree reordering. For example,

$$A \to (aABC, BxCA)$$

is such a rule, where the permutation is not separately written since it is clear that BCA is a permutation of ABC. This one rule describes the translation

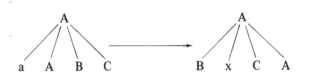

from the input side to the output side. On the (partial) input tree

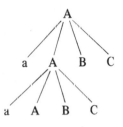

the sdts rule above effects translation to

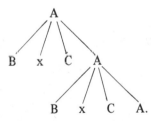

Abstractly, let t_1, t_2, t_3 denote trees and let τ denote the translation being performed by the sdts. Then

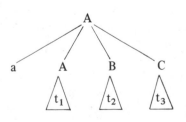

translates to

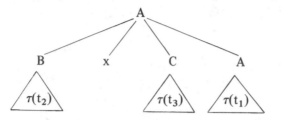

which demonstrates the subtree reordering. In applications to compiling, it is important that the external symbols on the input side and the output side are almost completely independent, allowing a considerable change of programming notation.

Consider the sdts rule

$$A \to (aBBA, BABb) \begin{pmatrix} 1 & 2 & 3 \\ 3 & 1 & 2 \end{pmatrix} .$$

In this case, the permutation must be specified to indicate which input B is connected to which output B. Another notation is

$$A \to (aB^{(1)} B^{(2)} A, \ B^{(2)} AB^{(1)} b)$$

which explicitly demonstrates the permutation of the subtrees rooted in B when carrying out the translation.

From each sdts rule $A \to (\alpha, \beta) (\pi)$, one finds the input production $A \to \alpha$ and the output production $A \to \beta$. Carrying this out for the entire sdts $S = (I, E_i, E_0, R, \sigma)$ results in the input grammar $G_i = (I, E_i, P_i, \sigma)$ and the output grammar $G_0 = (I, E_0, P_0, \sigma)$. Some theoretical properties of sdts are reported in Aho-Ullman (1972: 238–251) and in Baker (1973). Of greater interest in this survey are the computer algorithms for implementing sdts given in Aho-Ullman (1973: 730–757). It is also of interest to note that parsers may be viewed as particular forms of sdts (Aho-Ullman 1972: 263–275).

The notion of syntax-directed translation can be extended by removing the restriction that the internal symbols on the output side be a permutation of the internal symbols on the input side. The generalization is to allow for the duplication or elimination of subtrees in tree transformations. Both of these capabilities appear to be useful in describing grammatical transformation processes. It suffices to specify a rule of correspondence which shows how each internal symbol on the output side is related to some internal symbol on the input side. For example,

Input	*Output*
A → aBbcCD	A → xzCCEzBy

where the correspondence is given by

Input		*Output*
C ←	————————————	C
B ←	————————————	E
B ←	————————————	B

Note that D on the input side corresponds to no internal symbol on the output side. Therefore, the entire subtree below D is deleted when carrying out the transformation. Representing trees by triangles and the transformation by τ,

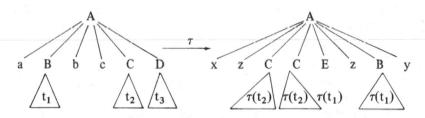

While these notations of translation are compatible with transformational grammar, the emphasis is different. The idea of translating from one language to another pervades the literature on syntax-directed translations, giving a bias to the results different from that in theoretical studies of transformational grammar such as Peters-Ritchie (1971, 1973a).

Certain 'natural' language understanding systems act as information retrieval devices in part. Conceptually, these programs consist of a 'natural' language parser, a possibly generalized syntax-directed translation which carries the input tree into a tree for the retrieval component, and a device to carry out the retrieval program generated by the syntax-directed translation. The systems reported by Green (1963), Woods (1972b, 1973b), Plath (1976), Coles (1968), Kellogg (1968), Simmons et al. (1968b), and Schwarcz et al. (1970) seem to fall into this theoretical framework. Other 'natural' language understanding systems have attempted to do deduction as the central understanding component. In this case, the syntax-directed translation produces statements in a predicate calculus which a theorem proving device acts upon. Systems which may be classified this way are reported in Biss (1971), Green-Raphael (1968), Palme (1971) and Sandewall (1971).

The sdts idea may be generalized still further to include the pairing of input grammar rules with output subtrees. For example,

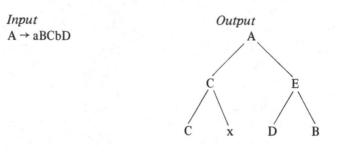

This has only the effect of introducing additional interior nodes in the output tree. While of some theoretic interest, I know of no useful application of this idea in compilers or 'natural' language understanding systems.

The sdts and their generalizations provide a generative description of tree transformations. Tree automata with output provide analytic descriptions of the same class. As is the case with languages, the automata point of view suggests methods for practical implementation. We simply sketch the tree automata view of transformations. For further details, see Thatcher (1973). An fra can be equipped with output which constructs the output tree from frontier to root during the course of the run up the input tree. Each partial output subtree may be thought of as being stored in a register. The register contents are connected as subtrees during each move of the fra. Suppose the fra has processed up through the subtrees t_1 and t_2 in the picture below, storing the translations $\tau(t_1)$ and $\tau(t_2)$ in two registers.

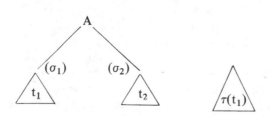

The automaton is now in states σ_1, σ_2 as indicated and the next move produces some state, say σ_3, at the node A. The fra contains a table giving the output subtree t, to correspond to the configuration

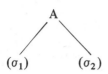

This output subtree specifies how the partial trees in the registers are to be combined with t to form the output at the node A. For example, the output might be

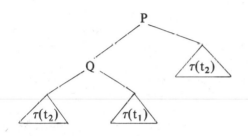

the translation of the input. This output is stored in a register, and the fra continues to move to the root. In this way, the fra with output can accomplish all of the previously mentioned forms of tree transformations. The theory is most elegantly expressed in Thatcher (1970). The advantage to this framework is the unification of a variety of results on this subject, many of which are considerably more obscure in the grammatical form.

The theoretical properties of syntax-directed translations in both grammatical and tree automata form have been thoroughly studied. Representative results are in Lewis-Stearns (1968), Aho-Ullman (1973), Thatcher (1970), Alagić (1975), Benson (1974b), Buttelmann (1974), Aho et al. (1969), Aho-Ullman (1969), Brainerd (1967), and Rounds (1968, 1970), although this list does not exhaust the papers on the subject. Worthy of mention here are the results which show the conditions under which a syntax-directed translation preserves the semantics. The semantics is taken to be functional, that is, the interpretation of each rewrite rule in each of the input and output grammars is a function in a common semantic domain. Benson (1974b) shows that there are very simple, but non-trivial, sufficient conditions under which the function computed by the interpretation of the translation of each input tree is equal to the function computed by the interpretation of the input tree itself. As a diagram,

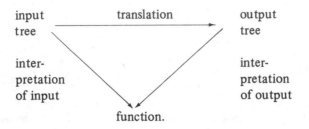

Buttelmann (1974) presents a procedure which usually finds a translation of interpreted trees in this sense.

The techniques of syntax-directed translations are of considerable value in the theory and practice of programming language compiler design. Unfortunately, the complexities of natural languages have forced designers of 'natural' languages to use ad-hoc techniques in order to capture appreciable portions of 'natural' language understanding. This seems reason enough to suggest that further research in tree automata and tree transformations is desirable. Out of a variety of theoretical techniques such as composition of automata, decomposition into subautomata and the like, some should find application in the design of 'natural' language understanding systems.

1.7 Parsing theory

The main application of formal language theory has been in the design of quality parsing algorithms. There is a substantial body of results, describing the properties of parsing algorithms and leading to the design of new parsers suited to particular classes of grammars. The main groupings of parsers are known, and the directions for further development are clear. A systematic and thorough treatment of all possible parsers is likely in the near future.

Parsing theory attempts to find one or more parsers for each class of grammars, find methods of simplifying these parsers, and to prove properties about the parsers. The most fundamental property of a parser is that it does, in fact, correctly parse. 'Correct parsing' is subject to several interpretations. Three such interpretations follow.

A parser P is *uniformly correct* for the class of grammars $\mathcal{G}$ if for every grammar G in $\mathcal{G}$ and every string $w \in L(G)$ it is the case that $P(G, w)$ is the set of all the syntactic structures for w in grammar G. Standard grammar classes studied are the type i grammars in the Chomsky hierarchy, the LR(k) and LL(k) grammars and a variety of other specialized classes.

A parser P is *correct for G* if it is uniformly correct for $\mathcal{G} = \{G\}$. That is, the parser works only for the grammar G, not accepting a grammar as a parameter.

A parser P is *partially correct* for the class $\mathcal{G}$ if for every grammar G in $\mathcal{G}$ and every string $w \in L(G)$, it is the case that P(G, w) is a non-empty set of *some* of the syntactic structure for w in the grammar G. Partially correct parsers are of interest in those practical applications in which syntactic ambiguity is not of interest.

Irrespective of the version of correctness used, the fundamental property of a parser is the ability to produce syntactic structures for strings relative to grammars. A common method to prove a parser correct is to begin with a class of grammars, prove properties about each grammar in the class, and use these properties as the control devices of the parser. The development of LL parsers, LR parsers, and precedence parsers are excellent examples of this (Aho-Ullman 1972: 334–426). Unfortunately, many parsers used in practice have not been proven correct. This causes no problem if the parser is indeed correct, but all too often there is an error in the design or implementation of the parser which a careful proof of correctness would have uncovered before the parser was implemented.

Other properties of interest are: the speed with which the parser can operate relative to the length of the input string, the size and complexity of the working storage used by the parser, the exact representation for the syntactic structures, and the size and style of tables necessary to encode the grammar. Parsing theory addresses these questions and not those of linguistic adequacy. The results in this body of theory are of great value in selecting a particular parser from among those considered adequate on linguistic or semantic grounds.

Bobrow's (1963, 1967) survey reviews early work on parsers. While these used a variety of notions of grammar, most of the recent work is solely within the framework of phrase structure grammar. The exceptions we have found will be noted. The interest here is in those parsing techniques which have been used, or may enjoy use, in 'natural' language understanding systems and to a lesser extent in compilers.

This section is then a compendium of parsers, organized in the first instance by the Chomsky hierarchy of grammar classes. As a general rule, the more restrictive the class of grammars accepted, the more efficient the parsing algorithm.

The most general class of grammars with a published parsing algorithm is the class of semithue grammars. A grammar is semithue if every rewrite rule originates at a non-null string and terminates at a non-null string. There are no other restrictions. The parser is the 'powerful parser' of M. Kay (Kay

1967, 1973; Benson 1969; Kaplan 1973a). A similar algorithm in Domolki (1968) is based on the non-phrase-structure grammar notion of Markov algorithms. Benson (1969) offers a partial proof of correctness for Kay's parser, but since the proof was not completed down to the last detail, the published algorithm contains a minor error. The correct algorithm has been used in the REL system (Thompson 1969), the ENT system (Benson 1973), the MIND system (Kay 1973) and in Kaplan's multi-syntactic processor (Kaplan 1973a, 1973b). A technically inadequate parser for semithue grammars was used in Thompson's early work (Craig et al. 1966). The Kay parser may be characterized as non-deterministic, left-to-right and reductive. Any parser which completes all parses in an ambiguous grammar is non-deterministic, at least in the sense that it gives several outputs for one input. The Kay parser does that and evidences other more technical forms of non-deterministic behavior. The parser is left-to-right in that it does as much reduction as possible before reading another input symbol. The parser directly reduces according to the grammar rules rather than using the grammar to form predictions of the form of the input. The Kay parser has been mildly popular despite its several defects. It is provably slow on context-free grammars — at least as slow as any of the context-free parsers. Specifically, its speed is of the order of k^n where n is the length of the input and k is a constant depending on the grammar. However, since n is small in the applications (always n < 100), this exponential behavior is apparently not a serious handicap. Still worse, the Kay parser will halt and produce answers on the recursive languages, while the grammars allowed by the parser are of the more general semithue type. Here the decidability results of language theory directly apply to practical problems. The theory shows that there is no way to characterize, by any finite means, all and only the recursive languages. Specifically, there is no algorithm which, when applied to a semithue grammar G, will determine whether or not L(G) is a recursive language. The users of the Kay parser perforce live dangerously, nor can one be safe with *any* parser for the semithue grammars. In practice there is no problem, since the parser is used on grammars which *do* generate recursive languages, but every change or addition to the grammar might cause it to 'run away'. Nor is this the end of the problems with the Kay parser. It can be shown that, in an important theoretic sense, the Kay parser is of maximal size in the amount of working storage (Benson 1974a). While this statement strictly only applies in a specialized theoretic sense, it is indicative of the complexity of parsing such a general class of grammars. There is strong reason to believe that one cannot do better in the case of semithue grammars. In spite of all this, the proponents of the Kay parser claim that its lack of grammatical restriction makes it a convenient tool for developmental work.

Several parsers for the context-sensitive grammars have been previously mentioned in connection with the proper notion of syntactic structures for this class of grammars. Apparently no 'natural' language understanding systems have been implemented using parsers in this class. Ghandour (1972) presents a parser for a class of formal systems which generate a superclass of the class of context-sensitive languages.

We turn to the class of context-free grammars. There are several important subclasses here. The first is the class of general context-free grammars itself. This is important because it allows for the ambiguity of natural language to be formalized, and this is a property that many 'natural' language under-standing program designers wish to incorporate in their systems (cf. Woods 1970b, 1972a, 1973a; Winograd 1972). The second class is the collection of LR grammars (Knuth 1965). These may be parsed deterministically and, therefore, both unambiguously and rapidly. The primary application is to programming language compilers, but specialized 'natural' language under-standing systems might well use this technique. The remaining classes are special cases of the LR grammars which offer additional advantages in speed and size. Again, the primary application is to compiler design.

For the class of general context-free grammars, the theory shows that, if pushdown techniques are used in the parser, then the parser must be non-deterministic. Since pushdown techniques amount to spreading out the tree over time instead of over space, it is clear that any parser for the general context-free grammars is inherently non-deterministic. There are many differ-ent parsers for this class. Those mentioned here are either of theoretic importance, used in at least one 'natural' language understanding system, or both. Palme (1971) surveys several general context-free parsers in relation to 'natural' language understanding systems. The current survey is rather more oriented toward the theory of these devices. Aho and Ullman (1972: 281–332) present several parsing algorithms in full detail.

There is an attempt to classify the general context-free parsers by the methods used to develop the parse, but a thorough taxonomy of parsers is not possible here. All the parsers reviewed here are left-to-right in the sense that as much processing as possible is completed before additional input is read. Determining what 'possible' means here is theoretically quite difficult. For some general results in the case of reductive parsers, see Benson (1970b). Techniques other than strict left-to-right (or strict right-to-left) are possible. Colmeraurer (1970) develops some of these based on generalized precedence relations.

The first subclass of the general context-free parsers are the reductive, or bottom-up, techniques. In this case, each time that the right side of a grammar rule is found in the input, the corresponding left side is substituted. There is usually no attempt to predict which sequence of reductions will eventually lead to the start symbol. Aho and Ullman (1972: 301–307) describe such a parser which requires time proportional to c^n for some constant c. Except for smaller constants, this is as slow as the Kay parser, which operates in much the same manner. Heidorn (1972, 1973a, 1973b) uses a reductive parser for the 'natural' language input to his simulation generator. No analysis of his exact techniques is reported.

The second subclass of the general context-free parsers are the predictive, or top-down, techniques. There are many predictive parsers which may be subclassified according to the search strategy used. The partial trees constituting the prediction form a search space in which the goals are the syntactic structures of the current input. As Palme (1971: 211) notes, the standard classification schemes of artificial intelligence apply to this space, giving a classification into the breadth-first methods, the depth-first methods and the heuristically guided methods. The heuristically guided methods are usually the best, since these techniques incorporate additional information about the language, perhaps in the form of probability distributions on the rewriting alternatives (Soule 1974). A variety of other useful heuristics are listed by Palme (1971: 212).

From the standpoint of current theory, the best pure search strategy parser is the breadth-first method of Earley (1970). At worst this parser requires time proportional to the cube of the length of the input, n^3. Furthermore, Earley's algorithm runs in time directly proportional to the input string length when run on a grammar which is LR. Earley's parser has been used by Coles (1968, 1969, 1972). Kochen (1969) also uses a breadth-first parser.

Breadth-first methods develop all parses in parallel. These algorithms carry all partial parsings in their working storage data structure. By the time the end of the input is reached, all possible parsings have been developed. These methods require rather clever techniques to encode the parse data in the working storage and some effort must be expended to recover the parse trees from the encoding. Earley's parser contains sufficient data to allow the trees to be recovered in either a top-down or bottom-up order. Early (1970) describes top-down recovery, and Aho and Ullman (1972: 328–330) describe bottom-up recovery. The top-down recovery requires only linear additional time while the bottom-up recovery requires time proportional to the square of the input length.

The depth-first pure strategy technique is considerably older. It first appeared as the backtracking or 'recursive descent' method (Bobrow 1963; Aho-Ullman 1972: 289–301). In this technique, a prediction is pushed through until it either fails to match the input or the entire input is matched.

In either case, the parser backs up to the previous decision point, makes the next possible choice in the list of choices, and continues to follow that pre-diction to a conclusion. Each time a parse is developed, it is emitted before the parser continues to hunt for the next potential parse. These recursive descent methods are theoretically slow; the time is exponential in the input length, time $= c^n$. The principal reason for the slow speed is that subtrees buried deep within a prediction are not remembered. If a subsequent pre-diction requires the same subtree, it must be entirely recreated. Despite the slow speed, the recursive descent methods offer considerable advantages for 'natural' language understanding systems. First, many 'natural' language understanding programs usually only require, or indeed can use, a single parse. Thus the first parse which satisfies semantic constraints suffices, and the parser is stopped after developing this parse. Stated another way, the partially correct parsers are the devices of interest in many 'natural' language understanding systems. The recursive descent parsers develop the first parse in linear time. If this is the semantically correct parse of the input, the re-cursive descent parsers give the appearance of being faster than the Earley algorithm. The second advantage of recursive descent is the ease with which heuristics can be added to modify the pure depth-first search for parses.

Before turning to the heuristically guided parsers, we note that there are a variety of methods which can be used to augment the pure reductive and the pure predictive parsers. None of these methods will cause the parser to run significantly slower on any grammar and will usually cause the parser to run significantly faster. These techniques are based solely on properties of the particular grammar in question, so do not qualify as heuristics in the same way as extra-grammatical considerations of semantics, frequency of production use, and the like.

We discuss only one of these, which may be used to augment any parsing algorithm. This is the use of k-look ahead. This technique was first advocated by Knuth (1965) and is explicated by Earley (1970) in connection with his parser. The idea is to let the parser look k symbols ahead into the input string beyond the point of active parsing. This additional information is frequently enough to determine that a particular production cannot be part of a complete parse. $k = 1$ is a typical practical value. The parser is to include a table of decisions. The rows are indexed by productions, and the columns are indexed by input symbols. The body of the table specifies whether the production can or cannot be used in a parse, depending on the next input symbol.

This explanation has oversimplified the actual use of k-lookahead, but nonetheless, an example is in order. Suppose the current prediction point is the internal symbol A. The parser is to determine if the rule $A \rightarrow aBC$ applies where a is a non-terminal symbol. An immediate check of the input, to see if a is actually present, suffices to determine whether A → aBC could possibly apply at this point. Now consider the rule A → DCC. In this case, there must be a prior calculation of all the external symbols which could possibly lead a string generated from D. If the actual input symbol is among these, then A → DCC is a potentially correct prediction. If not, then the entire search space leading from this prediction may immediately be discarded. For further discussion of k-lookahead, see Aho-Ullman (1972: 300, 306–307).

Other techniques depend on more complex properties of the grammar. In all these cases, the intent is to guide the search by eliminating those partial parses which are demonstratively incapable of completing to a parse of the input. Unfortunately, there is currently no theory which calculates the speed-up offered by these pre-calculation techniques. In practical cases it is clearly substantial, but I know of no theory other than the general results in Aho et al. (1974). An early attempt to use heuristics is described by Unger (1968).

Heuristically guided parsers have been used in a variety of 'natural' language systems, including Woods (1970b, 1972a, 1973a), Thorne et al. (1968), Bobrow-Fraser (1969), Winograd (1972), Thompson (1969), and Cohen (1974). The guidance is in part provided by the semantic rejection techniques discussed in section 1.6. In that section we considered the semantic rejection as a separate pass which is used only after the parsing is completed. Biss et al. (1971) imply that R2 runs semantic rejection as a separate pass. In other practice, it is interwoven with the action of the parser. This is easiest to implement in connection with a reductive parser, since the semantic rejection automaton runs from frontier-to-root. Each time the reductive parser finds a substring to reduce, the sequence of semantic states corresponding to that substring are passed to the semantic rejection device. If the substring passes the tests for semantic acceptability, the parser continues by actually performing the reduction. If the substring is rejected, the parser is reset to continue as if the substring was not possible to reduce. This technique drastically cuts down on the search space if the semantic tests are strong. In practice it is often necessary to complicate this ideal by giving the semantic rejection automaton access to the partial reductions already performed, so that more intelligent decisions can be made. This technique is used in REL (Thompson 1969) and ENT (Benson 1973).

The backtracking predictive parsers work from root-to-frontier, making the inherently frontier-to-root semantic rejection techniques a bit more difficult to apply. However, when a prediction actually matches some prefix of the input string, the semantic rejection automaton has the entire prediction available. It can then move up through the prediction and cause rejection to occur at any interior node in the available prediction. This allows the parser to backtrack through several levels at once, removing a considerable number of partial parses from further consideration. The ATN parser of Woods (1973a) has this type of ability. The disadvantage of predictive parsing over reductive parsing in this instance is that, in general, a sequence of many predictions, down to the frontier, must be made before the semantic fra can check any of them. Again, there is no body of theory to give guidance to the design of parsers which have an fra interwoven to provide rejection. Furthermore, for none of these alternatives is there a formal theory of how semantic restrictions affect parser speed. Woods (1970b: 605) offers comments on how the augmentation affects the speed in transition network parsing — a version of recursive descent — but these are overly restrictive in practice.

The heuristic of ordering the alternative rewrite rules applicable to each internal symbol by the likelihood of their use has been used for some time in compiler design. There are two possibilities here. The simplest idea is to provide a static, fixed ordering of the alternatives based on intuition and observation. Both Woods (1970b, 1972b) and Winograd (1972) use versions of this idea. Much more substantial is to use dynamic reordering of the alternatives based on the syntax and semantics of the prior input and some estimation of the probable course of the rest of the input. I know of no parsers which attempt this more ambitious heuristic, except possibly Woods' ATN parser (Woods 1970b: 605).

The last heuristic mentioned here is saving subtrees. It is heuristic, since not all the subtrees developed by a recursive descent parser are worth saving. Some mechanism must exist to choose those subtrees to be saved when the prediction in which they are embedded is to be abandoned. The string adjunct parser (Grishman 1973a, 1973b; Sager 1967, 1973) has this facility. Woods (1970b: 605) appears to consider this possible within the framework of the ATN parsing system, although his own 'natural' language understanding systems (Woods 1968, 1972b, 1973b) have not used this heuristic.

The subclass of deterministic context-free grammars, the LR(k) grammars, is of particular importance to programming language and compiler design. By definition, the deterministic context-free languages are those accepted by the deterministic pushdown automata. This means that they can be parsed in time directly proportional to the length of the input. Knuth (1965) claimed that the LR(k) grammars are exactly the grammars for the deterministic context-free languages. Harrison-Havel (1974) and Aho-Ullman (1973: 666—719) offer proofs of that fact. In particular then, the LR(k) grammars cannot generate ambiguous strings. While this is an extremely important property for programming languages, it seems unduly restrictive for 'natural' language understanding systems. However, for specialized applications of the 'research assistant' variety, the lack of ambiguity may, in fact, be a virtue, since the technical language admits but one interpretation in the appropriate technical sense. Sager (1972) discusses this point further.

The LR(k) parsers make use of a technique called shift-reduce parsing by Aho and Ullman (1972). The parser is capable of two kinds of moves, shifting and reducing. A *shift* is a transfer of an external symbol from the input to the top of the pushdown store. A *reduce* move corresponds to applying a context-free rewrite rule in reductive order. Reduce moves are only possible if the right side of a production appears on the top of the pushdown store and not even then if the k-lookahead forbids it. If the grammar is LR(k), then the k-lookahead shift-reduce parser can always deterministically decide whether a shift or a reduce (or *error*) is the next move to make. The LR(1) grammars are of greatest interest in programming language design. Lesk (1972) has proposed using an LR(1) grammar in a 'natural' language understanding system. LR parsing is surveyed by Aho and Johnson (1974).

The shift-reduce parsing algorithm has applications to other classes of grammars. There are subclasses of the LR(k) grammars which are of particular importance to programming languages due to the simplicity of structure so imposed. The simplicity is desired in programming languages, since it aids in human comprehension of the programs written in that language, and due to the smaller parsers required. One of the nicest classes is the class of SLR(k) grammars (DeRemer 1969a, 1969b, 1971; Aho-Ullman 1973: 621–662). There is reason to believe that the SLR(1) grammars provide the best parsing for programming languages, although I know of no use yet in 'natural' language understanding systems. Another and older subclass are the precedence grammars (Aho-Ullman 1972: 399–426; Gray-Harrison 1973) which have enjoyed considerable popularity in programming language design. Other sub-classes are presented by Aho and Ullman (1972: 426–455).

In fact, the shift-reduce techniques can be extended to some non-deterministic context-free languages by extending the complexity of the lookahead allowed (Čulik and Cohen 1973). The basic idea is to make two passes over the input. The first pass is by a finite-state automaton which determines certain regular set properties of the input string. The second pass is by a shift-reduce parser which uses, instead of fixed length k-lookahead, the regular set lookahead provided by the finite-state automaton. The grammars which can be deterministically parsed in this fashion are called LR-regular by Čulik and Cohen. As is frequently the case, the two passes can be over-lapped so that the finite-state automaton is running only a little ahead of the shift-reduce parser as both proceed down the input string. In spite of the additional complexity, this appears to be a very practical technique, since it is common to make a pass over the input to transform a character string into a string of lexical tokens. At the same time that this initial transformation is being performed, the necessary regular set properties could be computed. Irrespective of its eventual practical value, the LR-regular property is of theoretic interest, as it is currently the strongest test of unambiguity available.

The shift-reduce techniques constitute the deterministic reductive parsing algorithms. Deterministic predictive parsing is only possible on the class of LL(k) grammars which form a proper subclass of the LR(k) grammars. Even stronger, the class of languages generated by the LL(k) grammars is a proper subclass of the deterministic context-free languages. When doing deterministic parsing, reduction is more general than prediction. Nonetheless, a predictive parser meshes well with an interwoven sdts tree transformation so the programs implementing syntax-directed translations, as do some compilers, usually use predictive techniques. Aho and Ullman (1973: 742–745) illustrate this technique with an amusing translation of English to pig Latin. Gelb (1971) uses an LL parser in a 'natural' language problem-solving system. Grammatical transformations into LL form are considered in Rosenkrantz-Stearns (1970) and Hammar (1974).

Parsing theory provides a taxonomy of parsers. Within the classification, the theorems show the power of the parser and its time and storage complexity. We have not discussed storage complexity, that is, the functional variation of the working storage required as the input length grows, since this is only a practical restriction for the Earley parser. As the discussion makes clear, there are a variety of issues in parsing which have not yet been resolved. One important direction for the theory of parsing which has not yet been mentioned is to establish 'minimality' results. This should consist of procedures for determining of parsers whether or not they are minimal and algorithms to generate the minimal parsers for the interesting classes of grammars. Unfortunately, while the notion of minimality is precise for finite-state automata, there is no commonly accepted definition of minimality for parsers. Some first steps are reported in Benson (1974a). In particular, it is shown that the Kay parser is not minimal in a weak but theoretically important sense. Therefore, the Kay parser is not minimal for any reasonable definition of minimality. Certain grammar classes and parsing techniques are amenable to notions of minimality. Aho and Ullman (1973: 579–621) consider size reducing techniques which apply to the shift-reduce algorithms. Geller et al. (1974) suggest a variety of other minimality techniques aimed at the deterministic parsing algorithms.

As this brief survey suggests, theorists have paid the greatest attention to parsers suitable for use with programming languages, in part by inclination, but in large part because the problems are considerably more tractable. As these areas are completed, parsing theorists may turn their attention to the study of the more complex parsers used in 'natural' language understanding systems.

2. 'Natural' language practice

Our prime purpose in this brief section is to further expose those aspects of 'natural' language processing programs to which theory has contributed. In addition, we point out areas in which additional theory would be desirable and, indeed, appears possible. For the purposes of discussion, we divided the 'natural' language understanding systems into the syntax-directed programs and the pattern-match programs. This is a slightly artificial distinction, but provides a framework for the review. One might compare with the distinctions suggested in other compendia and reviews (e. g. Minsky 1968, 1970; Simmons 1965, 1966, 1967, 1970; Siklossy-Simon 1972; Schank-Colby 1973).

2.1 The syntax-directed model
In this paradigm there are four major stages to the processor. The first is the parser, accepting 'natural' language input and resulting in one or more syntactic structures. The second stage is a translator which converts the syntactic structure to a program in a command language. The third stage is the semantic and pragmatic component which carries out the command in order to retrieve data, remember facts, deduce consequences and the like, resulting in a collection of answers in an internal form. The final stage is an output generator which forms the reply to the input. Diagrammatically,

Syntactic-semantic component

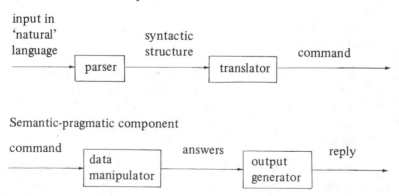

The syntactic-semantic component of the model has been thoroughly discussed in section 1. The parser feeds into the translator, which is abstractly an sdts or tree automaton with output. The resulting command may be tree-structured or it may be the frontier of the tree output by the translator stage. Depending on one's own view of the matter, the translator may be considered to be a semantic component resulting in a semantic structuring of the input string, or the translator may be considered as a transformation from syntactic surface structure to syntactic deep structure. This choice of terminology is irrelevant to the structuring of the actual processes at this stage, which are basically tree transformational. The actual form of the resulting 'commands' varies widely. The commands may be in a particular programming language designed for the purpose; they may be assertions in a logic system like the first-order predicate calculus; they may be sequences of subroutine calls, or other equivalent formulations of directions, commands and assertions to a data manipulator.

The semantic-pragmatic component contains those portions of the system which relate the now transformed input to the system's internal world view and particular universe of discourse. Whatever processing is done by the data manipulator is truly semantic and pragmatic in scope and intent. The answers resulting from the data manipulator are then passed to the output generator. Typically the answers have a rather complex structure which reflects the particular computer implementation techniques. These answer data structures are then formed into a linear string by the output generator. The output generation process may be an implementation of a particular linguistic theory. This aspect of 'natural' language processing is reviewed in section 2.3. We shall comment only briefly on the data manipulation stage, since the mechanisms used bear little relation to any aspect of formal language theory.

The syntax-directed model is intended as a clarifying abstraction of the mechanisms used by many 'natural' language understanding systems. Any particular understanding system will emphasize certain portions of the model, and in every case the information flow between the stages is not unidirectional, despite the diagrams. For example, the semantic rejection techniques imply the ability to look at the stored semantic and pragmatic data. Thus, semantic rejection could be delayed until the third stage, but efficiency requires that the parser make use of this information as soon as possible, so that the parser's search space will be rapidly narrowed. Similarly, the translator may not be capable of translating every possible syntactic structure that the parser is capable of producing. Again for efficiency, the translator should immediately report its inability back to the parser when such a partial parse is encountered. This suggests that the input acceptance phase blends across the first three stages, making use of the constraints provided by the second and third to guide the first. For reasons not detailed here, the output creation phase should be thought of as blending across the last three stages. As long as one keeps in mind the potential feedback to prior stages, the four stage model will suffice here. The model can be implemented in several ways. A common configuration is one in which each stage calls, as a subroutine, a subsequent stage or a portion of it to perform the desired tasks. This design lends itself to the interweaving of the actions of each stage.

The syntax-directed model is exactly the paradigm used in programming language compilers. In compilers there is little or no data manipulation necessary to produce the object program, except in the case of optimizing compilers. The optimizing compilers attempt to reorder the program elements to enhance the efficiency of the resulting object program. The syntax-directed model is very successful in explicating the structure of compilers, but programming languages are highly constrained, designed languages, and one cannot extrapolate from this success to the case of 'natural' language understanding systems. Each such understanding system needs to be evaluated on its own merits and defects without regard to the paradigm employed.

There are a variety of systems which employ this model. Among these are ZETA (Cohen 1974), NLPQ (Heidorn 1972, 1973a, 1973b), REQUEST (Petrick 1973, 1974a; Plath 1974a, 1974b, 1976), SHRDLU (Winograd 1972), LSNLIS (Woods 1972b, 1973b), R2 (Biss et al. 1971, 1972), the Proto-synthex work of Simmons and coworkers (Schwarcz 1967; Schwarcz et al. 1970; Simmons-Burger 1968; Simmons et al. 1966, 1968), REL (Thompson et al. 1968; Dostert-Thompson 1971, 1974; Dostert 1971), the data manager of Kellogg (1967, 1968, 1971), the Airline Guide (Woods 1968), GRANIS (Coles 1968, 1972), and the pioneering work of Green et al. (1968). The degree of syntactic ambition and range of acceptable inputs varies widely in this sample. Possibly the most syntactically capable of these are SHRDLU and LSNLIS, although this is certainly subject to dispute, since there are no commonly accepted measures of syntactic capability. However, these two are the most widely known of the syntax-directed 'natural' language understanding systems listed above, and for this reason are used here for a brief discussion of the contrasts between theory and practice.

LSNLIS used Woods' ATN parser (Woods 1970b, 1972a, 1973a), while SHRDLU uses a programmed variant of it. The ATN parser is basically a recursive descent general context-free parser. The actual design employs an augmentation to recursive descent methods which allows a variety of processes during the course of the parsing. A brief example is in order. The parser is always at a node in a transition network, maintaining a pushdown store of nodes to return to. Suppose a Noun Phrase is called for, putting the parser in the node *NP*. This begins a network of possible transitions, as the following diagram illustrates.

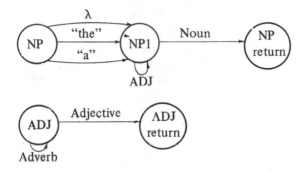

Beginning from *NP* there are three possible inputs: no input at all, a lambda transition, or either of the character strings *the* or *a*. In node *NP1* there are two possible transitions, the internal symbol *ADJ* or the lexical class *Noun*. Taking the *ADJ* transition causes *NP1* to be pushed on the top of the next-node store and the parser begins on the network headed by the label ADJ. With an input of *the red . . .*, the parser will arrive at the node *ADJ Return*, which causes the parser to pop the NP1 node from the next-node store and return to that node. If the input is *the red ball . . .*, the parser transits to *NP Return* and returns by another pop.

The augmentation consists of adding conditions to be satisfied on the transitions of the network, and commands to construct output during the course of a network traversal. The conditions may involve both syntactic and semantic checking, being in essence subroutine calls on arbitrarily complex functions. The augmentation can be viewed as introducing a semantic rejection tree automaton and a tree transformation automaton into the basic parsing process. The ATN schema provides a practical implementation of these theoretical concepts. In the LSNLIS application, the result of the tree transformation is viewed as a deep syntactic structure for the input.

SHRDLU uses the same techniques. In this case, the semantic rejection is accomplished by subroutine calls on portions of the semantic processor. These portions reject improbable combinations of concepts, giving the same effect as the restrictions on transitions in the ATN parser. During the course of surface structure parsing, the SHRDLU parser, in combination with semantic selection devices, generates a semantic case structure for the input. Abstractly there is no difference between the two programs. Both result in a transformed version of the surface structure as mediated by semantic considerations, and so are particular implementations of the theoretical class of 'parser + tree automata' devices. The distinctions reflect differing linguistic views, a matter of no interest to this survey. For thorough reviews of Winograd's work, see Clark (1974), and Petrick (1974b).

While these two 'natural' language understanding systems make explicit use of parsing theory and implicit use of tree automaton concepts, there is no theory which can be used to compare the differences in the way that the parsing and transformations are interwoven in these designs. What is needed is an algebraic structure theory for such devices which would be roughly comparable to that of Hartmanis-Stearns (1966) for sequential machines, and to that of Walter (1970) for grammars. (See Thatcher, 1970, 1973; Earley-Sturgis 1970 and Ricci 1973 for a few additional results tending in this direction.) Such a theory, if successful, would suggest the appropriate decomposition of the total syntactic-semantic component into subroutines for implementation.

In several respects then, the theory underlying the syntax-directed 'natural' language understanding systems is in strong accord with practice. An additional area is timing. If one assumes that the first parse generated is always a semantically appropriate one, then the parse time is linear with input length, using the recursive descent method. This assumption is plausible for the heuristically guided parsers in LSNLIS and SHRDLU. Tree automata operate in time linearly proportional to the input length so that the entire syntactic and transformational component operates in linear time, at least in theory and as a good approximation. Linear time is as fast as possible, although the constant of proportionality is always subject to improvement by both theoretical and practical programming advances. Unfortunately, the data manipulation stage, including those aspects of semantic rejection which require deductive mechanisms, has no such nice correlation with the length of the input. Finding fast, effective methods for this stage remains a serious theoretical problem, but not one in which formal language theoretic methods offer any appreciable guidance.

In spite of the practical and theoretical success of the syntax-directed model for 'natural' language understanding, there are several practical problems which currently admit of no theoretical solutions. Partial solutions exist in practice without measures of quality, speed or effectiveness. The most serious of these problems is the non-existence of a theoretical study of extensibility. Extensibility refers to the ability to define new words and phrases at will, and to establish new meanings for existing words and phrases, these meanings to apply in particular contexts. Thompson (1966, 1969, 1972) argues that this is a vital aspect of natural language which should be captured if 'natural' language understanding programs are to provide useful services as research assistants. REL (Thompson et al. 1969) is the most ambitious and successful attempt to provide extensibility in a 'natural' language system. While the extension mechanisms require a fair amount of linguistic sophistication on the part of the user, these skills are not beyond the capabilities of the serious practitioner of any research area. REL demonstrates the vitality and practicality of this approach to 'natural' language. Despite this success and the interest in extensibility for programming languages (Solnitseff-Yezerski 1974), there is no theoretical treatment of extensibility. A reasonable theory should suggest data representation techniques and the appropriate balance between extensibility and *a priori* syntactic and semantic structures.

Another such problem area is the treatment of discontinuous constituents such as the detached particle in verbs such as *drop . . . off* in sentences like *John dropped Mary off*. All the computer solutions I am familiar with are ad hoc, although Winograd's (1972: 100) solution is acceptable to a formal language theorist. The same sort of problems arise in treating conjunctions. Here again, the strict phrase-structure formalism fails to provide satisfactory solutions and specialized mechanisms are used by Woods and Winograd to treat this situation.

There are numerous semantic problems which reflect back into the particular choice of grammar implemented. This is a most reasonable way to design a syntax-directed 'natural' language understanding system, but, again, there is no theory on the relationships between syntax and semantics which aids in choosing the particular phrase-structure rules to implement. An algebraic structure theory would aid in choosing the proper grammar to support each particular collection of semantic routines. Since such a theory would be of value in compiler design as well, it is rather surprising that nothing substantial along these lines has been developed.

Because the syntax-directed model of 'natural' language understanding systems has been a successful paradigm, a variety of such programs has been developed. By our classification technique, these programs all share a common abstract structure based upon existing theoretical and linguistic principles. It is quite clear that the theoretical developments have strongly influenced these designs, both directly and indirectly. The programs listed previously differ more radically in the semantic-pragmatic component, ranging from the use of universal theorem-proving techniques (Biss et al. 1971) to highly pragmatic and specialized data retrieval and deductive techniques (Heidorn 1972). Despite this diversity, these programs are strikingly similar in their external behavior. With the sole exception of the Protosynthex work, they are all designed to act as research assistants in some field of endeavor other than linguistics or psychology. For example, LSNLIS answers questions posed by lunar geologists about the rock samples collected during the Apollo program. REL has been used by an anthropologist to ask sociometric questions based on his field data. REQUEST answers questions about *Fortune 500* business data. NLPQ is designed to help a system analyst set up a simulation of existing or proposed material flows. The input language in every case is admittedly limited, but is sufficiently rich and diverse to satisfy workers in the particular research area which the system was designed to support.

The success of these efforts is due in large part to the adaptability of the human user. If a particular syntactic form is not understood at all or understood in an odd manner by the program, the user quickly learns to phrase his requests in an acceptable manner, perhaps after a short period of initial frustration and annoyance. Yet, the learning involved in using these devices is considerably less than that required to program the computer directly, which requires an even more limited and fragile programming language. While the syntax-directed 'natural' language understanding efforts to date are experimental, the success of the syntax-directed paradigm has been demonstrated, and I expect that such 'research assistants' will soon be widely available to those who can afford the rather substantial computer costs. Petrick (1976) has a somewhat different, but also optimistic view.

In summary, there remain a variety of important areas in the design of 'natural' language understanding systems which would benefit from further theory. Siklóssy and Simon (1972: 46) agree with my own view in stating:

"The concerns usually designated by 'syntax' and 'semantics', respectively, are not distinct but are mingled along a continuum, with the syntactic component clearly dominating at one end and the semantic component dominating at the other end. This view has been imbedded in much computer science research on language for about a decade and is steadily gaining wider acceptance in formal linguistics today. Little interest attaches to formal definitions that attempt to distinguish sharply between the two components".

Nonetheless, any computer implementation of this continuum is forced to segment the process into discrete components. Some are accepted as syntactic, others as semantic with room in between for argument. The theorist takes these arguments — for example, whether the result of tree transformation is syntactic deep structure or semantic case structure — as beside the point. What is required is an algebraic structure theory — a decomposition theory — which will offer insight into the most efficient and conceptually elegant methods of segmenting the entire understanding process. Ideally, such a theory would offer as much to the entire understanding process as formal language theory currently offers to the initial stages.

2.2 The pattern-match model

The pattern-match model is sufficiently general to cover almost every computation. The model is simply: every time a pattern is matched by the input, do something. While this general statement includes the syntax-directed models, our intent is to exclude those programs which parse in the phrase structure sense. Instead, the patterns discovered in the input are used directly to effect semantic computations in some form. Since the organization is not syntax directed, there is almost no applicable theory. Nonetheless, we briefly survey some 'natural' language understanding programs of this type to see what theory might soon be developed.

The basic idea of pattern matching is to discover key words and phrases within the input which then implicitly analyze the sentence. The patterns are arranged in accordance with the needs of the particular semantic processor. Thus, they need have no relationship to the usual linguistic conceptions of sentence structure and grammar. For example, *the father of* could be a pattern which, if found in the input, could cause the immediately following word to be treated by a special semantic routine dealing with knowledge about fathers. The pattern-matching becomes considerably more complex when word classes are used, and certain patterns are directly replaced in the input. The replaced patterns may cause further matches, and so on. With this generality, pattern-matching and replacement is equivalent in generality to semithue rewriting systems, but without the notions of syntactic structure surveyed in section 1.

This paradigm has a variety of advantages. It is directly related to computer programming, being particularly easy in the COMIT and SNOBOL/SPITBOL programming languages, as these languages were designed to facilitate the writing of pattern-matchers. Despite this, the most interesting and complexly structured work has been done in LISP, no doubt due to LISP's major orientation toward semantic information processing. The paradigm avoids many of the parser's travails. For example, the traditional word classes such as Adjective, Noun, Verb prove to be of little use in parsers, since so many words lie in two or more of the classes. (However, see Thorne et al. 1968.) Considerable portions of the complexity of natural language are avoided by tailoring the patterns to the particular fragmentation useful to the semantics of the particular universe of discourse. The patterns may be discontinuous, which can easily resolve the annoying problem of treating detached particles, questions of anaphora, and other of the non-immediate constituent aspects of language.

Examples of 'natural' language understanding systems which use this paradigm are those of Weizenbaum (1966), Bobrow (1968), Raphael (1968), Charniak (1969), Ramani (1971), McCalla-Sampson (1972), Colby and co-workers (Colby 1973, 1974; Colby-Smith 1969; Colby et al. 1972, 1974), Schank and coworkers (Goldman 1975; Rieger 1974; Russell 1972; Schank 1972a, 1972b, 1973a, 1973b, 1973c; Schank-Rieger 1974; Schank-Tesler

1969, 1970; Schank et al. 1972), Shen and Krulee (1973), and Wilks (1968, 1972, 1973a, 1973b, 1975). Several of these programs are particularly oriented toward semantics with little attention to the breadth of 'natural' language input. Of those with breadth, the work of Colby, Schank and Wilks is of the greatest interest for our purposes.

Schank claims that the analysis of 'natural' language should be oriented directly and immediately to finding a semantic deep case structure for the input. His version is called 'conceptual dependency'. This system is rather thoroughly worked out in the references cited above, although there remains a considerable amount of linguistic research to fill out the details of his system. Since the linguistic framework is so complete, it is possible to pose a number of mathematical questions about conceptual dependency which could lead to a suitable mathematical theory of the subject. For example, Schank and Tesler (1969, 1970) have attempted to parse input directly to conceptual dependency structures. That is, the parser moves directly to deep case structures without an intervening surfacial syntactic structure and transformation. As far as I know, there has been no attempt by Schank's group or by formal language theorists to measure the relative efficiencies of these two approaches. Using the difficulty of context-sensitive parsing as a guide, one suspects that the attempt to go directly to conceptual structures is less efficient than proceeding to conceptual structures via surface structure and transformations; however, this remains only a guess until an appropriate comparative theory is worked out. As another example, conceptual dependency theory points up the fact that there are an enormous number of possible structures for language, ranging from very shallow syntactic structure to very deep semantic structure. Within this range, I would place conceptual dependency as a moderately deep case structure capable of a wide range of expression. Several theoretical questions arise. Can this intuitive idea of 'range' be made precise? If so, how does the choice of particular structures along the range affect the design and performance of 'natural' language understanding systems? These questions are difficult, and one should not expect answers to be forthcoming soon. Perhaps several years' more experience with a variety of 'natural' language understanding programs designed along widely differing lines will be necessary before the theoretical questions can even be properly posed.

Colby and coworkers have devised a computer model of paranoid personalities, PARRY. Since PARRY is a psychological simulations model, it is possible to subject it to numerous tests of adequacy (Colby et al. 1972; Colby-Hilf 1974). This is the only 'natural' language understanding system which has been subjected to scientific evaluation. Results show that PARRY can understand its input sufficiently well over a sufficiently broad range of linguistic complexity and subject matter to thoroughly validate the approach taken in its design. Unfortunately, the linguistic competence of PARRY is buried in the program and the various papers about this work fail to adequately explain the linguistic aspects. Apparently, PARRY, in its most recent manifestations, has been influenced by conceptual dependency theory, although earlier verions were without a well-formulated syntactic-semantic theory. PARRY's linguistic tasks are eased by searching for key emotive words which cause PARRY to respond in ways characteristic of its internalized delusional complexes. Thus, when the input contains such a key word, the rest of the sentence can be ignored. While this method leads to persuasive dialogs between psychologists and PARRY, it contributes little to the development of non-paranoid 'natural' language understanding systems. It is difficult to find any influence of formal language theory in the design of PARRY.

Wilks' work is oriented toward obtaining a semantic network of the inter-relationships between sentences in a corpus. The techniques involve matching a Subject-Verb-Object prototype to sentences and then using various semantic processing methods to establish the interrelationships between the words and phrases used in different sentences. Despite Wilks' disclaimers (Wilks 1972, 1975), his methods are strongly related to a syntactic analysis of individual sentences which uses semantic features similar to syntactic-semantic devices such as Count Noun/Mass Noun distinctions and the like. (See Shapiro 1974 for a review of Wilks 1972.) Wilks' pattern-matching methods, while distinct from immediate constituent phrase structure grammar, appear to be suscep-tible to a similar theoretical treatment. Again, an analysis of the relative efficacy of Wilks' methods and syntax-directed methods would be of interest.

Despite the lack of mathematical syntactic theory in these three projects, all seem to rely on the idea of finding a 'kernel sentence' within the input. After the kernel is found, the various modifiers and qualifying phrases are hung on the appropriate portion of the representation of the kernel sentence. This framework is of significant advantage in programs such as PARRY which must always keep up its end of the conversation, never dropping into com-putereze to explain inability to parse or to understand. As long as the kernel is correctly understood, the modifications can be totally ignored and a realistic reply still generated. If 'kernel sentences' is an appropriate abstraction of this work, then the development of string adjunct grammars (Joshi et al. 1972, 1975) may provide the theoretical method most in keeping with the pattern-matching 'natural' language understanding systems.

Until such time as the mathematical theory of formal languages develops to include these 'natural' language understanding systems, they remain ad hoc. Without the extra-linguistic framework of theory, these programs are

148   David B. Benson

difficult to describe, since there are no convenient mathematical abstractions
with which to explain portions of the total system and the methods by which
the portions combine to form that total. For processes as complex as these,
neither a verbal description nor a computer program listing suffices. There
must be an intermediary of mathematical theory. In the syntax-directed model,
the theory sets up the overall staging of the program and suggests what is and
what is not possible in that scheme. A particular linguistic theory then provides
additional structure in the form of parsing used, the type of transformations
and features to be included and so on. Finally, the exact, detailed choices of
transformations, features, words, etc. to be included are specified in the
program itself. The pattern-match programs have no such hierarchy of description ranging from general to concrete. Therefore, the knowledge gained
by the devising of such 'natural' language understanding systems is significantly
more difficult to transmit than is the case in the syntax-directed systems. In
view of the success of programs such as PARRY, perhaps theorists will take
some interest in devising suitable abstract models of the pattern-matching
approach to 'natural' language understanding systems.

2.3 Semantics and sentence generation
We briefly consider the semantic and answer generation processes used in the
'natural' language understanding systems being surveyed. The semantic data
manipulation used in these programs varies widely, but the general processes
are addition, deletion, retrieval and deduction. Certain inputs are commands
to add new data to store, others to delete data already stored. Data modification combines deletion with addition. Retrieval refers to gathering facts from
the store while deduction refers to finding inferences from the data explicitly
in the memory. These matters are currently subject to intensive research on
the part of philosophers (Bar-Hillel 1971; Davidson-Harman 1972; Rescher-
Urquhart 1971), psychologists (Lindsay 1963, 1971; Miller et al. 1960),
linguists (Bartsch-Vennemann 1972; Chafe 1970; Fillmore 1968; Jackendoff
1972; Weinreich 1972), logicians (Bogan-Niiniluoto 1971; Church 1964;
Scott 1972), and computer scientists (Biss et al. 1972; Bruce 1972; Derksen
et al. 1972; Fikes 1970; Green-Raphael 1968; Isard-Longuet-Higgins 1971;
Mishelevich 1971; Nilsson 1971; Quillian 1968, 1969; Sandewall 1971;
Siklóssy 1972; Simmons 1973; Krägeloh-Lockemann 1974), to cite but a few
representative papers and collections not previously mentioned. None of this
work is particularly oriented toward formal language theory, but there are
aspects of it which are mathematical and capable of undergoing theoretical
treatment. This can only help to enrich the possibilities for applicable formal
language theory. As the semantic and pragmatic features of language understanding become better understood, the earlier stages can be pointed rather

more directly toward eliciting the essentials of language information flows and transformations.

Interest has recently been directed toward the development of case grammars for use in 'natural' language understanding systems, stemming largely from Fillmore's (1968) paper. The early BASEBALL program of Green et al. (1963) used a restricted notion of case grammar to express the commands for the retrieval component. Currently, the interest lies in far more expressive case systems, but the idea is as old as the first attempt at 'natural' language understanding by Green et al. There is an outstanding need for a suitable mathematical theory of case grammars. While Bruce (1973) has taken a first step here, a fully articulated theory could support a comparative study of parsing to case structures. Since semantic case structure can be reached from sentences via surface parsings and transformations, or can be reached by semantic parsing in the style of Schank and Tesler, a comparative study should show which is the more efficient procedure.

Within the semantic-pragmatic component itself, some systems use semantic networks, while others require a predicate calculus representation. Semantic networks are traversed by 'net' automata — not a well defined notion as yet — while sets of axioms in a predicate calculus are acted upon by automatic theorem proving programs. Although Simmons and Bruce (1971) have established some of the connections between these two methods, a substantial theory would show the conditions under which one or the other notation was the more advantageous. As part of such a theory, an appropriate notion of net automaton, perhaps as an extension of tree automaton, would need to be developed. Closely associated with these ideas are the beginnings of the mathematical theory of computation (Brainerd-Landweber 1974; Manna 1973, 1974), which will eventually contribute to the design of semantic information processing in 'natural' language understanding systems.

Reply generation, in one form or another, is done by all 'natural' language understanding systems. The programs designed to act as information retrieval research assistants frequently reply in laconic lists of the requested data, (Thompson et al. 1969; Woods 1973b; Kellogg 1968; Plath 1976), surely sufficient for those purposes. Of greater interest in this survey are the programs which attempt to reply in complete sentences (Schank 1973; Colby 1973; Wilks 1973a, 1973b; Heidorn 1972; Simmons-Slocum 1972; Schwarcz et al. 1970).

Using Schank's conceptual dependency theory, Goldman and Riesbeck (1973) have developed a sentence paraphraser. In this device the semantic network articulating the conceptual dependencies of an input sentence is traversed in varying orders to provide several paraphrases of the input. At least in the abstract, Wilks' French translation and Colby's PARRY operate in the same fashion: some form of semantic data is selected to choose the particular output sentences.

Simmons and Slocum (1972) explicitly use a grammar to control the generation process. Heidorn (1972) does likewise, with the additional interesting feature of using essentially the same grammar for both input and output. In this case, a paragraph of text is generated to describe the proposed simulation model developed during a dialog between the user and NLPQ. The paragraphs demonstrate a surprising coherency and style in this particular subject area. Simmons and Slocum's (1972) paper offers the most accessible and detailed description of reply generation using a mediating grammar. The grammar is written as a transition network just like those used by the Woods ATN parser (1970b). In input analysis the final choice of transition arc followed is fundamentally dependent on the input. Here, the choice of transition arc is dependent upon the semantic network being articulated. The LISP program to carry out the generation is surprisingly simple in view of the complexity of generating a coherent paragraph. The burden of complexity has been placed in the semantic network and in the grammar. This choice of simple program and rich data networks is appropriate to Simmons and Slocum's goals, but immediately leads to the question of what division among semantics, grammar and generation program is the most efficient. Heidorn's success, using very similar techniques to those of Simmons and Slocum, suggests that placing the complexity in the grammar and the semantics enables the system designer to devise a rather sophisticated system. Nothing is said about the resulting efficiency and it may be that theory has something to offer here. Tree transformation theory seems remarkably close to the syntactic guidance methods of Simmons and Slocum, suggesting that an appropriate variation of sdts or tree automata may provide explanatory power in this stage.

2.4 Conclusion

Formal language theory has clarified the problem of selecting a grammar type. The results on syntactic structures, semantic correspondences and parsers all strongly suggest that context-free grammars are the most appropriate vehicle for the expression of syntax in compilers and 'natural' language understanding programs. The results on tree automata and sdts tree transformations are suggestive, but currently do not provide the depth of guidance for practical transformation methods that parsing theory provides for practical parsers. Sentence generation hasn't been touched by the theorists, but should be. Delving into semantic-pragmatic information processing, formal language theory offers almost no insight. The methods used are semantic and deductive, and formal language theory, by its very scope and intent, contributes little.

The general undecidability results remain valid in semantic domains as well, suggesting that overly general approaches to semantics and deduction are doomed to failure. As the mathematical theory of semantic computation begins to ripen, we may expect to see rather more attention paid to the feasibility and economics of various approaches to semantic understanding.

The original impetus for formal language theory arose from linguistic considerations. This impetus continues today, largely due to the interest in compilers, although natural language linguistical considerations continue to play some part in the development of mathematical theory (Gross et al. 1973). I expect that the growing interest in 'natural' language understanding systems will cause theorists to study the problems raised here as well as a host of other issues there has been no space to explore. As the theories unfold, the 'natural' language understanding systems will become more precisely structured with a greater understanding of what are good design choices.

Note

* Research supported in part by National Science Foundation grant GJ-43495.

References

Aho, A. V.
    1968   "Indexed grammars – an extension of context-free grammars", *Journal of the Association for Computing Machinery* 15.4: 647–671.
    1969   "Nested stack automata", *Journal of the Association for Computing Machinery* 16.3: 383–407.
Aho, A. V. – J. E. Hopcroft – J. D. Ullman
    1969   "A general theory of translation", *Mathematical Systems Theory* 3.3: 193–221.
Aho, A. V. – S. C. Johnson
    1974   "LR parsing", *Computing Surveys* 6.2: 99–124.
Aho, A. V. – J. D. Ullman
    1968   "The theory of languages", *Mathematical Systems Theory* 2.2: 97–126.
    1969   "Translations on a context free grammar", *Proceedings of the Association for Computing Machinery Symposium on Theory of Computing* (Marina del Rey), 93–112.
    1972   *The theory of parsing, translation, and compiling, Volume I: Parsing* (Englewood Cliffs, NJ: Prentice-Hall).
    1973   *The theory of parsing, translation, and compiling, Volume II: Compiling* (Englewood Cliffs, NJ: Prentice-Hall).
Aho, A. V. et al.
    1974   *The design and analysis of computer algorithms* (Reading, MA: Addison-Wesley).

Alagić, Suad
    1975   "Natural state transformations", *Journal of Computer and System Sciences*
              10.2: 266–307.
Bach, Emmon
    1967   "*Have* and *be* in English syntax", *Language* 43: 476.
Baker, Branda S.
    1973   "Generalized syntax-directed translation, tree transducers, and linear space",
              Technical Report 18–73 (Harvard University).
Bar-Hillel, Y. (Editor)
    1971   *Pragmatics of natural language* (Dordrecht, Holland: D. Reidel).
Bartsch, R. – T. Vennemann
    1972   *Semantic structures* (Frankfurt: Athenäum Verlag).
Benson, D. B.
    1969   "The algebra of derivations and a semi-thue parser", *Proceedings of the
              24th National Association for Computing Machinery Conference*, 1–9.
    1970a   "Syntax and semantics: A categorical view", *Information and Control* 17:
              145–160.
    1970b   "Syntactic clues", *Institute of Electrical and Electronics Engineers Con-
              ference Record 11th Annual Symposium on Switching and Automata
              Theory*, 133–138.
    1973   "Introduction to ENT 2210 and ENT Database 2201", CS-73-006 (Pull-
              man, WA: Computer Science Department, Washington State University).
    1974a   "An abstract machine theory for formal language parsers", *Acta Informatica*
              3.2: 187–202.
    1974b   "Semantic preserving translations", *Mathematical Systems Theory* 8.2.
    1975a   "The basic algebraic structures in categories of derivations", *Information
              and Control* 28.1: 1–29.
    1975b   "Some preservation properties of normal form grammars", CS-74-024
              (Pullman, WA: Computer Science Department, Washington State University).
Biss, K. O. – R. T. Chien – F. A. Stahl
    1971   "R2 – a natural language question-answering system", *American Federa-
              tion of Information Processing Societies Conference Proceedings* 38:
              303–308.
    1972   "A data structure for cognitive information retrieval", *International Journal
              of Computer and Information Sciences* 1.1: 17–28.
Bobrow, D. G.
    1963   "Syntactic analysis of English by computer – a survey", *Proceedings of
              the American Federation of Information Processing Societies Fall Joint
              Computer Conference* 24 (New York: Spartan), 365–387.
    1967   "Syntactic theory in computer implementations", *Automated Language
              Processing*, edited by H. Borko (New York: John Wiley and Sons), 217–
              251.
    1968   "Natural language input for a computer problem-solving system", in: *Semantic
              information processing*, edited by M. L. Minsky (Cambridge, MA: M. I. T.
              Press), 146–226.
Bobrow, D. G. – J. B. Fraser
    1969   "An augmented state transition network analysis procedure", *Proceedings
              of the International Joint Conference on Artificial Intelligence* (Bedford,
              Mass.: Mitre Corporation), 557–568.
Bogan, R. J. – Ilkka Niiniluoto (Editors)
    1971   *Logic, language and probability, Selection 4th International Congress for
              Logic, Methodology, and Philosophy of Science, Bucharest* (Dordrecht,
              Holland: D. Reidel).

Book, Ronald V.
  1973   "Topics in formal language theory", in: *Currents in the theory of computing*, edited by A. V. Aho (Englewood Cliffs, NJ: Prentice-Hall), 1–34.
Brainerd, Walter Scott
  1967   *Tree generating systems and tree automata* (Ann Arbor, MI: University Microfilms).
Brainerd, W. S. – L. H. Landweber
  1974   *Theory of computation* (New York: John Wiley and Sons).
Bruce, Bertram C.
  1973   "A model for temporal references and its application in a question answering program", *Artificial Intelligence* 3: 1–25.
  1973   "Case structure systems", *Proceedings of the 3rd International Joint Conference on Artificial Intelligence* (Palo Alto: Stanford Research Institute), 364–371.
Buttelmann, H. W.
  1974   "Semantic directed translation of context free languages", *American Journal of Computational Linguistics* Micro 7.
  1975   "On the syntactic structures of unrestricted grammars", to appear in *Information and Control*.
Chafe, Wallace L.
  1970   *Meaning and the structure of language* (Chicago: The University of Chicago Press).
Charniak, E.
  1969   "Computer solution of calculus word problems", *Proceedings of the International Joint Conference on Artificial Intelligence* (Washington, D. C.), 303–316.
Chomsky, N.
  1956   "Three models for the description of language", *Institute of Radio Engineers Transactions of Information Theory* IT2: 113–124.
  1959   "On certain formal properties of grammars", *Information and Control* 2: 137–167.
Church, Alonzo
  1964   "The need for abstract entities in semantic analysis", in: *The structure of language: Readings in the philosophy of language*, edited by Fodor and Katz (Englewood Cliffs, NJ: Prentice-Hall), 437–445.
Clark, H. H.
  1974   Review of *Understanding natural language* by T. Winograd, *American Scientist* 62.1: 118–119.
Cohen, Philip R.
  1974   "A prototype natural language understanding system", Department of Computer Science, TR-64, University of Toronto.
Colby, Kenneth M.
  1973   "Simulations of belief systems", in: *Computer models of thought and language*, edited by R. C. Schank and K. M. Colby (San Francisco: W. F. Freeman & Co.).
  1974   *Artificial paranoia: A computer simulation of paranoid processes* (New York: Pergamon Press, Inc.).
Colby, K. M. – F. D. Hilf
  1974   "Multidimensional evaluation of a computer simulation of paranoid thought", in: *Knowledge and cognition*, edited by L. Gregg (Potomac, MD: Lawrence Ehrlbaum & Associates).
Colby, K. M. – D. C. Smith
  1969   "Dialogues between humans and an artificial belief system", in: *Proceedings of the International Conference on Artificial Intelligence*, 319–324.

154   David B. Benson

Colby, K. M. et al.
  1972   "Turing-like indistinguishability tests for the validation of a computer simulation of paranoid processes", *Artificial Intelligence* 3: 199–221.
  1974   "Pattern-matching rules for the recognition of natural language dialogue expresions", *American Journal of Computational Linguistics* Micro 5.
Coles, L. Stephen
  1968   "An on-line question-answering system with natural language and pictorial input", in: *Proceedings of the 23rd National Association for Computing Machinery Conference*, 157–167.
  1969   "Talking with a robot in English", in: *Proceedings of the 1st International Joint Conference on Artificial Intelligence, Washington, D. C.*, 587–596.
  1972   "Syntax directed interpretation of natural language", in: *Representation and meaning: Experiments with information processing systems*, edited by H. A. Simon and L. Siklóssy (Englewood Cliffs, NJ: Prentice-Hall), 211–287.
Colmeraurer, A.
  1970   "Total precedence relations", *Journal of the Association for Computing Machinery*, 17.1: 14–30.
Craig, J. A. et al.
  1966   "DEACON: Direct English Access & CONtrol", *American Federation of Information Processing Societies Conference Proceedings* 29 (Washington, D. C.: Spartan Books), 365–380.
Čulik, Karel II – Rina Cohen
  1973   "LR-regular grammars – an extension of LR(k) grammars", *Journal of Computer and Systems Sciences*, 7.1: 66–96.
Daly, Richard T.
  1974   *Applications of the mathematical theory of linguistics* (The Hague: Mouton & Co.).
Davidson, D. – G. Harman (Editors)
  1972   *Semantics of natural language* (Dordrecht, Holland: D. Reidel).
DeRemer, F. L.
  1969a   "Generating parsers for BNF grammars", *American Federation of Information Processing Societies Conference Proceedings* 34: 793–800.
  1969b   *"Practical translators for LR(k) languages* (Ph. D. Thesis) (Cambridge, MA: M.I.T.)
  1971   "Simple LR(k) grammars", *Communications of the Association for Computing Machinery* 14.7: 453–460.
Derksen, J. A. et al.
  1972   "The QA4 language applied to robot planning", *American Federation of Information Processing Societies Conference Proceedings* 41: 1181–1192.
Domolki, B.
  1968   "A universal compiler system based on production rules", *BIT* 8.4: 262–275.
Dostert, B. H.
  1971   "REL – an information system for a dynamic environment", *REL Report 3* (Pasadena: California Institute of Technology).
Dostert, B. H. – F. B. Thompson
  1971   "The syntax of REL English", *REL Report 1* (Pasadena: California Institute of Technology).
  1974   "The REL system and REL English" in: *Computational and mathematical linguistics, Proceedings of the 1973 International Conference on Computational Linguistics, Pisa, Italy*, edited by A. Zampolli (Firenze: Casa Editrice Olschki).

Earley, Jay
    1970   "An efficient context-free parsing algorithm", *Communications of the Association for Computing Machinery* 13.2: 94—102.
Earley, Jay — Howard Sturgis
    1970   "A formalism for translator interactions", *Communications of the Association for Computing Machinery* 13.10: 607—617.
Edmundson, H. P.
    1967   "Mathematical models in linguistics and language processing", in: *Automated Language Processing*, edited by H. Borko (New York: John Wiley & Sons), 33—96.
Feldman, J. A. — D. Gries
    1968   "Translator writing systems", *Communications of the Association for Computing Machinery* 11.2: 77—113.
Fikes, R. E.
    1970   "REF-ARF: A system for solving problems stated as procedures", *Artificial Intelligence* 1.1/2: 27—120.
Fillmore, Charles J.
    1968   "The case for case", in: *Universals in linguistic theory*, edited by E. Bach and R. T. Harms (New York: Holt, Rinehart and Winston), 1—88.
Fischer, M. J.
    1968   "Grammars with macro-like productions", *Institute of Electrical and Electronics Engineers Conference Record, 9th Symposium on Switching and Automata Theory*, 131—142.
Friedman, Joyce
    1969   "A computer system for transformational grammar", *Communications of the Association for Computing Machinery* 12.6: 341—348.
Friedman, J. et al.
    1971   *A computer model of transformational grammar* (New York: American Elsevier).
Gelb, Jack P.
    1971   "Experiments with a natural language problem-solving system", *2nd International Joint Conference on Artificial Intelligence* (London, British Computer Society), 455—462.
Geller, M. M. et al.
    1974   "Production prefix parsing", *Automata languages and programming: Proceedings of the 1974 Conference Saarbrücken*, edited by J. Loeckx (New York: Springer-Verlag).
Ghandour, Z. J.
    1972   "Formal systems and analysis of context sensitive languages", *Computer Journal* 15.3: 229—237.
Ginsburg, S.
    1966   *The mathematical theory of context-free languages* (New York: McGraw-Hill).
    1974   *Algebraic and automata-theoretic properties of formal languages* (New York: American Elsevier).
Ginsburg, S. et al.
    1969   "Studies in abstract families of languages", *Memoirs of the American Mathematical Society #87* (Providence, RI: American Mathematical Society).
Goldman, Neil M.
    1975   "Sentence paraphrasing from a conceptual base", *Communications of the Association for Computing Machinery* 18.2: 96—106.

Goldman, Neil M. and C. K. Riesbeck
    1973   "A conceptually based sentence paraphraser", *AIM*-196 (Stanford University).
Gray, J. N. – M. A. Harrison
    1972   "On the covering and reduction problems for context-free grammars", *Journal of the Association for Computing Machinery* 19.4: 675–698.
    1973   "Canonical precedence schemes", *Journal of the Association for Computing Machinery* 20.2: 214–234.
Green, C. C. – B. Raphael
    1968   "The use of theorem-proving techniques in question-answering systems", *Proceedings of the 23rd National Conference of the Association for Computing Machinery*, 169–181.
Green, B. F. et al.
    1968   "BASEBALL: An automatic question answerer", in: *Computers and thought*, edited by E. A. Feigenbaum and J. Feldman (New York: McGraw-Hill), 207–216.
Greibach, S. A.
    1970   "Full AFL's and nested iterated substitution", *Information and Control* 16.1: 7–35.
Griffiths, T. V.
    1968   "Some remarks on derivations in general rewriting systems", *Information and Control* 12: 27–54.
Grishman, Ralph
    1973   "Implementation of the string parser of English", in: *Natural language processing, Courant Computer Science Symposium 8*, edited by R. Rustin (New York: Algorithmics Press), 89–109.
Grishman, R. et al.
    1973b   "The linguistic string parser", *American Federation of Information Processing Societies Conference Proceedings* 42: 427–434.
Gross, M. – M. Halle – M.-P. Schützenberger (eds.)
    1973   "The formal analysis of natural languages", *Proceedings of the First International Conference* (The Hague: Mouton & Co.).
Gross, M. – A. Lentin
    1970   *Introduction to formal grammars* (New York: Springer-Verlag).
Guiliano, V. E.
    1972   "In defense of natural language", *Proceedings of the Association for Computing Machinery National Conference* (New York: Association for Computing Machinery) 1074.
Halpern, M.
    1966   "Foundations of the case for natural-language programming", *Proceedings of the American Federation of Information Processing Societies 1966 Fall Joint Computer Conference*, 639–649.
Hammer, Michael M.
    1974   "A new grammatical transformation into deterministic top-down form", *Proceedings of the 6th Association for Computing Machinery Symposium on Theory of Computation* (New York: Association for Computing Machinery), 266–275.
Harrison, M. A. – I. M. Havel
    1974   "On the parsing of deterministic languages", *Journal of the Association for Computing Machinery* 21.4: 525–548.
Hartmanis, J. – R. E. Stearns
    1966   *Algebraic structure theory of sequential machines* (Englewood Cliffs, NJ: Prentice-Hall).

Hays, David G.
  1967   *Computational linguistics* (New York: American Elsevier).

Heidorn, George E.
  1972   "Natural language inputs to a simulation programming system" (NPS-55HD72101A) (Monterey: Naval Postgraduate School).
  1973   *Simulation programming through natural language dialogue* (IBM Research RC 4535) (Yorktown Heights: IBM).
  1973b   *English as a very high level language for simulation programming* (IBM Research RC 4536) (Yorktown Heights: IBM).

Hill, I. D.
  1972   "Wouldn't it be nice if we could write computer programs in ordinary English — or would it?", *Honeywell Computer Journal* 6.2: 76–83.

Hopcroft, John E. — J. D. Ullman
  1969   *Formal languages and their relation to automata* (Reading, MA: Addison-Wesley).

Hotz, G.
  1966   "Eindeutigkeit und Mehrdeutigkeit formaler Sprachen", *Elektronische Informationsverarbeitung und Kybernetik* 2.4: 235–247.

Hotz, G. — V. Claus
  1972   *Automaten-Theorie und formale Sprachen III. Formale Sprachen* (Mannheim: Bibliographisches Institut).

Isard, S. — H. C. Longuet-Higgins
  1971   "Question-answering in English", *Machine Intelligence 6* (New York: American Elsevier), 243–254.

Jackendoff, Ray S.
  1972   *Semantic interpretation in generative grammar* (Cambridge: M. I. T. Press).

Johnson, W. L. et al.
  1968   "Automatic generation of efficient lexical processors using finite state techniques (A tutorial)", *Communications of the Association for Computing Machinery* 11/12: 805–813.

Joshi, A. K.
  1973   "A brief survey of some mathematical results relevant to natural language processing", in: *Natural language processing, Courant Computer Science Symposium 8*, edited by R. Rustin (New York: Algorithmics Press), 1–24.

Joshi, A. K. et al.
  1972a   "String adjunct grammars, Part I", *Information and Control* 21.2: 93–116.
  1972b   "String adjunct grammars, Part II", *Information and Control* 21.3: 235–260.
  1975   "Tree adjunct grammars", *Journal of the Computer and Systems Sciences* 10.1: 136–163.

Kaplan, Ronald M.
  1973a   "A general syntactic processor", *Natural language processing, Courant Computer Science Symposium 8*, edited by R. Rustin (New York: Algorithmics Press) 193–241.
  1973b   "A multi-processing approach to natural language", *American Federation of Information Processing Societies Conference Proceedings* 42: 435–440.

Kay, Martin
  1967   *Experiments with a powerful parser* (RM-5452-PR) (Santa Monica: Rand Corp.).
  1973   "The MIND system", in: *Natural language processing, Courant Computer Science Symposium 8*, edited by R. Rustin (New York: Algorithmics Press), 155–188.

158   David B. Benson

Kellogg, C. H.
1967   "Designing artificial languages for information storage and retrieval", in:
        Automated language processing, edited by H. Borko (New York: John
        Wiley and Sons), 325–367.
1968   "A natural language compiler for on-line data management", *American
        Federation of Information Processing Societies Conference Proceedings* 33
        (New York: Spartan Books), 473–492.
Kellogg, C. H. et al.
1971   "The converse natural language data management system: Current status
        and plans", *Proceedings of the Symposium on Information Storage and
        Retrieval*, (New York: Association for Computing Machinery) 33–46.
Klein, S. – M. A. Kuppin
1970   "An interactive heuristic program for learning transformational grammars",
        Computer Studies in the Humanities and Verbal Behavior 3.3: 144–162.
Klima, Edward S.
1964   "Negation in English", in: *The structure of language: Readings in the
        philosophy of language* (Englewood Cliffs, NJ: Prentice-Hall), 246–323.
Knuth, D. E.
1965   "On the translation of languages from left to right", *Information and
        Control* 8.6: 607–639.
1968   "Semantics of context-free languages", *Mathematical Systems Theory*
        2.2: 127–146. Also see *Mathematical Systems Theory* 5.1: 95–96.
1971   "Examples of formal semantics", in: *Symposium on semantics of
        algorithmic languages*, edited by E. Engeler (*Lecture Notes in Maths.*
        #188) (New York: Springer-Verlag), 212–235.
Kochen, M.
1969   "Automatic question-answering of English-like questions about simple
        diagrams", *Journal of the Association for Computing Machinery* 16.1:
        26–48.
Krägeloh, K.-D. – P. C. Lockemann
1974   "Retrieval in a set-theoretically structured data base: Concepts and
        practical considerations", in: *International Computing Symposium 1973*,
        edited by A. Gunther et al. (Amsterdam: North-Holland).
Kuno, S. – A. G. Oettinger
1963   "Multiple path syntactic analyzer", *Information Processing 1962*, (Amster-
        dam: North Holland).
Kuno, S.
1967   "A context sensitive recognition procedure", *Mathematical Linguistics
        and Automatic Translation* (Report NSF-18, Computation Lab.) (Cam-
        bridge: Harvard University).
Kuroda, S.-Y.
1969   "A topological study of context-free languages", in: *Journées d'études
        sur l'analyse syntactique*, edited by T. Nivat (Fontainebleau).
1973a   "Généralisation de la notation d'équivalence de grammaires: Une methode
        topologique", in: *The formal analysis of natural languages, Proceedings
        of the First International Conference*, edited by Gross, Halle and Schützen-
        berger (The Hague: Mouton & Co.), 362–371.
1973b   "On structural similarity of phrase-structure languages", in: *Automata,
        languages and programming*, edited by M. Nivat (New York: American
        Elsevier), 467–474.
Lesk, Michael A.
1972   *Semantic analysis of English text: A preliminary report* (= *Computer
        Science Technical Report 9*) (Murray Hill, NJ: Bell Telephone Labs.).

Lewis, P. M. II – R. E. Stearns
 1968   "Syntax directed transduction", *Journal of the Association for Computing Machinery* 15.3: 464–488.
Lindsay, R. K.
 1963   "Inferential memory as the basis of machines which understand natural language", in: *Computers and thought*, edited by E. A. Feigenbaum and J. Feldman (New York: McGraw-Hill), 217–233.
 1971   "Jigsaw heuristics and a language learning model", in: *Artificial intelligence and heuristic programming*, edited by N. V. Findler and B. Meltzer (Edinburgh University Press), 173–189.
Maibaum, T. S. E.
 1974   "A generalized approach to formal languages", *Journal of Computer and Systems Sciences* 8.3: 409–439.

Manna, Z.
 1973   "Program schemas", in: *Currents in the theory of computing*, edited by A. V. Aho (Englewood Cliffs: Prentice-Hall) 90–142.
 1974   *Mathematical theory of computation* (New York: McGraw-Hill).
Marcus, Solomon
 1967   *Algebraic linguistics: Analytical models* (New York: Academic Press).
McCalla, Gordon, I. – Jeffrey R. Sampson
 1972   "MUSE: A Model to Understand Simple English", *Communications of the Association for Computing Machinery* 15.1: 29–40.
Miller, G. A. et al.
 1960   *Plans and the structure of behavior* (New York: Henry Holt and Co.).
Minsky, Marvin (Editor)
 1968   *Semantic information processing* (Cambridge: M. I. T. Press).
Minsky, Marvin
 1970   "Form and content in computer science", *Journal of the Association for Computing Machinery* 17.2: 197–215.
Mishelevich, D. J.
 1971   "MEANINGEX – A computer-based semantic parse approach to the analysis of meaning", *American Federation of Information Processing Societies Conference Proceedings* 39: 271–280.
Modesitt, K. L.
 1972   *ELIJAH: An approach to natural language programming* (Ph. D. Thesis, Computer Science Department) (Pullman, WA: Washington State University).
Montgomery, C. A.
 1972   "Is natural language an unnatural query language?", *Proceedings of the Association for Computing Machinery National Conference* (New York: Association for Computing Machinery) 1075–1078.
Napper, R. B. E.
 1966   "A system for defining language and writing programs in 'natural English'", in: *Formal Language Description Languages for Computer Programming*, edited by T. B. Steel, Jr. (Amsterdam: North-Holland), 231.
Nilsen, D. L. F.
 1972   *Toward a semantic specification of deep case* (The Hague: Mouton & Co.).
Nillson, Nils
 1971   *Problem-solving methods in artificial intelligence* (New York: McGraw-Hill).
Palme, J.
 1971   "Making computers understand natural language", in: *Artificial Intelligence and Heuristic Programming*, edited by N. V. Findler and B. Meltzer (Edinburgh University Press), 199–244.

Peters, P. Stanley — R. W. Ritchie
   1971   "On restricting the base component of transformational grammars", *Information and Control* 18.5: 483–501.
   1973a   "On the generative power of transformational grammars", *Information Sciences* 6: 49–83.
   1973b   "Context-sensitive immediate constituent analysis: Context-free languages revisited", *Mathematical Systems Theory* 6.4: 324–333.
Petrick, S. R.
   1973   "Transformational analysis", in: *Natural language processing, Courant Computer Science Symposium 8*, edited by R. Rustin (New York: Algorithmics Press), 27–41.
   1974a   "Semantic interpretation in the REQUEST system" in: *Computational and mathematical linguistics, Proceedings of the 1973 International Conference on Computational Linguistics, Pisa, Italy*, edited by A. Zampolli (Firenze: Casa Editrice Olschki).
   1974b   Review of *A procedural model of language understanding* by Terry Winograd, *Computing Reviews* 15.8: #27005.
   1976   "On natural language based query systems", to appear in *IBM Journal of Research and Development*.
Plath, Warren J.
   1974a   "Transformational grammar and transformational parsing in the REQUEST system", in: *Computational and mathematical linguistics, Proceedings of the 1973 International Conference on Computational Linguistics, Pisa, Italy* edited by A. Zampolli (Firenze: Casa Editrice Olschki).
   1974b   "String transformations in the REQUEST system", *American Journal of Computational Linguistics* Micro. 8.
   1976   "The REQUEST SYSTEM", to appear in *IBM Journal of Research and Development*.
Platt, J. T.
   1971   *Grammatical form and grammatical meaning: A tagmemic view of Fillmore's deep structure case concepts* (Amsterdam: North-Holland).
Quillian, M. R.
   1968   "Semantic memory", in: *Semantic information processing*, edited by Minsky (Cambridge: M. I. T. Press).
   1969   "The teachable language comprehender: A simulation program and theory of language", *Communications of the Association for Computing Machinery* 12.8: 459–475.
Ramani, S.
   1971   "A language based problem-solver", *2nd International Joint Conference on Artificial Intelligence* (London: British Computer Society), 463–473.
Raphael, B.
   1968   "SIR: A computer program for semantic information retrieval", in: *Semantic Information Processing*, edited by M. Minsky (Cambridge: M. I. T. Press), 33–145.
Rescher, N. — A. Urquhard
   1971   *Temporal logic* (New York: Springer-Verlag).
Ricci, G.
   1973   "Cascades of tree-automata and computations in universal algebra", *Mathematical Systems Theory* 7.3: 201–218.
Rieger, C.
   1974   "Understanding by conceptual inference", *American Journal of Computational Linguistics* Micro. 13.
Rosenkrantz, D. J. — R. E. Stearns
   1970   "Properties of deterministic top-down grammars", *Information and Control* 17.3: 226–256.

Rounds, William C.
1968   *Trees, transducers, and transformations* (Ann Arbor, MI: University Micro-
        films).
1970   "Mappings and grammars on trees", *Mathematical Systems Theory* 4.3:
        257–287.
Russell, Sylvia W.
1972   *Semantic categories of nominals for conceptual dependency analysis of
        natural language* (= AIM-172) (Stanford University).
Sager, Naomi
1967   "Syntactic analysis of natural language", in: *Advances in Computers 8*,
        edited by F. Alt and M. Rubinoff (New York: Academic Press).
1972   "Syntactic formatting of science information", *American Federation of
        Information Processing Societies Conference Proceedings* 41: 791–800.
1973   "The string parser for scientific literature", in: *Natural language processing,
        Courant Computer Science Symposium 8*, edited by R. Rustin (New York:
        Algorithmics Press), 61–87.
Salomaa, Arto
1973   *Formal languages* (New York: Academic Press).
Sammet, J. E.
1966   "The use of English as a programming language", *Communications of
        the Association for Computing Machinery* 9: 228–230.
1972   "An overview of programming languages for specialized application areas",
        *American Federation of Information Processing Societies Conference
        Proceedings* 40: 299–311.
Sandewall, W.
1971   "Representing natural language information in predicate calculus", *Machine
        Intelligence 6* (New York: American Elsevier), 255–277.
Savitch, Walter J.
1973   "How to make arbitrary grammars look like context-free grammars", *Society
        of Industrial and Applied Mathematics Journal of Computing* 2.3: 174–182.
Schank, Roger C.
1972a   "Conceptual dependency: A theory of natural language understanding",
        Cognitive Psychology 3: 552–631.
1972b   *Adverbs and belief* (= AIM-171) (Stanford University).
1973a   "The conceptual analysis of natural language", in: *Natural language pro-
        cessing, Courant Computer Science Symposium 8*, edited by R. Rustin
        (New York: Algorithmics Press), 291–309.
1973b   "Identification of conceptualizations underlying natural language", in:
        Computer models of thought and language, edited by R. C. Schank and
        K. M. Colby (San Francisco: W. F. Freeman & Co.).
1973c   *The fourteen primitive actions and their inferences* (= AIM-183) (Stan-
        ford University).
Schank, R. C. – K. M. Colby (Editors)
1973   *Computer models of thought and language* (San Francisco: W. H. Freeman
        & Co.).
Schank, Roger C. – Charles J. Rieger
1974   "Inference and the computer understanding of natural language", *Artificial
        Intelligence* 5.4: 373–412.
Schank, Roger C. – L. G. Tesler
1969   "A conceptual parser for natural language", in: *Proceedings of the Inter-
        national Joint Conference on Artificial Intelligence*, edited by Walker
        569–578.
1970   "A conceptual dependency parser for natural language", *Statistical Methods
        in Linguistics 6*.

Schank, R. C. et al.
1972   *Primitive concepts underlying verbs of thought* (= AIM-162) (Stanford University).

Schnorr, C. P.
1969   "Transformational classes of grammars", *Information and Control* 14.3: 252–277.

Schnorr, C. P. – H. Walter
1969   "Pullbackkonstruktionen bei Semi-Thuesystemen", *Elektronische Informationsverarbeitung und Kybernetik* 5.1: 27–36.

Schwarcz, Robert M.
1967   "Steps toward a model of linguistic performance: A preliminary step", *Mechanical Translation and Computational Linguistics* 10.3/4.

Schwarcz, R. M. et al.
1970   "A deductive question-answer for natural language inference", *Communications of the Association for Computing Machinery* 13.3: 167–183.

Scott, Dana
1972   "Continuous lattices", in: *Toposes, algebraic geometry and logic*, edited by F. W. Lawvere (*Lecture Notes in Mathematics* #274) (New York: Springer-Verlag).

Shapiro, Stuart A.
1974   Review of *Grammar, meaning and the machine analysis of language* by Y. A. Wilks, *American Journal of Computational Linguistics* Micro. 1: 46–50.

Shen, Stewart N. T. – Gilbert K. Krulee
1973   "Solving linear programming problems stated in English by computer", *Proceedings of the Association for Computing Machinery Annual Conference* (New York: Association for Computing Machinery), 299–303.

Shepard, C. D.
1969   "Languages in general algebras", *Proceedings of the First Association for Computing Machinery Symposium on Theory of Computing* (New York: Association for Computing Machinery), 155–163.

Siklóssy, L.
1972   "Natural language learning by computer", in: *Representation and meaning: Experiments with information processing systems*, edited by H. A. Simon and L. Siklóssy (Englewood Cliffs: Prentice-Hall), 288–338.

Siklóssy, L. – H. A. Simon
1972   "Some semantic methods for language processing", in: *Representation and meaning: Experiments with information processing systems*, edited by H. A. Simon and L. Siklóssy (Englewood Cliffs: Prentice-Hall), 49–65.

Simmons, R. F.
1965   "Answering English questions by computer: A survey", *Communications of the Association for Computing Machinery* 8.1: 53–70.
1966   "Automated language processing", in: *Annual review of information science and technology, vol. 1*, edited by Carlos A. Cuadra (New York: Interscience Publishers, Inc.).
1967   "Answering English questions by computer", in: *Automated language processing*, edited by H. Borko (New York: John Wiley & Sons), 253–289.
1970   "Natural language question-answering systems: 1969", *Communications of the Association for Computing Machinery* 13.1: 15–30.
1973   "Semantic networks: Their computation and use for understanding English sentences", in: *Computer models of thought and language*, edited by R. C. Schank and K. M. Colby (San Francisco: W. R. Freeman & Co.).

Simmons, R. F. – B. C. Bruce
 1971   "Some relations between predicate calculus and semantic net prepresenta-
           tions of discourse", *Second International Joint Conference on Artificial
           Intelligence* (London), 524–530.
Simmons, R. F. – J. F. Burger
 1968   "A semantic analyzer for English sentences", *Mechanical Translation and
           Computational Linguistics* 11, 1/2: 1–13.
Simmons, R. F. – J. Slocum
 1972   "Generating English discourse from semantic networks", *Communications
           of the Association for Computing Machinery* 15.10: 891–905.
Simmons, R. F. et al.
 1966   "An approach toward answering English questions from text", *American
           Federation of Information Processing Societies Conference Proceedings*
           30: 357–363.
 1968   "A computational model of verbal understanding", *American Federation
           of Information Processing Societies Conference Proceedings* 33: 441–456.
Solnitseff, N. – A. Yezerski
 1974   "A survey of extensible languages", *Review of Automatic Programming*,
           7.5.
Soule, S.
 1974   "Entropies of probabilistic grammars", *Information and Control* 25.1:
           57–74.
Stanat, D. F.
 1972   "Approximation of weighted type 0 languages by formal power series",
           Information and Control 21.4: 344–381.
Stearns, R. E. – P. M. Lewis II
 1969   "Property grammars and table machines", *Information and Control* 14.6:
           524–529.
Thatcher, J. W.
 1967   "Characterizing derivation trees of context-free grammars through a
           generalization of finite automata theory", *Journal of Computer and
           System Sciences* 1: 317–322.
 1970   "Generalized sequential machine maps", *Journal of Computer and
           Systems Sciences* 4.4: 339–367.
 1973   "Tree automata: An informal survey", in: *Currents in the theory of
           computing*, edited by A. V. Aho (Englewood Cliffs: Prentice-Hall), 143–
           172.
Thompson, F. B.
 1966   "English for the computer", *American Federation of Information Pro-
           cessing Societies Conference Proceedings* (Washington, D. C.: Spartan
           Books), 349–356.
Thompson, F. B. et al.
 1969   "REL: A Rapidly Extensible Language system", *Proceedings 24th Na-
           tional Conference of the Association for Computing Machinery*, 399–417.
Thompson, F. B. – B. H. Dostert
 1972   "The future of specialized languages", *American Federation of Informa-
           tion Processing Societies Conference Proceedings* 40: 313–319.
Thorne, J. et al.
 1968   "The syntactic analysis of English by machine", *Machine Intelligence* 3,
           edited by D. Michie (Edinburgh University Press).
Unger, S. H.
 1968   "A global parser for context-free phrase structure grammars", *Communica-
           tions of the Association for Computing Machinery* 11.4: 240–247.

164   David B. Benson

Walter, H.
1970   "Verallgemeinerte Pullbackkonstruktionen bei Semi-Thuesystemen und
        Grammatiken", *Elektronische Informationsverarbeitung und Kybernetik*
        6.4: 239–254.
1974   "Topologies on formal languages", to appear in *Mathematical Systems
        Theory*.
Weinreich, U.
1972   "Explorations in semantic theory" (= *Janua Linguarum, series minor* 89)
        (The Hague: Mouton).
Weintraub, K. Kathryn
1968   "The English relative clause", *Mechanical Translation and Computational
        Linguistics* 11.3/4.
Weizenbaum, Joseph
1966   "ELIZA – A computer program for the study of natural language communi-
        cation between man and machine", *Communications of the Association for
        Computing Machinery* 9.1: 36–45.
Wilks, Yorick
1968   "On-line semantic analysis of English texts", *Mechanical Translation and
        Computational Linguistics* 11.3/4.
1972   *Grammar, meaning and the machine analysis of language* (London: Rout-
        ledge & Kegan Paul).
1973a   "The Stanford machine translation project", in: *Natural language pro-
        cessing, Courant Computer Science Symposium 8*, edited by R. Rustin
        (New York: Algorithmics Press), 243–290.
1973b   "An artificial intelligence approach to machine translation", in: *Computer
        models of thought and language*, edited by R. C. Schank and K. M. Colby
        (San Francisco: W. F. Freeman & Co.).
1975   "An intelligent analyzer and understander of English", *Communications
        of the Association for Computing Machinery* 18.5 (May 1975) 264–274.
Winograd, T.
1972   *Understanding natural language* (New York: Academic Press).
Woods, W. A.
1968   "Procedural semantics for a question-answering machine", *American Federa-
        tion of Information Processing Societies Conference Proceedings* 33:
        457–471.
1970a   "Context-sensitive parsing", *Communications of the Association for
        Computing Machinery* 13.7: 437–445.
1970b   "Translation network grammars for natural language analysis", *Communica-
        tions of the Association for Computing Machinery* 13.10, 591–606.
1972a   "An experimental parsing system for transition network grammars", *Bolt,
        Beranek and Newman Report* 2362.
1972b   "The lunar sciences natural language information system", *Bolt, Beranek
        and Newman Report* 2378.
1973a   "An experimental parsing system for transition network grammars", in:
        Natural language processing, Courant Computer Science Symposium 8,
        edited by R. Rustin (New York: Algorithmics Press), 111–154.
1973b   "Progress in natural language understanding – an application to lunar
        geology", *American Federation of Information Processing Societies Con-
        ference Proceedings* 42: 441–450.

HERBERT G. BOHNERT and PAUL O. BACKER

Automatic English-to-logic translation in a simplified model

A study in the logic of grammar

Preface

This paper was originally issued in 1967 as Research Paper RC-1744 by the IBM Watson Research Center (jointly sponsored by IBM and the Air Force Office of Scientific Research [contract AF 49 (638)–1198]). Since then, its general thesis (that symbolic logic provides the best starting point for the logico-semantic analysis of natural language) has become independently familiar. The interchange between logicians and linguists, which was in its infancy at the time, has since become an extensive literature. But despite both the interchange and the considerable substantive progress that has been made, this paper continues to merit attention on several levels. On the programmatic level, its plan of stepwise elaboration, beginning with the grammar of logic itself and moving toward English by successive incorporation of regularized devices of natural grammar, beginning with the humblest, poses a significant alternative both to logical analysis of selected, "interesting" locutions, and to analysis in terms of linguistic productions and transformations, which have yet to make firm contact with logic. On the level of syntactic representation, its placer-demand scheme provides an attractively natural way of characterizing "telescoped" or "factored" forms of English that other grammars leave out of account. On the level of specific analyses, its treatment of determiners as longscope and shortscope (i. e., as yielding quantifiers of different length scopes, according to definite rules), and of nested relative clauses, are among several which have independent interest. Finally, the role and value of computers in such research is made especially evident.

1. The logic of grammar: Motives and methods

The grammar of any natural language appears exasperatingly illogical to any but the most unreflective native speaker. Therefore, the phrase in our subtitle,

"The logic of grammar", may sound naive. Yet underlying the evolutionary welter of conflicting rules, we sense the existence of basic communicative tasks, independent of any language in detail, but important for each language to find some way of doing: tasks such as naming, predicating, negating, and so on.

With a systematic inventory of what these basic tasks are, we could proceed in our study of various languages by studying the corresponding devices which each had developed, evaluating the efficiency and economy of each. Even when conflicting ways of doing the same task occur within a language, consistent rules can be separated out, made explicit, and studied as to the consequences of following each exclusively within the general framework, noting advantages and disadvantages, and possibly gaining some insight into why each has survived.

Thus, both in the generic communicational tasks and in the specific consequences of limited grammatical rules, there seems a basis for a *rational* analysis of grammar. Justification of the term "logic" in a narrower sense may be momentarily postponed.

The idea of analyzing a language in this way is not new. The very terms of ancient grammatical analysis, "dative", "ablative", "genitive", reflect an attempt to provide such a task analysis of grammatical features. In more recent times, the Danish philologist, Otto Jespersen, made a serious effort of this sort, perhaps the last within the framework of linguistics proper, which he called the notional, as opposed to the formal, approach to grammar (Jespersen 1927). The difficulty of carrying out such ideas bred an understandable skepticism among later linguists. The pendulum swung to *de facto* description with behaviorists such as Bloomfield and structuralists such as Harris.

The current broad drive toward exact syntactic description via generative and transformational grammars, initiated by Chomsky, inherited this skepticism, and at the outset stressed the independence of syntax from questions of communicative function or meaning (Chomsky 1961: 2). More recently, however, there has been increasing concern with the problem of relating each syntactic structure to a so-called deep structure which is intended to bear some closer relation to meaning than the apparent, or surface syntax admits (see Postal 1964; Chomsky 1965). This suggests that the pendulum may have begun a swing back toward something like Jespersen's notional analysis.

Thus "Barking dogs don't bite" and "Parallel lines don't meet" appear to have the same surface syntax. Yet the transformation which changes the first sentence into the equivalent "No barking dog bites" yields "No parallel line meets" when applied to the second, which is unintelligible. This is said to reveal a difference in deep structure in the originally given strings. But, in order to say exactly what the difference is, a system for representing deep structures must be found.

It is a thesis of the present study that an appropriate system of representation is already at hand. It is the notation of modern logic. It provides the needed inventory of basic tasks naturally and comprehensively. Indeed, the very terms used earlier to suggest the existence of basic tasks — "naming", "predicating", "negating" — belong to the basic vocabulary of logic, and its notation provides a systematic representation of them. Lest it be thought suitable only for such elementary notions as those mentioned, it should be borne in mind that it suffices for the formulation of all mathematics and hence for any formalized scientific theory. Even aspects of grammar which are not purely logical (but still notional in Jespersen's broader sense), such as tense, which is based on the physical concept of time, can be represented in logical notation with the help of explicit time symbolism, as will later be seen. It is in this sense that our use of the term "logic" seems appropriate.

This is not to say that current logical theory is adequate to represent all known grammatical devices. There are well-marked problem areas remaining, e. g., modalities, indirect discourse, causal locutions, etc. But its representational powers are, for example, quite equal to exhibiting the difference in deep structure in the two sample sentences given earlier. "Barking dogs don't bite" can be paraphrased:

1. For every x, if x is a dog and x is barking, then x does not bite (anything).

"Parallel lines don't meet" can be paraphrased:

2. For every x, for every y, if x is a line and y is a line and x is parallel to y, then x does not meet y.

Logicians will recognize these reformulations as corresponding to a familiar logical notation, revealing the difference to involve, among other things, the *relational* demands of "parallel" and "meets".

As the example suggests, our proposal is not merely the modest one that logical symbolism be used to systematize talk *about* the structure of sentences (Fodor-Katz 1964), but the more ambitious one that the sentence's deep structure be represented by an actual paraphrase in the notation of logic.

This idea, *per se*, is also not new. Not only have logicians from Aristotle, through the Stoics, Descartes, and Leibniz, analyzed specific sentence structures in the logical terms of their day, but Russell's writings give linguistic analyses in the modern symbolism he helped create; and later logicians, e. g., Quine, have contributed greatly to this development (Quine 1960a, 1960c).

While linguists have hardly begun to tap logic's potential even at this level, it remains true that such analyses so far have remained piecemeal. A grammar is, after all, a system of rules, and the logician's suggestions can only be evaluated adequately in terms of their operation within a system. Rudolf Carnap was apparently the first to suggest the possibility of approximately representing some part of a natural grammar by a logistic system[1], and was followed by Hans Reichenbach who made important suggestions for such work in this direction (Reichenbach 1947, ch. 7).

To the extent that a natural grammar can be approximated by a logistic model, an additional advantage is gained in being able to carry over to that part of natural grammar the integrated system of semantical concepts that have been developed for such systems by Tarski, Carnap, Bar-Hillel (1952) and others, e. g., designation, truth, consequence, information content, generality ("width") of predicates, and, of course, sameness of meaning, or synonymity, a concept pre-supposed in any discussion of deep structure.

Bar-Hillel (1954) urged these advantages upon linguists but was rebuffed by Chomsky (1955). Later, however, Chomsky has taken a more moderate wait-and-see attitude, along with his increasing interest in the deep structure problem.

Logistic modelling is admittedly a formidable task and even with its rationale fully accepted, it might normally be expected to be undertaken with reluctance. The advent of computers, however, has provided new incentive. There is obvious need to communicate with machines in as natural and flexible way as possible. This need has, together with the possibilities of machine translation and retrieval of information from natural language texts, already fostered a surge of research in natural language. So far, this has been almost entirely in the purely syntactic, transformational grammar tradition, with little attempt to relate the machine parses produced to logical representations. At the same time, however, there has been an impressive development of machine deduction based directly on logic (an early, and still impressive example: Wang's program (1960) which proved all three hundred and fifty of the first order theorems of *Principia Mathematica* in 8.4 minutes). The potentialities of a computer system which would translate from English, not just to a linguistic parse, but to logical notation thus became apparent to many writers independently in a fairly short time-period (cf. Williams 1956; Bohnert 1961; Cooper 1963).

There have, in fact, already been several computer programs written which translate from English-like sentences into logic; some linked with a deduction program permitting deductive solutions of problems posed in English. Perhaps the most advanced so far is that of Darlington (1965). In most of these, however, the focus has been on the practical possibilities with the analysis of grammar a secondary consideration. Typically, the exact part of grammar being modelled is not explicitly specified (though implicit in the program, after a fashion). While further development of these practical possibilities will in itself call for a deeper analysis of the logic of grammar, with embodiments in computer programs, there are strong reasons why the purely scientific analysis of grammar, logical as well as purely syntactic, should organize itself around the computer, as astrophysics once organized itself around the spectograph.

Quite aside from its obvious advantages of speed, it provides an almost indispensable check on the operation of proposed rules within a *system*. As might be expected, proposed grammatical rules interact, often in ways difficult to foresee. The computer, doing exactly what it is told, acts as a merciless critic. By the same token, when a program finally checks out over an intended range of sentences, it constitutes evidence of rule compatibility beyond that of even the most scrupulous human examination. A further, less direct, reason is that technical features of the underlying programs, such as the specific sorts of string manipulations or list structures required, seem rich in insight into basic features of linguistic information handling in machines, and perhaps in the human brain. While proper caution is called for here, such considerations might, in the long run, prove at least equally important.

With these motivations, the present study has embodied its basic logico-grammatical models in computer programs. The procedure has been to begin with a very roughly Englishlike language, English I, whose grammar is essentially that of elementary logic itself (similar to the representation provided for in the barking dogs-parallel lines comparison). This is in accord with the thesis that the tasks performed by elementary logical notation do, in fact, represent a linguistically basic repertoire. For this language, the principal task is providing a program which recognizes grammaticality (translation to logical symbolism being a simple dictionary operation). From there we proceeded to construct languages (i. e., by giving exact definition of sentencehood in terms of appropriate auxiliary concepts) which were progressively more Englishlike, each one accompanied not only by a recognition program, but by a program which translates it back to a standard logical notation. Thus our procedure might be described by saying that we start with deep structure and work toward surface syntax, rather than the other way around.

It may be felt that although an algorithm which translates to standard logical notation might provide a useful deep structure representation, and even a logic (as it does, if one rules that the logical relations which hold between sentences are just those that hold between their logical translations), it falls short of what one might expect of a logistic *model* of L. One might expect a logistic model of a natural language to resemble it not only in its basic syntactic categories and formation rules, but also in its logic, or transformation rules. There should be a "natural" logic, it might be urged, formulated in terms of the natural language forms, not their translations, and these should lead to a "natural" deep structure representation quite different from the artificial notation of logic. This is a reasonable aspiration and our more indirect procedure may be regarded as a roughhewn prolegomenon to such a finer modelling. This first step seems an almost mandatory one, however. We know that standard logic works, so to speak, and we can feel confident that the logic of a certain English device has been really understood if its translation to standard notation can be shown to be uniformly possible. It is hard to see how such confidence could be otherwise obtained. Indeed, any proposed more natural logic could hardly be justified itself except by some proof that it also provided a representation logically equivalent with the standard notation version.

From another viewpoint, the use of standard logic notation provides a valuable generality in its very non-resemblance to natural languages. It is strongly neutral with respect to the grammatical features that typically distinguish one natural language from another. Such notation does not distinguish between nouns, verbs, or adjectives. It has no declensions, genders, or rules of agreement. It has no tense, person, mood, or number. (Leibniz was perhaps the first to insist on the logical dispensability of such devices.) Yet the intended effect of these features can be paraphrased within the framework of this one, exact, very general grammar, as we shall try to show. It has often been remarked that grammatical studies have been badly warped by a tendency to force Latin tense and case paradigms on languages which had no corresponding mechanisms. Logic may suffer from its own provincialism but, if so, it is at least a far broader one.

Our treatment of syntactic ambiguity is another feature which may at first repel linguists. Our policy has been, when faced with such an ambiguity, to rule somewhat arbitrarily in favor of a single interpretation. More exactly, our formation rules alone "generate" well-formed strings which are ambiguous in the syntactic sense that their generation could have been accomplished in more than one way. Our recognition and translation rules, however, involve a transformation of each string to an unambiguous form. Our selection of an interpretation in this sense is guided not only by consideration of what the most "natural" interpretation might be, but also by whether there exists in our grammar an alternative, reasonably natural, way of expressing the rejected interpretation. This is to give any given model language as much referential capacity as possible, admittedly a normative rather than a descriptive consideration. The policy of "artificial" univocality, however, is in keeping with the methodological attitude expressed in the opening paragraphs: When faced by conflicting rules, make each explicit and follow out the consequences of adhering to each exclusively. Our present policy amounts to the initial step of following one rule in each case. Nothing prevents later exploration of other consistent readings, nor of constructing programs which successively yield a given range of possible readings. A more basic, though probably more arguable, reason is the belief that the vexing problems of ambiguity are not especially profound in principle and that they tend to confuse and obscure deeper syntactic or logical problems.

The present approach, then, represents a confluence of linguistics, logic, philosophical language analysis, and computer science, and it is addressed to specialists in all of these fields. With these distinct audiences in mind, care is taken to make the main line of discussion understandable to those without special training in logic or computer science. In fact, the grammar of logical notation will itself be informally developed first, so that the linguistic reader may have a fair opportunity to evaluate for himself the claims here put forward for it. Similarly, informal descriptions of the program algorithms will precede more technical treatments; informal characterizations of the model languages considered will accompany formal constructions, etc.

These procedures are, of course, not intended to substitute for courses in logic, training in programming, nor even as full preparation for following the technical portions in detail.

2. The grammar of logic: Predicating, compounding, generalizing

This section gives an informal overview of the syntax of typical logical notation and some of the questions it raises for the logical analysis of natural grammar.

2.1 Elementary predication

A central grammatical conception in all language, natural or artificial, is that of applying a predicate to a subject, or subjects, i. e., of "saying something about something". Its clearest manifestation is in ascribing some property to a single named object, e. g., "David is hungry". When the predicate is used to assert a relation between two objects (i. e., when it is *dyadic* in the terminology of logic), e. g., "David killed Goliath", "Boulogne is north of Paris", or among three objects (triadic), "Cleveland is between New York and Chicago", the situation need not be much more complex syntactically. All that is required is to specify the relation, name the participants in the tableau, and distinguish their role in it.

In a typical logic notation (one we will use), the attribute or relation is represented by a single capital letter (subscripted when the alphabet gives out), while the participants in the tableau (always a fixed number for a given predicate, called its *degree*) are named by single small letters (also possibly subscripted) trailing the predicate letter. The role of the participants in the tableau is fixed by the order in which the letters occur. Thus "a is between b and c" could be rendered as "Babc". I. e., if "a is between b and c" is rendered as "Babc", then "Bbac" would have to mean "b is between a and c", and "Bcba" would have to mean "c is between b and a". A predicate of degree n, followed by n *names* (small letters) is said to be an elementary (atomic) sentence (of the given notation).

2.2 Compounding

Compound sentences are built up by either of two methods:

1) (*parenthesis*, or infix, *notation*) introducing symbols for the *connectives* "or", "and", etc. with parentheses to avoid ambiguous grouping;

2) (*Polish* prefix *notation*) introducing symbols corresponding somewhat to English groupers "Either", "Both", etc. The two methods are illustrated below using small letters, beginning with "p", to stand for whole subsentences. Note that negation, acting on a single sentence, can be regarded as either connective or grouper.

Polish notation	Parenthesis	Rough Englishlike analogy
Np	~p	Not p
Bpq	(p · q)	Both p (and) q
Epq	(p v q)	Either p (or) q
Ipq	(p ⊃ q)	If p (then) q
BpEqr	(p · (q v r))	Both p (and) Either q (or) r
BEpqr	((p v q) · r)	Both Either p (or) q (and) r
EBpqr	((p · q) v r)	Either both p (and) q (or) r

The grouping letters here have been changed from Lukasiewicz's original 'Polish' notation to provide a mnemonic correlation with the English words on the right, to which we shall assign similar grouping functions in Englishlike languages.

2.3 Generalizing

Next we consider logic's means of obtaining *general sentences*, i. e., those which in English are typically expressed with the help of terms like "every" and "some". The required indefiniteness is obtained by introducing a new syntactic category: (individual) *variables*: $x, y, z, x_1, y_1, z_1, \ldots$ These act

like names syntactically. More exactly, if we lump names and variables together as (individual) *terms*, an n-degree predicate followed by n terms constitutes an elementary (or atomic) *formula*. These "indeterminate" formulas,
in turn, can be compounded, as atomic sentences were, into compound (or
molecular) formulas. Formulas containing variables can be transformed into
meaningful sentences of the system by applications of the *universal quantifier*,
"A", and the *existential* quantifier, "E", by admitting a rule that one may
prefix any formula, e. g. (Px v Qxy), by a quantifier followed by a variable
e. g., Ax(Px v Qxy), and still have a formula provided the original formula
did not already contain a subformula in which a quantifier is immediately
followed by the same variable (which would cause an ambiguity). The significance of the resulting formula is most easily conveyed by the following
paradigms:

> Ax _____   For every x, _____
> Ex _____   There exists (at least one) x such that _____
>   or   For some x, _____ ,

where the dash stands for the original formula, whose reading is, in itself,
not altered by prefixing the quantifier. In the paradigm shown, the variable
"x" is used but only as illustration. Any variable is admitted. The variable
following the quantifier is said to be bound in the formula to which it is
prefixed. Here parentheses again serve to prevent ambiguity. Thus in
(Ax(Px v Qx) v Rx) the "x" in "Rx" is not bound. It is said to be outside
the *scope* of the quantifier. The other occurrences of "x" are bound. A
variable unbound in a given formula is said to be *free* in that formula. In
order for a formula to have determinate meaning, then, all its variables must
be bound, in which case it is called a *sentence* of the system.

Interpreting a formalized language of that sort, i. e., giving it a *semantics*
as well as a *syntax*, requires among other things, that a *universe of discourse*
be specified (e. g., connected material objects, space-time regions, mass-
points) so that, e. g., when a sentence is prefixed by 'Ax' its universal claim
is indeed definite. The variables in such a notation are then said to *range over*
the universe of discourse.

By careful attention to the degree of predicates, the exact reading of
connectives, quantifiers, and their scopes, these simple syntactical means
can be combined to express complex sentences. Initial illustrations have
already been given in the barking dogs-parallel lines examples. A further
example will be given here.

Consider the sentence "A chain is no stronger than its weakest link". We
can symbolize the needed vocabulary and make clear the assignment of
roles to places in the predicational sequence by presenting each predicate

in a full atomic formula with distinct variables and matching it with a quasi-English paraphrase in which the same (variable) letters appear in the intended role:

Cx	x is a chain
Lxy	x is a link of y
Sxy	x is stronger than y

We shall need no other terms. In particular, we shall need no special symbolization for the superlative nor for the effect of the possessive pronoun. The latter is implicit in the decision to regard "link of" as a dyadic relation. The sense of the superlative "weakest" can be spelled out in terms of the comparative "stronger than". The given sentence can be rendered:

$$AxAy \ (Cx \cdot (Lyx \cdot {\sim}Ez \ (Lzx \cdot Syz)) \supset {\sim}Sxy) \ .$$

This can be stiffly but intelligibly read as follows:

"For every x for every y (if x is a chain and (y is a link of x and not (there is at least one z such that z is a link of x and y is stronger than z)) then not x is stronger than y".

Parentheses are retained to keep the grouping obvious. A somewhat more natural version would be:

"For any chain, x, and any of its links, y, such that there exists no link z, of x, stronger than y, chain x is not stronger than link y".

And of course the most natural of all is the original sentence.

The system we have so far described is referred to by logicians by various phrases: the first order predicate calculus, quantification theory, the restricted, or lower, functional calculus. While a more exact characterization could of course be given, it is hoped that enough has been said to convey an idea of its basic syntactical resources: 1) fixed-degree-fixed-order predication involving names and variables, 2) negating and compounding formulas according to some unambiguous scheme of grouping, 3) expressing generalized propositions by binding variables with quantifiers.

2.4 Problems for the logical analyst

Each of these features presents problems to the logical analyst of natural language:

1) How does a given language indicate role in a predication? How and to what extent does it achieve flexibility in predicational word order?

How can apparent variations in predicate degree be assimilated to a fixed degree system?

2) What devices does a given language have to indicate grouping? When a language compounds not only sentences, but subjects, objects, predicates, etc., can its syntax be analyzed sufficiently to be translated into logic's simpler system?

3) By what means does a given language express generality? Natural languages do not have anything quite like variables. Even pronouns, which have often been likened to variables, often fail to appear in general sentences, e. g., "Bees buzz" (universal), "Mary had a little lamb" (existential).

These are among the questions with which this study will be concerned. Though fundamental, they do not, of course, exhaust the problems of language nor the resources of logic. In particular, it may help to round out this preliminary survey of the grammar of logic to remark that logical systems more powerful than the first order calculus (which are needed in varying degree of strength for various parts of mathematics (and for analysis of even very elementary quantitative locutions in natural language)) will usually differ *syntactically* from the first order calculus, if at all, only in introducing new classes of *variables* (ranging over more abstract entities; sets, functions, numbers, etc.).

Certain forms of logic may employ a few other syntactical forms such as term-forming operators or function-symbols, but these are, in principle, eliminable. While we anticipate calling upon all the logical and syntactical resources of advanced logic (in analyzing quantitative locutions, abstract terms, modal auxiliaries (*may*, *must*, etc.)), the three features we have described, i. e., predicating, compounding, and generalizing, remain basic.

3. The grammar of English I and II

This central section of the report describes the grammar of our model, English II, alongside that of the more logic-like English I. Some of the notation is that of the SNOBOL program which processes the sentences of English II and translates them into English I preparatory to representation in parenthesis and Polish notation. The discussion is divided into grammatical topics. In each part a preliminary informal treatment is given to motivate the formalism of the rules which follow. The rules themselves constitute a self-contained recursive definition of the well-formed expressions of the language.

3.1 Predication

English I and II are restricted to third-person singular forms. They use a single tense, typically present, though simple past is sometimes used in the printout examples. Predicates are assigned a degree as in logic. In English II, predicates are also assigned a traditional category: Verb, Adjective, Noun. In elementary predication, these take the forms displayed in the following paradigm:

verb	Don runs	Don does not run
adjective	Don is tall	Don is not tall
noun	Don is a runner	Don is not a runner

After translation from English II to English I these settings are lost. The uncategorized English I equivalents are:

Don runs	Not Don runs
Don tall	Not Don tall
Don runner	Not Don runner

The copulas "is" and "does" are not regarded as verbs in English II but as part of the syntactical setting of adjectives and nouns. Whether a full, consistent analysis of the natural English copula is possible is not yet known. It is not attempted here. But one of the typical problem areas, the conflict between the predicative and identity use of "is", is discussed in a later section.

When a predicate (of any category) is of higher than first degree it often occurs in a pattern with other words, here called the *placers* of the given predicate, shown italicized below:

verb	George gives Fido *to* Don	x gives y *to* z
adjective	George is taller *than* Don	x (is) taller *than* y
	A is between B *and* C	x (is) between y *and* z
noun	Fido is a gift *from* George *to* Don	x (is a) gift *from* y *to* z

Placers will often belong to the traditional category of prepositions, but they need not (as in the case of "than" and "and" above). Webster's classifies "than" as a conjunction (1) but its defining entry is "Indicating the second member of a comparison expressive of inequality". I. e., its function is simply that of a placer. Note also its typical role in "A writer than whom no sage was wiser wrote 'Isagoge'", an example whose translation may be seen in the printout (Appendix B, Example 15).

Prepositions, on the other hand, do not always serve as placers. They often have a straight predicational use, in which their copular setting is not different from that of adjectives, as in the "between" example above. For this reason, such prepositions can occur in English II classified as (non-monadic) adjectives, while at the same time appearing as part of the placer pattern of other predicates. While it would be premature to deny all validity to the traditional category of preposition, this division of prepositional uses at least partly into those of idiomatically fixed placers and adjectives suggests that some revision of the concept is in order.

The use of placers to distinguish participants in the predicational tableau is a syntactical alternative to the use of order alone. Like the case system of an inflected language, e. g., Russian or Latin, it permits more flexible word order. English, indeed, does not take full advantage of its possibilities, since subject, and usually object, are not marked by placers and hence are frozen in position, in ordinary usage. Such fuller advantage could be seen, e. g., in a form of logical notation which introduced a special set of placer terms, e. g., $a_1, a_2, \ldots, a_i$, rewriting a four-place predicate M x y z w as follows:

$$M\ a_1 x\ a_2 y\ a_3 z\ a_4 w$$

With these placers, order could be shifted so that, e. g., "a_3 George a_1 John M a_2 William" would mean the same as "M John William George". Even here, however, complete freedom is not attained since *positionals* (placer-with-argument) of one predicate could not be allowed to stray among those of another. In contemplating the bookkeeping that would be required to permit complete freedom one quickly sees it would be prohibitively complex, if possible at all.

The advantages of some flexibility in word order, on the other hand, are by no means limited to rhetorical considerations. Some of its abbreviatory value will become clear in the later discussion of "factoring". A glimpse of its full theoretical significance may be seen in Quine (1960b) and in any treatment of combinatorial logic. Other devices for increasing flexibility in English and English II include the active-passive option and the use of converses (*husband*, *wife*).

English II, as so far described, then, admits proper names and predicates of three categories, verb, adjective, and noun, each with an accompanying pattern of placers, e. g., "x gives y to z". These are specified by the program user at the time of a machine run, forming a temporary dictionary. In compiling the dictionary, the program represents the pattern in a special form called the *demand* (since it indicates a demand of a predicate for arguments that must be filled to form a sentence). Such a dictionary can be regarded as an enumerative definition of expressions of the form "P is a predicate of category C with demand D" and of the term "name", thereby providing the first step in the recursive definition of "sentence" (of English II). Strictly speaking, of course, each different dictionary determines a different language, so that English II grammar should be regarded as a language *frame* rather than a fully determined syntax.

It may help to fix ideas at this point if we become more specific about notation, and especially about representation of the demand.

3.2 Notation

Several closely parallel notations are used. There is spelled-out English I and II and a parallel symbolic form. Thus "mHaL" is the symbolic form corresponding to "Mary had a little lamb". The use of upper and lower case in the symbolic form conforms to the usage of logic, in which individuals are represented by lower case, attributes by upper case letters. This conformity to logical rather than English usage is motivated by the possible interest of the notation for purely logical use, i. e., as a valuably terse notational addition to logic itself.

As in logical notation, furthermore, the use of mnemonic first letters (e. g., "m" for Mary) is admitted only in informal use. It is unwieldy for syntactical definitions and proofs, and for machine programs. Instead, proper names become "y_1", "y_2", . . . and predicates become subscripted "H"'s. These subscripted symbols are assigned, in fact, by the SNOBOL program in the order in which the experimenter enters them. One should distinguish, incidentally, between the transient symbolic language which has a finite number of subscripted "y"'s and "H"'s, corresponding to a given dictionary, and the theoretically convenient, unchanging, maximal symbolic language for which the infinite class of all subscripted "y"'s are names, etc. The recursive rules of English II, taking "name" and "predicate" as defined, apply to either, as does that part of the machine program which deals with the symbols only; but the input recognizer, which rejects non-dictionary words, causes the program as a whole to apply just to the experimenter's temporary language.

A further minor variation in representation is caused by the fact that the program handles only capitals and that subscripts must be raised to the main print-line. Thus, names appear as "Y1", "Y2", etc. Predicates will actually appear, e. g., as "H1.2", "H2.1", "H3.3", etc., where the first numeral is sequentially assigned and the second categorizes the predicate as verb(1), adjective(2), noun(3).

3.3 Demand

We come now to the program's representation of the predicational pattern, i. e., the *demand*. Such a pattern could be represented simply by the sequence of placers if each argument had an explicit placer. But since English has no subject placer, often no object placer, and sometimes even no indirect object placer ("John gave Mary a toy"), "null" placer symbols are introduced. The null placer symbols are "P0.1", "P0.2" . . . etc., where the zero indicates the null status and the second numeral stands for an argument position. Real placers, as encountered in the experimenter's predicational patterns, are assigned the symbols "P1.1", "P1.2", etc. The form of the demand used by the program, then, is a sequence of real and null placers, each followed by a slash. Thus the demand of "gives" with the pattern "x gives y to z" would be P0.1/P0.2/P1.5/, assuming that the placer "to" were the fifth placer encountered in the given dictionary. It is this representation of the demand that is to be understood in the formal syntactic rules to be given presently.

3.4 Compounding: The grouping problem

English I, like logic, can compound only formulas. There are no compound subjects, predicates, etc. To achieve unambiguous grouping it simply uses "not", "both", "either" and "if" like Polish groupers, but it retains the redundant associated connectives "and", "or", "then", as shown on the notation comparison table of the foregoing logic section (see under 2.2).

There is often a clumsy pile-up of groupers in English I (e. g., "Both either p or q and r and s"). But the system is, of course, unambiguous.

English II, like natural English, permits connectives unaccompanied by groupers. This leads to syntactic ambiguity, but it need not lead to semantic ambiguity if rules are applied during the reading which supply missing groupers. This is the method of the present program, which supplies groupers according to a precedence system.

Such techniques are familiar not only to logicians but more recently to programmers, in their handling of algebraic expressions where parentheses are omitted (Floyd 1963).

In the basic method, each connective is given a number called its precedence strength (in order from strongest to weakest: "not", "and", "or", (if) "then", "if and only if"), with the proviso, roughly speaking, that an ungrouped sentence "breaks" at its weakest connective. Thus "p and q or r" would break at "or" rather than at "and". That is, it would be grouped ((p and q) or r). English I groupers would accordingly be inserted: "Either both p and q or r".

In the case of repeated connectives, grouping is to the right, e. g., "p v q v r" becomes (p v (q v r)) or "either p or either q or r". This treatment of "or" and "and" as strictly dyadic may seem an artificiality of logic forced on language by the present approach. It may be artificial but it is not forced by logic *per se*. Systems of logic which permit nondyadic, expanding "and" and "or" expressions have been developed (Cook 1965) and may be resorted to when a finer modelling of natural language is called for, e. g. when measures of syntactic complexity in the sense of Bar-Hillel et al. (1963) become a focus of attention.

While the precedence system described above provides the general principle for the English II compounding-grouping system, there is a further refinement.

The precedence system is extended by introducing two additional connectives whose logical roles are still those of "or" and "and" but whose strength in the precedence system is altered. Thus, "or else" is introduced as a weaker "or" and "and furthermore" is introduced as a weaker "and". The grouping effect is shown in the following comparisons:

"p and q or r" is construed as $((p \cdot q) \vee r)$

while

"p and furthermore q or r" is construed as $(p \cdot (q \vee r))$.
"If p then q or r" is construed as "$(p \supset (q \vee r))$"

while

"if p then q or else r" is construed as $((p \supset q) \vee r)$.

These additional low strength connectives help in avoiding pile-ups of groupers. Without them, the grouping in the last example above would have to be made explicit by groupers:

"Either if p then q or r".

The rendition of these low precedence connectives by *longer* phrases is prompted by two plausible linguistic conjectures.

The first is that in spoken English, grouping is often effected by shifts in speed or by use of pauses. That is, if, in reading "p and q and r or t" we read it "p and q" pause "and r or t" the hearer tends to understand it as the independent assertion of p and q with an assertion of the disjunction "r or t", e. g., $(p \cdot q) \cdot (r \vee t)$; while if we read it "p" pause "and q and r or t" the hearer understands it as $p \cdot ((q \cdot r) \vee t)$, especially if "q and r" are read quickly.

The second conjecture is that words like "else", "furthermore", "moreover", etc., act as written counterparts of verbal pauses, allowing a certain mental "closure" to set in; something like mentally adding a right-hand parenthesis, sealing off what has been said from involvement with any connectives to follow.

The method of multiple precedences can be extended further, of course, by introducing, e. g., "it is not the case that" as a low precedence negation, etc. And it can be altered to study the naturalness of other rankings. The basic ranking actually used was: "not", "and", "or", "then", "or else", "and furthermore".

The machine representation of groupers and connectives can be seen in Table I, where they are displayed in order of their precedence. The precedence number is the first numeral, the function number the second. Thus the representation of "and furthermore" as C3.8 shows it to have low precedence, 3, but to function like "and", 8.

Table I   Logical terms

English I or II	machine symbolic	text symbolic	SNOBOL
Not	N	~	G9.9
Both	B	B	G8.8
And	.	.	C8.8
Either	E	E	G7.7
Or	V	v	C7.7
If	I	I	G6.6
Then	=*	⊃	C6.6
Or else	V*	v*	C4.7
And furthermore	.*	.*	C3.8
For every	A	A	Q1
For some	S	E	Q2
(variables)	Z1, Z2, . . .	x, y, z, x, y	Z1, Z2
Is	is	is	H1.1
Was	is	is	H1.1
Every	D1	e	D1
A	D2	a	D2
An	D2	a	D2
Any	D3	u	D3
Some	D4	s	D4
No	D5	n	D5
Which	W1	w	W1
Who	W2	w	W2
Whom	W3	w	W3

The general principle of the grouping program (a SNOBOL 3 function GRU(S)) is easily given. Each time a grouper is encountered its function number is entered in a pushdown. When a connective is encountered its function number is compared to that in the pushdown. On match, the pushdown is popped up (i. e., the demand of the grouper is satisfied) and the string between the grouper and connective is enclosed by parentheses. On no match, the connective goes on a "hunt" leftward through the string matching its precedence with that of each connective encountered (but skipping parenthesis-enclosed strings) until either (1) it comes to the beginning of the sentence, whereupon its corresponding grouper is placed at the head of the sentence, enclosing the traversed string by parentheses, or (2) it encounters a weaker connective whereupon it inserts its own corresponding grouper to the immediate right of the weaker connective, and encloses the traversed string with parentheses. After each such operation a new sentence is sought. If, when the end of the string is reached, there are no claims left in the pushdown, the string is wellformed and fully grouped. The parentheses or groupers are then edited out depending on whether Polish or parenthesis notation is desired.

Since the grouping-by-precedence system described is quite general, English II uses its GRU function to group compound subjects, predicates, etc. and it is to this topic we next turn.

3.4.1 Compounding terms

The sentence "George or Donald answered", in the diagramming method of high school memory[2], would be rendered as follows:

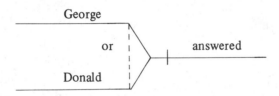

Logical notation does not admit compound subjects, and it pays for the simplicity of its rules in the clumsiness of its sentence structures. The sample sentence must be changed to "George answered or Donald answered" before direct translation into such notation (e. g., as Ag v Ad) is possible.

If we grant the primacy of logic's grammar, the English compound subject may be thought of as the result of *factoring* out the repeated predicate "answered". And the more primitive sentence may be thought of as attained from the more compact English sentence by *distribution* of the predicate over the compound subject.

This algebraic analogy may be seen more graphically if we imagine introducing a notation for compound subjects into logic in such a way that a "factoring law" establishes the equivalence:

$$A(g \vee d) \equiv Ag \vee Ad$$

Compound direct and indirect objects also occur in English, of course, and can be similarly handled. A sentence of the form "a gives b or c to d and e" with the traditional diagram:

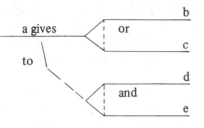

can be thought of as the result of successive factorings. The original "primitive" sentence can be recovered by successive distributions, as follows:

1.   a gives b to d and e or a gives c to d and e .

2.   a gives b to d and a gives b to e or a gives c to d and a gives c to e.

In the augmented logical notation, letting "G" stand for "gives", we would have the equivalence:

$$G(a, (b \lor c), (d \cdot e)) \equiv ((Gabd \cdot Gabe) \lor (Gacd \cdot Gace))$$

Formally, to construct a logic notation of this sort in which factoring and distribution would be possible we should have to alter the usual logic syntax so as to make compound individual expressions acceptable arguments for predicates, e. g. (a v (b · c)) as an argument to a predicate P, making P(a v (b · c)) a well-formed formula.

We now take the corresponding step in our recursive construction of English II. Instead, however, of merely defining "compound name" we introduce a more general word, "term" whose meaning will be extended by later steps in the recursion. Informally speaking, "term" will ultimately embrace all expressions which form acceptable arguments for English II predicates.

The required clauses for the recursion are the following:

1. Names are terms.

2. If a and b are terms, then so are the following:
   not a, both a and b, either a or b   (grouped forms)
   a and b, a or b,   (ungrouped forms)
   a and furthermore b, a or else b   (low precedence forms).

In this formulation, and others like it to follow, *any* letters, capital or small, or strings of them, may be used (as "a" and "b" have been here) as metalinguistic variables ranging over strings. In certain contexts some words

will be used without quotes to refer to themselves. The context will always
make clear what is meant.

Also, further statements belonging to the recursion will be abbreviated
by use of the symbols shown in Table I. Thus, the preceding list of forms
could have been presented as

Na, Ba.b, Eavb, a.b, avb, a.*b, av*b

with the agreement that a symbol corresponds to the spelled word followed
by a blank.

Terms, then, so far, consist of names and combinations of names, e. g.,
"George", "Charles and either Donald or Estelle and furthermore Arnold"
are counted among the terms of English II.

3.4.2 Compounding fragments

Besides compound subjects, objects, and indirect objects, traditional grammar
also recognizes compound *predicates* as in "George runs or walks". Indeed
all traditional categories are presumably compoundable.

Natural language factoring can, however, produce compounds which
correspond to no traditional category. Thus when an indirect object is
factored out as in:

"George sent the card and Tom wired the bouquet to Estelle", the string
"George sent the card and Tom wired the bouquet" does not constitute a
compound subject, or predicate, but a compound "sentence-with-missing-
indirect-object".

The corresponding logical notation would seem to be (Sgc. Wtb)e which
should distribute to Sgce · Wtbe.

To handle factoring in general, then, we appear to need a way of handling
fragments, i. e. expressions which *would* be well-formed sentences if they
were not defective in certain argument positions.

It was for the purpose of setting up such a needed calculus of fragments
that we introduced our concept of *demand*, which we can now extend to
fragments by a recursive process based on the demands assigned to the
predicates by the dictionary.

Similarly, the categories are extended to strings other than predicates.
Thus "either boy or girl" will be called a noun. "Noun phrase" may be used
in informal discussion, but it is not required in the recursion.

Throughout the following recursive stipulations it should be borne in
mind that "predicate" is reserved just for the words entered on dictionary
cards. Also, by the noun "demand" we always refer to a string of machine
symbols, possibly null which the recursion proceeds to associate with the

strings called fragments (though we shall continue to use "demand" more informally, both as noun and verb in accompanying explanations).

One null placer will be said to be *less than* another if its place number is less. E. g., PO.2 will be said to be less than PO.4. In this sense, we can also speak of the *lowest null placer* in a given demand.

We now proceed with the recursion, numbering the stipulations, 3, 4 . . . etc., as sequels to stipulations 1 and 2 given in 3.4.1.

3. If P is a predicate of demand D and category C then it is also a fragment with the same demand and category.

4. If t is a term and F is a fragment whose demand contains PO.1 then

tF, t does not F   (if F is a verb fragment) ⎫
t is F, t is not F   (if F is an adj fragment) ⎬
t is a F, t is not a F   (if F is a noun fragment) ⎭

are fragments whose demands are obtained by deleting PO.1/ and whose category remains that of F in each case, provided that such deletion does not leave the demand null; if null demand does result, the "filled" fragment is assigned the category of sentence.

5. If t is a term, p a non-null placer, F a fragment whose demand contains p then Fpt is a fragment whose demand is obtained by deleting p/ from the demand of F, and whose category is that of F, provided that such deletion does not leave the demand null, otherwise, a sentence.

6. If t is a term, F a fragment in whose demand a lowest null placer, p, exists but with p $\neq$ PO.1 then Ft is a fragment whose demand is obtained from that of F by deleting p/, and whose category is that of F, provided that such deletion does not leave the demand null, otherwise, a sentence.

7. If t is a term, F a fragment whose demand does not contain PO.1, p the lowest null placer in the demand of F, then tF is a fragment whose demand is obtained from that of F by deleting p/ and whose category is that of F provided that such deletion does not leave the demand null, otherwise, a sentence.

8. If t is a term, p a non-null placer, F a fragment whose demand contains p but not PO.1 then ptF, Fpt are fragments whose demand is obtained from that of F by deleting p/ and whose category is that of F provided that such deletion does not leave the demand null, otherwise, a sentence.

9. If F and G are fragments of identical category and demand then

NF, BF.G, EFvG, F.G, FvG, F.*G, Fv*G

are fragments of the same category and demand, provided that this does not result in a final term of F being separated from a first term of G by a connective. In such a case, the same compounds may be formed but with a comma preceding the connective.

10. If F and G are sentences then IF $\supset$ G is a sentence.

3.4.3 Informal explanation of the foregoing rules

Stipulation 3 simply includes predicates among the fragments and thus establishes some fragments, at least, as having a given demand.

4. says in effect that if you prefix a term to a fragment which demands a subject, in the copular setting required by the given category, you get a fragment which does not demand a subject. In this way, the concept of demand is extended from predicates such as "beats", with the demand PO.1/PO.2/ to strings such as "John beats" which would get the reduced demand PO.2/. Examination of later clauses will reveal that no other way of deleting a subject demand is provided other than use of the proper copular setting specified in stipulation 4. The category concept is extended to include *sentence*.

5. says that terms with a demanded non-null placer can always be added behind any fragment; e. g., suppose "takes" has the pattern x takes y from z to w, then to the fragment "John takes George" one may add "to NY" and then "from Chicago" to get the permuted, but understandable, pattern "John takes George to NY from Chicago".

6. says that placerless terms can also be added behind but they will be interpreted as filling the lowest placerless position demanded, but never that of subject. E. g., assume the placerless pattern "John gives George Fido" for "gives". Then adding Fido to the fragment "John gives" whose demand is PO.2/Po.3/, deletes the lowest placer, PO.2, i. e. that which accompanies the indirect object in this pattern.

7. says that when a fragment has a subject already, placerless terms may be added in front if they can be regarded as satisfying a lowest placerless demand at the fragment.

8. says that placed terms may be added before or after a fragment demanding them, provided it already has a subject.

With each concatenation of the above sorts to a fragment, its demand becomes less. This permits a certain "adjustment" of fragments so that they can form compounds under stipulation 9. Thus, "x gives y to z" is a triadic pattern with demand PO.1/PO.2/TO/ while "x waves to y" is a dyadic pattern with demand PO.1/TO/ (where "to" has been left uncoded for readability). But "gives Fido" is a fragment with demand PO.1/TO/which is the same as that of "waves" which permits the compound "gives Fido and waves" with the same demand. With the remaining demands satisfied, e. g., "George gives Fido and waves to Mary", we have an English II sentence.

The clause in 9. about the comma is to avoid ambiguity in a sentence such as "Albert likes Betty and Cathy and Dora likes Ernest".

In view of the characterization of "sentence" as a fragment with null demand in the foregoing stipulations, it might seem that "sentence" was now defined and that the characterization of English II was therefore completed. We would indeed have defined, at this point, a language of names and predicates, with factoring and grouping. This language, called LFG (LOGOS with Factoring and Grouping), was programmed separately and reported on in an earlier report[3]. Actually, of course, the stipulations have only established that filled fragments are among English II sentences; further stipulations could specify other forms. The extension to general sentences (e. g., universal and existential) undertaken in the next section, however, proceeds instead to extend the concepts *term* and (noun) *fragment*.

Before proceeding with the extension to general sentences, it may be helpful to sketch the procedure whereby sentences involving just factoring with names and predicates would be transformed to English I and to discuss some general points of interest in factoring. Stipulation 10 here will later be renumbered to come last (see Appendix A).

The transformation takes place, roughly speaking, in the following steps:

1. Recognition of compound individual expressions, assigning working names to each so that the sentence is rewritten with these names, without apparent compound individuals.

2. Build-up of a dictionary of recognized fragments with their demands until the sentence can be represented as a truth-function of filled fragments.

3. Distribution within each filled fragment of the individual "working names" so that each simple predicate is finally the sole predicate in its own filled fragment.

4. Successive distribution of each simple predicate over the compound individual expressions which are its actual arguments. (The first two steps are actually carried out in a single sweep of the sentence.)

It is worth pausing at this point to present some general observations on factoring.

One point of interest in factoring is that it represents a purely syntactical abbreviatory device. Throughout the history of logic, the central abbreviatory device has been that of defining a new term to stand for a longer expression.

In factoring, no new term is introduced. Instead, rules are added which permit expansion with the help of the already available logical connectives. Furthermore, this purely syntactical expansion has no pre-set limit. A defined term, on the other hand, permits only a single fixed saving.

A second point is that factoring can often replace the need for variables in logic or pronouns in natural language. Thus Ax(Px ⊃ Qx) can be abbreviated to A(P ⊃ Q). Also, in "You saw John and I saw him", the "him" is eliminated in the factorization "You and I saw John". Factoring when coupled with some way of representing permutations of predicates (e. g., converses) can, in fact, obviate variables altogether.

Factoring, as mentioned, can also act as a grouping device. Thus, A is P or A is Q and B is Q is ambiguous without a precedence system. With the present precedence system, it would be grouped A is P or (A is Q and B is Q). But, if the grouping (A is P or A is Q) and B is Q were intended, at least one explicit grouper would be needed. (Both) Either A is P or A is Q and B is Q. However, factoring can achieve this grouping without using groupers: A is P or Q and B is Q.

This grouping function of factoring may well play a vital role in human comprehension of linguistic communication, since abstract thought quite apparently operates by bunching complexities into simpler units for batch processing. For example, the (factored) input of Example 21 in Appendix B seems definitely easier to understand than the distributed output.

In natural language, factoring produces many more kinds of fragments than those mentioned. There are, as already remarked, compounds belonging to every syntactical category and every fragment of such categories. Even proper names are fragmented and factored: "Dr., Mrs., and Joanna Brown".

Factoring occurs also with the logical connectives acting like relations having whole sentences as arguments. Thus "A if and only if B" can be regarded as a factored form of "A if (B) and (A) only if B." It is even possible to regard the legal "A and/or B" as short for "A and or B" which could be a factorization of "(A and B) or (A or B)" where the "or" is read in the exclusive sense. That is, in symbols:

$$A((.) \not\equiv (\not\equiv)) B \equiv (A.B) \not\equiv (A \not\equiv B) [\equiv A \vee B]$$

Logicians sometimes informally factor out quantifiers, e. g., "AxyzEwuv Rxyzwuv" for "AxAyAzEwEuEvRxyzwuv".

It is apparent that no syntactical device is immune to factorization, whether it plays any independent semantic role or not. It is not known whether a general rule could be given, even for a relatively simple language, that would accomodate every possible unambiguous factorization.

When iterations grow very large, even factoring is not enough and the sentence form itself tends to be abandoned in favor of lists, tables, etc., in which the factored predicate, or magnitude designation, appears only as a heading. Nevertheless, even here an understanding of the factoring phenomenon may at least throw some light on the exact communicational role of lists and tables and correctly indicate their place in the more general framework of communication in sentence form.

We now return from these informal observations on factoring to the methods used for the formulation of universal and existential sentences in English I and II.

3.5 General sentences

To express general propositions (universal and existential), English I uses variables, $z_1, z_2, z_3, \ldots$ and quantifiers, "For-every" and "For-some", symbolized and coded as shown in Table I (see 3.4), so that English I is essentially a spelled-out version of predicate calculus in Polish notation, but with the retained connectives and predicational pattern described earlier.

English II uses no variables. It expresses generality with determiners: every, no, any, a, some; and the relative pronouns: which, who, whom. The latter permit formation of dependent clauses, nested and compounded.

We proceed forthwith to give the formational stipulation for determiners, followed by examples and a preliminary discussion of the intended logico-semantical functions of determiners.

3.5.1 Determiners

10. If d is a determiner and N is a noun fragment whose demand consists just of PO.1/ then dN is a term.

Such new sorts of terms include "every nation", "a pilot", "some friend of George", "any gift from Schmidt to Casey", "no shipment from either Tabu or Uuno to Manila or Djakarta". Such terms can, under the already given stipulations, fill any argument position in a predicate or a compound fragment. We also get such terms as "every associate of any Senator", "no flight between Tabu and any entrepot of an ally of any nonSEATOnation". Such examples can be manufactured for any given length by iterated use of predicates of other than first degree, though of course human users would not tend to avail themselves of such possibilities. With respect to the run-together name "nonSEATOnation", it should be remarked that not only does the present program require single-word names but that it can also not admit hyphens due to a conflict between our dictionary handling technique and a certain restriction in the SNOBOL 3 systems (string names may not use hyphens). But an easy, though slightly machine-time-expensive, elaboration of technique can remove both this and the single word-name restriction.

In order to translate English II sentences containing general terms involving determiners into English I sentences which express generality by the quantifier variable system, it is clear that the translating program must, when encountering a determiner, generate a variable as yet unused in the given translation process, substitute it in the argument place where the general term appeared, and then, in some way, insert both (1) a quantifier followed by the variable, and (2) a qualifying phrase containing the new variable specified by the (possibly very complex) noun which follows the determiner, somewhere in the sentence, together with appropriate scope indications.

As may be expected, each determiner requires a special rule.

While the full treatment of determiners in English II can not be described until the grammar specification is completed, the basic principles of their use can be illustrated in the framework of a simpler language in which neither copular settings, factoring, nor relative pronouns are admitted. We shall call this simplification of English II, L II. For its exact characterization see Bohnert (1962b).

For diagrammatic clarity, we use the determiner symbols shown in Table 1, e. g.,

e	every
a	a
u	any
s	some
n	no

in conjunction with the other "text symbolic" symbols, shown there, and with informally chosen predicate letters. Thus,

"Every businessman gambles"

might be represented as

eBg .

In English I, the corresponding sentence

"For every z_1 if z_1 businessman then z_1 gambles" could be represented as $Az_1 \, Iz_1 \, B \supset z_1 \, G$

or in parenthesis notation

$Az_1(Bz_1 \supset Gz_1)$.

As shown in these representations, "Every man gambles" has the form of a simple subject predicate sentence with the general term "every man" as subject. The logic versions, on the other hand, show it as a generalized compound sentence, in this case the universalization of an if-then (or *conditional* or *implication*) formula.

Following the steps outlined, the transformation may be carried out by

1. generating a variable, e. g., z_1;

2. substituting it for the general term, getting $z_1 G$;

3. placing the new variable, as subject, in a qualifying phrase provided by the general term, giving us $z_1 B$;

4. and, following the special rule for e, placing these pieces, with 1 and, in the conditional word order shown, universalized.

The rule for e will also require that the insertion of this qualifying quantified clause take place *within* whatever context the whole predicational unit which contains the general term itself occurs in. Thus, suppose we provide a context consisting only of a preceding negation, e. g. "Not every businessman gambles" or NeBG. The stated context rule requires the insertion of $Az_1 Iz_1 B$ within the context of eBG, i. e., *after* the negation. This gives

$$NAz_1 Iz_1 B \supset z_1 G$$

or in parenthesis form

$$\sim Az_1 (Bz_1 \supset Gz_1)$$

which is, of course, the normal logical rendition of the given sentence.

In order to state the last rule more fully, and similar rules for the other determiners, it will be convenient to symbolize the (possibly null) leading and following contexts as M and W respectively, and let dRS stand for a single predicational pattern, without inversions of the dictionary-given word order, in which dR *is the first general term to appear* (where d is the determiner being studied). This notation may be illustrated by the following:

Suppose "If George rejects every best seller then contract 17 terminates" is symbolized as

$$IgReB \supset cT$$

Then eB is the first general term in the predicational pattern gReB, which is, then, represented eBS, where S does not represent a predicate, but rather a metalinguistic transformation on eB. Applying the same transformation to z_7 for instance, we would have

$$z_7 S \to gRz_7$$

or in words, the S-transform of z_7 is the string "George rejects z_7".

The whole sentence, then, may be symbolized as M eBS W, where M, the leading context, stands just for "if", and W, the following context, stands for "then contract 17 terminates".

In stating the rules with the help of this symbolism we shall assume that the leading context, M, is either the null string or free of general terms, having already passed through the *determiner elimination* process which is being recursively characterized. In the same vein, in the transformation symbolism, dRS, in which the general term dR is the first such term to occur, we admit the possibility of earlier argument positions being occupied by variables resulting from earlier determiner elimination steps (whose quantifiers and qualifying clauses are already in the leading context string represented by M). Thus, the rules to be stated picture, so to speak, a moment in a left-to-right sweep of a given sentence when "the next" general term to be eliminated is encountered and then exhibit the result of the described single elimination step. Such elimination always involves generation of a variable not yet used in previous eliminations. (The present program does this simply by counting steps and concatenating the next numeral to z, e. g. $Z1$, $Z2$, etc.). The generated variable (letter and numeral) is represented by z in the schematism below.

The rules for determiner elimination in the simplified illustrative language are the following:

Rule for e (every)
    M eRS W → M AzIzR z S W
            M Az(zR zS) W

Rule for u (any)
    M uRS W → AzIzR ⊃ M zS W
            Az(zR ⊃ M zS W)

Rule for a (a, an)
    M aRS W → M EzBzR . zS W
            M EZ(ZR . zS) W

Rule for n (no)
    M nRS W → M AzIsR ⊃ NzS W
            M Az(zR ⊃ ∿ zS) W

Rule for s (some, in the sense of "some certain")

M sRS W → EzBzR . M zS W

Ez(zR . M zS W) .

The two readings on the right correspond to English I and parenthesis notation, respectively, except for the leading argument variation in the parenthesis notation.

We now study the effect of these rules in a number of examples, showing first a possible input sentence, which we will call stage 1, *s*l, shown both in symbolized and spelled form. Then come the transformations *s*2, *s*3, . . . which occur each time a determiner is encountered in reading the latest transform from the left. The last numbered transform in each sequence is the resulting parenthesis form sentence. Subsequent unnumbered transformations, marked with an arrow, are sometimes carried out according to transformation rules of logic itself to bring the result into a more readable form. Occasionally a further transformation will be given, back into English II or natural English for purposes of comparison, but this is meant informally since the reverse translation algorithms have not been stated.

1. *s*1: eBG   Every businessman gambles.
   *s*2: Ax(xB ⊃ xG)

2. *s*1: mHaL   Mary has a lamb.
   *s*2: Ex (xL.mHx)

3. *s*1: jReB   John reads every bestseller.
   *s*2: Ax(xB ⊃ jRx)

4. *s*1: jRuB   John reads any bestseller.
   *s*2: Ax(xB ⊃ jRx)   (Equivalent to 3)

5. *s*1: ∿jReB   John does not read every bestseller.
   *s*2: ∿Ax(xB ⊃ jRx)

6. *s*1: ∿jRuB   John does not read any bestseller.
   *s*2: Ax(xB ⊃ ∿jRx)   i. e., John reads no bestseller.

In 3 and 4, "every" and "any" seem to have the same meaning. But in other contexts, such as the negative forms of 5 and 6, their meanings diverge. It is the merit of our rules that this seeming discrepancy is shown to be the result of the straightforward operation of simple rules for each sign. The essential distinction between the two rules concerns the scope of the implied operator and the location of the qualifying clause. The idea harks back to Russell, who likens the behavior of "any" to free variables and that of "every" to bound variables. The idea has been touched upon and developed somewhat by various writers since then (Quine, Carnap) but apparently has not been incorporated in any formalized natural language model.

As a further example of a context in which the meanings of "every" and "any" diverge, but in a way accounted for by our rules, consider 7 and 8 below. Here a small liberty is taken with the symbolism in that "W" is meant to stand for the whole sentence "War occurs" or "There is a war". The analysis of such a sentence is inessential to the point being illustrated.

7. $s1$: eSH ⊃ ∿W   If every soldier stays home, there is no war.
   $s2$: Ax(xS ⊃ xH) ∿W

8. $s1$: uSH ⊃ ∿W   If any soldier stays home, there is no war.
   $s2$: Ax(xS ⊃ (sH ⊃ ∿W))
   → Ax(xS . xH ⊃ ∿W)
   → Ex(xS . xH) ⊃ ∿W
   → aSH ⊃ ∿W   i. e., If a soldier (at least one) stays home, there is no war.

Both in English and in the model language, 7 is a truism and 8 is a "falsism". These sentence forms are shown in Appendix B in the variation "If every guest declines then the party fails", "If any guest . . ." etc.

Just as the narrow scope "every" is accompanied by the broadscope "any", we would expect the narrow-scope a to have a broadscope correlate with the existential operator. As shown in the rules given earlier, "some", symbolized s, has been given this role. This reads well in many test contexts. However, actual English often prefers other locutions, such as "a certain" to effect the lengthening of scope. Some of the examples below may sound more clearcut if "a certain" is substituted for "some".

9. $s1$: ∿jKaG   John does not know a girl.
   $s2$: ∿(Ex(xG . jKx))
   → Ax(xG ⊃ ∿jKx)
   → jKnG   John knows no girl.

10. $s1$: ∿jKsG   John does not know some (certain) girl.
    $s2$: Ex(Gx . ∿jKx)   There is a girl John does not know.

Examples 9 and 10 exhibit the effect of short and long scope in a and s, as examples 5 and 6 did for e and u, in the simple context of negation. It is admitted that English is less compelling in its scope readings for these words than for "every" and "any", but they seem to hold up in many complex contexts such as those next considered. (Part of the problem of a word like a is that it presumably has other functions to perform, such as that of providing reference for later occurrences of definite singulars as described in Quine (1960).)

11. s1: eFaWFsG   Every friend of a ward boss is a friend of some
    s2: Ax(xFaW $\supset$ xFsG)   gangster (or of a certain gangster).
    s3: Ax(Ey(yW . xFy) $\supset$ xFsG)
    s4: Ez(zG . Ax(Ey(yW . xFy) $\supset$ xFz))   i. e. There is at least one
                                               gangster z such that every
                                               friend of a ward boss is a
                                               friend of z.

12. s1: eFsWFaG   Every friend of some ward boss is a friend of
                               a gangster.
    s4: Ey(yW . Ax(xFy $\supset$ Ez(zG . xFz))   By similar steps.

Examples for n:

13. s1: jRnB   John reads no bestseller.
    s2: Ax(xB $\supset$ $\sim$jRx)   equivalent to example 6

14. s1: nSRuB   No student reads any bestseller.
    s2: Ax(xs $\supset$ $\sim$xRuB)
    s3: Ay(yB $\supset$ Ax(xS $\supset$ $\sim$xRy))
    $\rightarrow$ Ay(Ax(yB . xs $\supset$ $\sim$xRy))

15. s1: nSRaB   No student reads a bestseller.
    s2: Ax(xS $\supset$ $\sim$xRaB)
    s3: Ax(xS $\supset$ $\sim$(Ey(yB . xRy))
    $\rightarrow$ Ax(Ay(xS . yB $\supset$ $\sim$xRy))   equivalent of 14.

16. s1: nSRsB   No student reads some (certain) bestseller.
    s2: Ax(xS $\supset$ $\sim$xRsB)
    s3: Ey(yB . Ax i xS $\supset$ $\sim$xRy)

17. s1: nSRnB   No student reads no bestseller.
                              (awkward but intelligible)
    s2: Ax(xS $\supset$ $\sim$xRnB)
    s3: Ax(xS $\supset$ $\sim$(Ay(yB $\supset$ $\sim$xRy))
    $\rightarrow$ Ax(xS $\supset$ Ey(yB . xRy))   i. e., Every student reads a bestseller.

It should be emphasized that the above determiner rules apply only to languages simplified in the way described. When factoring is admitted, for example, the order in which grouping, distribution, and determiner elimination steps are carried out is crucial to the "reading" of the sentence. Choosing the best possible sequence of operations becomes, indeed, one of the most complex problem areas in this approach to the logic of grammar.

Nevertheless, the rules shown illustrate the basic conception to be followed, and already shed some light on some interesting linguistic questions. We have already seen above the "every-some" ambivalence of "any" accounted for in terms of scope; also the scope lengthening effect of phrases like "a certain" or "some certain".

Now we turn to the further questions: one concerning an important ambiguity of "is" and the other an odd phenomenon associated with the active-passive transformation.

3.5.2 "Is": Predication and identity

"Is" is notoriously ambiguous. We shall not attempt a catalogue of all the meaning variations linguists, lexicographers, and logicians have found in it (e. g. identity, genidentity, class membership, class inclusion, existence, location, synonymy, etc.) but shall consider just the conflict between the "is" of identity (as in "Venus is (identical with) the nearest planet") and the predicational "is" used in ascribing a property to something, e. g. "Mt. Everest is high" (not *identical* with high). This clash may already have disturbed the reader of this study in finding "a star" treated as a term in a context such as "A star rose", while in "Betelgeuse is a star" the "is a" is swept away as mere syntactical setting, leaving "Betelgeuse star", in English I, as a simple predication with star as predicate.

Suppose that in the latter example "is" is read as identity (symbolized by "=" and that "a star" is treated as a term, i. e., as the second argument in the dyadic identity relation. Then "Betelgeuse is a star" may be symbolized $b = aS$. Using the determiner elimination rule for "a" we have

$$Ez(zS . b = z)$$

or "For some z, z is a star and b is (identical with) z". This can be shown to be logically equivalent to the simpler predication bS, or "Betelgeuse (is a) star".

Such a proof, interestingly enough, can not be carried out in the simple first order logic we have so far used but only in *first order logic with identity*, a somewhat stronger system which, while still syntactically first order, requires a special set of axioms for identity. Taking the obvious equivalence of meaning for granted, however, we can verify that the proposed identity reading for "is" consistently reacts with general terms in a way consistent with our decision to treat them as terms. That is, in a language without adjectives (which require the predicational reading) we could always read "is" as identity. The point may be illustrated by recasting earlier examples.

$s1$: eB = aG   Every businessman is a gambler.
$s2$: Ax(xB ⊃ x = aG)
$s3$: Ax(xB ⊃ Ey(yG . x = y))
→   Ax(xB ⊃ xG)   Which is equivalent to example 1, as it should be.
$s1$: eFaW = aFaG   Every friend of a ward boss is a friend of a gangster.
$s2$: Ax(xFaW ⊃ x = aFaG)
$s3$: Ax(Ey(yW . xFy) ⊃ x = aFaG)
$s4$: Ax(Ey(yW . xFy) ⊃ Ez(zFaG . X = z))
$s5$: Ax(Ey(yW . xFy) ⊃ Ez(Ew(wG . zFw) . x = z))
→   Ax(Ay(yW . xFy ⊃ Ew(wG . xFw)))   i. e., Every friend of any ward boss is a friend of a gangster.

This representation also has a certain historical interest for logicians. (Others are invited to skip this brief digression.) Ancient laws of the syllogism are phrased with the concept of a *distributed* term. A class term is said to be distributed in one of the four traditional propositional forms, if the proposition says something about each member of the class. It is also said that it is just the subjects of universal sentences and the predicates of negative sentences which are the distributed terms, that is, the underlined terms below, in the traditional AEIO scheme.

A. Positive Universal
   All *P's* are Q's

E. Negative Universal
   No *P's* are *Q's*

I. Positive Particular
   Some P's are Q's

O. Negative Particular
   Some P's are not *Q's*

Just why the italicized terms are said to be distributed in the sense that the proposition says something about each member is not equally clear in all cases. It is obvious enough for the A case. It becomes clear in the E case for the P term at least when it is rendered in modern symbolism as Ax(xP ⊃ ∿xQ), since this makes the universal quantifier explicit. This then clarifies then Q term also when the equivalent contrapositive, "no Q is P" is symbolized in turn.

But the Q term in the O case is symbolized as Ex(xP . ∿xQ) and no usual transformation turns up a prefixed universal quantifier; one does show up, however, if we express the four propositions in our English II singular general terms with determiners, with "is" read as identity, and with a rule (adopted in English II) that when a negated term (syntactically permitted in our earlier recursive stipulations) is encountered at a certain argument position, the negation is transferred from the term to the predication in which it stands, before its determiner is eliminated. We illustrate the effect of our general-terms-with-identity parse on all four cases, but direct special attention is paid to the O case.

A. $s1$: $eP = aQ$ Every P is a Q
   $s2$: $Ax(xP \supset x = aQ)$
   $s3$: $Ax(xP \supset Ey(yQ . x = y))$
   $\rightarrow$ $AxEy(xP \supset (yQ . x = y))$

E. $s1$: $nP = aQ$ No P is a Q
   $s2$: $Ax(xP \supset \sim x = aQ)$
   $s3$: $Ax(xP \supset \sim Ey(yQ . x = y))$ (short scope rule for a)
   $\rightarrow$ $AxAy(xP . yQ \supset \sim x = y)$

I. $s1$: $aP = aQ$ a P is a Q
   $s2$: $Ex(xp . x = aQ)$ (Same transformations occur for
   $s3$: $Ex(xP . Ey(yQ . x = y))$ "some P is a Q" $sP = eQ$.)
   $\rightarrow$ $ExEy(xP . (yQ . x = y))$

O. $s1$: $aP = \sim aQ$ a P is not a Q
   $s2$: $Ex(xP . x = \sim aQ)$
   $s3$: $Ex(xP . \sim x = aQ)$ Transfer of negation when negated term
                                           is encountered)
   $s4$: $Ex(xP . \sim Ey(yQ . x = y))$ (Short scope rule for a)
   $\rightarrow$ $ExAy(xP . yQ \supset \sim x = y)$ (Same transformation results from *Some*
                                           P is not a Q)

It will be noticed that in each of the final formulas a universal quantifier appears in the prefix corresponding exactly to those terms which have been called distributed.

Unfortunately, "is" *is* ambiguous and presents an obstacle. It might be urged that since "is" acts predicationally before adjectives and could be consistently, if clumsily, interpreted as "=" before general terms, proper names (and other items not yet entering our analysis such as "the" phrases, pronouns, functors), that a systematic dependence on context could be built into a sufficiently orderly model of English. This may be so but there would be at least considerable clumsiness in devising a system which would take a compound of adjectives and general terms, such as "Smith is experienced, able, a negro, and a war veteran" and shift treatments of "is" during distribution.

It is because of such difficulties that English II has admitted certain crudities in its handling of "is a".

3.5.3 When the active-passive transformation involves general terms

"John likes Mary" means the same as "Mary is liked by John". This seems, at first glance, an instance of a general rule that "x likes y" means the same as "y is liked by x". But we then note that "No girl is liked by every boy" is different in meaning from "Every boy likes no girl". At first glance, it appears we must either abandon the general rule of active-passive equivalence or attempt to force the same meaning on the two general term sentences. Luckily there is a way in which we can have both our rule and the apparent exceptions too. Since our underlying logic uses variables, our rule could be stated using them just as given above. But we have not specified a logic for English II except by saying that the logical relations which hold between English II sentences are just those which hold between their translations into logic (by the program). In particular, we have not broadened the under-lying logic by adding a rule that general terms of English II may be sub-stituted for variables (e. g. in any law of logic or any definition).

Thus, in the formula "x likes y if and only if y is liked by x" we can not substitute the general terms "no girl" or "every boy". The only way to study the logical relation between the two sentences is to translate each into its logical equivalent by sequential elimination of determiners and compare the results. When we do this, we discover that we have exhibited the very differ-ence of meaning we instinctively felt in the first place. In the following elimina-tion process we symbolize the passive formation of L (likes) by $\breve{L}$ (is liked by).

$s1$: nG$\breve{L}$eB   No girl is liked by every boy.
$s2$: Ax(xG $\supset$ $\sim$x$\breve{L}$eB)
$s3$: Ax(xG $\supset$ $\sim$(Ay(By $\supset$ x$\breve{L}$y)))
$\rightarrow$ Ax(xG $\supset$ (Ey(By . $\sim$x$\breve{L}$y)))

$s1$: eBLnG   Every boy likes no girl.
$s2$: Ax(xB $\supset$ xLnG)
$s3$: Ax(xB $\supset$ Ay(Gy $\supset$ $\sim$xLy))
  Ax(Ay(xB .. yG $\supset$ $\sim$xLy))

A similar explanation (within a higher order logic) can be given for the variation between: "Everyone in this room speaks two languages", "Two languages are spoken by everybody in this room". In these, and similar examples, we see evidence that the order of occurrence of indefinite singular terms or other quantificational idioms in English sentences has much the same significance as the order of operators in a sentence of formal logic, and that the present left-to-right scan technique accurately preserves this parallelism.

3.5.4 Relative pronouns and dependent clauses

The grammatical "power" of English II will now be advanced by the incorporation of dependent clauses introduced by the relative pronouns "who", "whom", and "which". These in turn are then used to make a further broadening of the concept of term. As in earlier sections, the stipulations are given first, and then illustrated and discussed.

11. If w is a relative pronoun and F is a fragment whose demand consists just of PO.1/ then

    wF   (if F is a verb) ⎤
    w is F   (if F is an adj) ⎬ is a relative clause.
    w is a F   (if F is a noun) ⎦

It should be noted that the relative clause rules extend the term concept but do not, independently, extend the fragment concept. They do not, for example, admit a monadic fragment such as "civilian who informed or soldier who deserted or official against whom a complaint was filed". Such a combination would seem to be admitted by a rule of the following form, acting together with the fragment combination rule:

If F is a fragment with demand PO.1, R a relative clause then FR is a fragment with demand PO.1.

While such fragments occur in English, their analysis within the present system raises certain problems akin to the scope problems within general terms discussed in Quine (1960a). The above rule, in any case, will not do, since while one application might produce the permissible "civilian who informed", iterated application would produce, e. g., "civilian who informed who informed who deserted against whom . . ." etc.

3.5.5 Prepositional phrases

Before leaving the syntax of relative clauses, it should be remarked that the familiar grammatical category of *prepositional phrases* consists largely, if not entirely, of relative clauses from which the relative pronoun has been dropped along with any copular setting with the placer, if any, which had accompanied the relative pronoun removed to the end of the clause.

12. If w is a relative pronoun and F is a fragment whose demand consists just of p/, p ≠ PO.1, then

    pwf   (if p is not a null placer) ⎤
    wF   (if p is a null placer)   ⎦ is a relative clause.

13. If R and S are relative clauses then
    R. S, RvS are relative clauses.

14. If d is a determiner, n a name, F a fragment of the noun category whose
    demand is just PO.1/, and R a relative clause, then dPR, nR are terms.

These stipulations may be illustrated as follows:

Simple applications of 11: "which hurts", "who is present", "who is a
musician".
Simple applications of 12: "over whom Napoleon triumphed", "which
George bought", "to whom George gave a toy".
Simple applications of 13: "from which coffee is exported and to which
iron is imported", "which radios or from which a flare is fired".
Simple applications of 14: "every bill which is outstanding", "no student
who lacks a pass", "George who is a musician".
More general relative clause: "to whom George or Anne gave a toy which
buzzes or an instrument which plonks or toots or who was backstage".
More general term: every man or woman or child who was present or to
whom an invitation to every theater which participated was sent".
Consider the example: "Every stoplight between a school crossing intersection and a certain intersection near a department store is on auto-control".
The prepositional phrases are easily, if inelegantly, transformed into relative-
pronoun-introduced relative clauses as follows: "Every stoplight which is between an intersection which is a school-crossing and a certain intersection
which is near a department store is on auto-control".
Just as the grouping of the program is able to insert missing groupers, so
an additional branch could either convert prepositional phrases to dependent
clauses or, working directly, subject them to the analogous transformation.
The details must, however, be left for future investigation.

3.5.6 Translational principle for relative pronouns

The principle underlying our translation technique for relative pronouns can
be put informally as follows. When a relative pronoun, possibly preceded by
a placer, is encountered in a left-to-right sweep during what we shall call the
determiner elimination phase of the processing, its immediate predecessor
will be either a formula in which a variable has just replaced a determiner by
a preceding determiner elimination or it will be a proper name. Following
the relative pronoun there will be a fragment whose demand (always a single
placer) will already have been computed. The relative pronoun is, then,
replaced by the preceding name or variable. This, with the accompanying
placer, if any, is then shifted to the argument position indicated by the

demand of the following fragment (if it is a simple predicate, otherwise it, *with* the fragment, form a new fragment with null demand to await a later distributional phase). This formula is added by inserting the "both" grouper and the "and" connective.

Consider the sentence "every child to whom a toy is given is happy", or

eC to w aT is G is H .

The first determiner elimination step yields:

AxIxC to w aT is G $\supset$ xH.

Preceding the to w is a formula in which x has just replaced the determiner e. The fragment "a toy is given" demands a to y completion. More exactly, its demand is TO/, with the dictionary revealing that in the natural order TO is the third position marker. The preceding x then replaces the w and the positional to x is shifted to its natural position, giving the well-formed formula

a toy is given to x, or, aT is G to x.

Forming the conjunction, the sentence becomes

AxIBxC . aT is G to x $\supset$ xH

Elimination of the determiner a now yields

AxIBxC . EyByT. y is G to x $\supset$ xH

i. e., "for every x if both x child and for some y both y toy and y is given to x then x happy".

The rules for eliminating relative pronouns can be given in the symbolism earlier employed to describe determiner elimination:

$$M zS_1 pwS_2 W \rightarrow M BzS_1 . pzS_2 W$$
$$M zS_1 wS_2 W \rightarrow M BzS_1 . zS_2 W$$

where both S_1 and S_2 are predicational transformations, as S alone was in the determiner elimination rules.

3.6 The recognition-translation method

The task of constructing a mechanical recognition method for a recursively defined set of strings is seldom easy (and may be impossible: the class of first

order theorems is recursively definable but it is known that the problem of
finding a first order decision method, i. e., a mechanical method for recognizing
theorems, is recursively unsolvable). For English II the problem is solved, but
the method requires techniques and concepts not obvious from the recursive
stipulations given.

The method used involves several major phases, most of them involving
iterations or recursions of levels corresponding to the various sorts of nesting
that may appear in an English II sentence.

The first phase is simple enough. It translates the spelled input into the
SNOBOL code (thereby checking that all the words encountered belong to
the logical vocabulary or the temporary dictionary). The SNOBOL code is
needed not only for its brevity but for the syntactical information that is
packed into each code word, precedences, categories, etc.

The second, or parse, phase analyzes the input string by an aggregating
process in which it

1. lumps terms together, giving each maximal string of terms it encounters
   an auxiliary symbol beginning with an "I" (for individual) which it thereafter treats as a proper name. This is, of course, a recursive process since
   terms may contain general terms and dependencies which may contain
   further general terms, etc. Therefore, the auxiliary I symbols are coded
   according to a level system;

2. picks out a given momentary level in a sequence of substrings which we
   shall call *fractions*. Each fraction consists of a single dictionary predicate
   accompanied by whatever arguments and groupers are not separated from
   the predicate by connectives. Thus in

   A both gave B and sold C to D

"A both gave B" and "sold C to D" are fractions.

By consulting the dictionary-given demands of the predicates in each fraction and computing the demands of the fractions (disregarding imbedded
groupers), it identifies which fractions can merge with which to form
fragments whose demands it computes in turn until the string under consideration can be regarded as a compound of minimal-length, null-demand
fragments called L-atoms to each of which the parser assigns an auxiliary
symbol beginning with an L and numbered according to its level and position.

The result of this phase is to exhibit the sentence as a Boolean combination of simple predications but with the "names" and "predicates" involved
being auxiliary symbols actually representing, e. g., compounded general terms,

fragments, etc. A temporary dictionary is built up for such auxiliary predicates, assigning them (computed) demands.

The third phase eliminates determiners and relative pronouns according to the general principles stated earlier, but working from the inmost and lowest level components outward. Copulas are tailored away in the process.

The fourth is the distribution phase. Within each filled fragment the individual "working names" are distributed to the components of the fragment, until each simple predicate is finally the sole predicate in its own filled fragment. The individual terms represented by the working names are now Boolean combinations of proper names and variables. The predicates are distributed over these compound individuals.

The fifth, or output phase, by minor trimmings and replacements translates the transformed SNOBOL string into the format desired: English I, parenthesis notation, Polish notation, or parenthesis notation in which the elementary predications (atoms) are spelled out.

4. Conclusion

In this final section we review the accomplishments of the project, the insights gained, and the difficulties encountered, and comment on the theoretical and practical potential of logic-based, machine-implemented analyses of natural grammar of the type here exemplified.

Speaking first in a general way, we have shown by example that syntactical ambiguity (in the sense of current linguistics, i. e., the well-formedness of a string can be established by more than one sequence of formation rule applications) need have little relation with semantic ambiguity for a machine, provided that its read-parse algorithm is equipped with adequate resolution rules (e. g., of grouping, scope, distribution, etc.). This raises a serious question as to whether formation rules alone provide an adequate explication of "grammar". It may be claimed that such ambiguity-resolving parse algorithms step beyond syntax into semantics, but actually they make use only of syntactical information (if it be granted that the association of numbers such as degree and precedence with elements of vocabulary is not a semantical step).

We have demonstrated to our own satisfaction that the embodiment of parsing algorithms in a computer program is an almost indispensable heuristic procedure. Not only have program runs repeatedly revealed subtle errors in algorithms which showed up only in examples too complicated to have been analyzed by hand, but is has, on occasions, provided valuable positive suggestions as to possible simplifying paraphrases. One example concerned the ambiguity in the scope of a relative pronoun following a compound expression. In the following two sentences, for example, the scope of "who" varies:

1. Any Ph. D. or applicant who has seven years experience is eligible for the job.

2. Any instructor or professor who has taught seven years is eligible for a sabbatical.

In the first, "who" refers only to the applicant; in the second, "who" distributes to both instructor and professor. In accord with the policy of selecting only one out of several competing rules for English II, we chose the first sentence as our paradigm, but then had difficulty in finding an economical paraphrase for the idea expressed in the second. Later, a slight change in the program for another reason had the unintended effect of reversing our decision on this point, and an example involving compound general terms provided us with a possible paraphrase for the *first* sentence, i. e.,

> Any PhD and any applicant who has seven years experience is eligible for the job.

This is not graceful English, but it is understandable, not cumbersome, and translates to the correct logical formulation, and thus serves our approximative purpose for the present stage of modelling.

At other times, we have been led to more deliberate heuristic use of the program, e. g., when the grammar becomes too complex to permit examination of all consequences of a new change. This was particularly the case in testing rules governing negation, since in English II, negation appears in many contexts, negated names, negated predicates, negated general terms, negated compounds, negated fragments, negations imbedded in dependent clauses, etc.

Speaking more particularly, we have explored the natural language correlates of the logical concepts of degree, grouping, quantification, scope. We have embodied and coordinated, in a single machine-parse system, several longstanding suggestions of logicians:

1) That the logical concept of predicate *degree* offers a basis for a unified understanding of the role of cases and prepositions, the transitive-intransitive distinction, the active-passive relationship and related phenomena (especially stressed by Reichenbach);

2) That words like "if", "either", "both", act like truth-functional groupers (most recently remarked on by Quine);

3) That "any P" behaves logically like an unquantified variable restricted to the domain P (Russell);

4) That pronouns perform, to some extent, the function of variables in logic.

In following the first line of suggestions (concerning degree), we have been led to the concept of *placer* as a basic grammatical function category as yet little recognized by grammarians. The phrase "grammatical function category" may be understood, for present purposes, by reference to familiar remarks of grammarians such as that in such-and-such a context a certain phrase *functions* adverbially. With the placer concept, we may say that prepositions often *function* as placers (as do words belonging to other traditional categories: the "and" of "between x and y") but that they also may function as independent dyadic predicate adjectives ("x is *in* y").

We have amplified the second line of suggestions with our grouper-avoiding system of precedences, extended by our conjecture that the grouping effect of such phrases as "and furthermore" may be modelled by a system of multiple precedences.

The third line of suggestions, concerning "any", has been amplified so as to make variations of quantifier *scope* a primary consideration in the analysis of natural language. Thus the effect of "some", in the sense of "some certain", is attained with our long-*scope* rule.

Indeed, the very idea of translating general terms into expression involving quantifiers and variables raises the question of the *order* of quantification, in a way little suggested by traditional grammar itself.

Our scope rules, together with our rule for quantifying according to the left-to-right order in which general terms are encountered, have enabled us to demonstrate a unified algorithm which automatically and correctly interprets (1) the "puzzling" variation in the meaning of "any", depending on context, and (2) the "puzzling" variation in meaning when the active-passive transformation is carried out with general terms instead of names (as in the "No girl is liked by every boy" — "Every boy likes no girl" example).

The fourth area of suggestion (concerning pronouns and variables) has been entered only to the extent of incorporating the relative pronouns "who", "whom", and "which", thus permitting the formation of (indefinitely nested) dependent clauses. What Quine has called the "cross-referencing" function of variables is exemplified here to the extent that a relative pronoun triggers pick-up of a variable already generated by a preceding general term.

Other relative pronouns, such as "when", "where" can be handled similarly in simple extensions of English II in which time and place variables are admitted along with time-dependent predicates. In present English II, they can be paraphrased by "time which", "place which", etc.

Indefinite pronouns, such as "something", "everybody", etc. can be included by an extra step in the scan process which would divide such words, making them into general terms, e. g., "some thing", "every body", etc., where, of course, "thing", "body", etc. would be included as monadic predicates in the dictionary. Since this method produces redundant clauses, however, a more direct method should be used.

The successful handling of relative pronouns places us not too far from being able to accept and analyze a large class of prepositional phrases, namely, those which can be regarded as formed by dropping a relative pronoun and its setting, as in "the boy (who was) by the window". Analyzing such forms is, of course, a restoration process, and hence may not be trivial.

It must be admitted, however, that since (third person) personal pronouns are not included in English II, it has less expressive power than English I (and the predicate calculus). That is, there are formulas of logic which have no English II paraphrase, e. g., AxAy(Rxy ⊃ Sxy). The exact class of formulas which English II can paraphrase has not yet been exactly characterized. It is obviously not limited to the monadic calculus since De Morgan's relational "horse's head" argument can be expressed in it. This sort of problem, which may be called that of the *articulateness* of a given language is little investigated by linguists, apparently because they are committed to the view that any natural language can express any thought. In this, however, they seem not to be considering a synchronic or "snapshot" account of a given language, but rather to be reflecting on the capacity of native speakers to stretch their linguistic resources as needed.

A characterization of the articulateness of English II has not been attempted since its articulateness may be easily increased in many ways (e. g., by permitting it to include English I as a sublanguage). Steps toward including personal pronouns have been taken but will not be described here.

Besides the four areas of logical suggestion, there have been developments of more purely syntactical interest. Our grammar has been based on the observation, already tacitly made by Lewis Carroll in having Alice commended for her eyesight in being able to see *nobody* on the road, that general terms act syntactically like proper names (perhaps because of a historically natural syntactical inertia). This treatment of general terms was found to shed considerable light on the variation in the meaning of "is", as between identity and predication, and upon some long puzzling terminology in traditional syllogistic, concerning "distributed terms". The ambiguity in "is" did, however, prevent the inclusion in English II of certain factored expressions occurring in normal English in which general terms and predicates are mixed together.

In constructing the system, we were forced to the recognition of natural syntactic units, the *fragments*, not heretofore recognized, and to develop a calculus of *demand* computation to account for the ways in which they can be combined and analyzed. The concept of demand and its calculus, applied here only to English II, may prove a valuable paradigm for the analysis of a broad class of natural and artificial grammars. (The system has a certain resemblance to cancellation grammars of the Ajdukiewicz, Lambek, Bar-Hillel-Gaifman types, but it is more closely tied to the logical import of the expressions analyzed.)

In order to carry out the computation of demands in a way requiring no backtracking, a further grammatical unit was recognized: the *apparent fragment*, together with a technique for grouping these together into minimal distribution units (the L-atoms). This technique also should be of value for parsing systems of this sort.

The demand concept may also be easily extended to embrace *sort* distinctions, e. g., permitting "John admires courage" but ruling out "Courage admires John". Such a system was developed for English II but not incorporated in the actual program since rejection of such categorial errors did not, at this stage, seem an important enough objective to justify the additional storage space and machine time required.

For theoretical linguistics, then, we hope to have made a respectable case for the existence of a promising field of investigation: the logic of natural grammar, and to have provided by example some worthwhile methodological principles and procedures, emphasizing the role of the computer and the value of logical notation as a consistent, broadly articulate, indeed almost inevitable, form of deep-structure representation.

The practical significance of logic-based, Englishlike languages will, we feel sure, ultimately be great — in law, in computer-assisted teaching and research, and in information retrieval. Its nearer term importance depends on factors hard to predict: the progress of machine inference techniques, the progress of computer software and hardware technology, and the progress of logic itself.

Notes

1. Carnap (1937). The famous quote from the Introduction is reproduced once again: "The method of (logical) syntax . . . will not only prove useful in the logical analysis of scientific theories — it will also help in the logical analysis of the word languages . . . The direct analysis of these, which has been prevalent hitherto, must inevitably fail, just as a physicist would be frustrated were he from the outset to attempt to relate his laws to natural things — trees, stones, and so on. In the beginning, the physicist relates his laws to the simplest of constructed forms; to a thin straight lever, to a simple pendulum, to punctiform masses, etc. Then, with the help of the laws relating to these constructed forms, he is later in a position to analyze into suitable elements

the complicated behavior of real bodies, and thus to control them. One more comparison: the complicated configurations of mountain chains, rivers, frontiers, and the like, are most easily represented and investigated by the help of geographical coordinates — or, in other words, by constructed lines not given in nature. In the same way, the syntactical properties of a particular word-language, such as English, or of a particular sub-language of a word-language, are best represented and investigated by comparison with a constructed language which serves as a system of reference."

   While this quote has received sharp criticism from Chomsky (1955), the basic point that analysis of grammatical forms may profit from idealization seems sound.
2. Originating, apparently, in Reed-Kellogg (1888). We are indebted to Prof. D. W. Emery, University of Washington, for this historical reference.
3. See Bohnert items, and Bohnert and Backer (1965) in References. Since the preparation of this report, a shortcoming was found by Paul Backer in the recognition algorithm, causing it to reject certain well-formed strings. For this reason, detailed accounts of the recognition and translation algorithms have been withheld pending correction. For a discussion of the difficulty and steps toward its resolution see Backer (1966).

References

Backer, P.
   1966   "The recognition problem in LOGOS", International Business Machines (Internal Publication, RC-1682).
Backer, P. — H. Bohnert
   1965   "Computer analysis of compound expressions", International Business Machines (unpublished).
Bar-Hillel, Y. — R. Carnap
   1952   "An outline of a theory of semantic information", *Technical Report* 247, (Research Laboratory of Electronics: Massachusetts Institute of Technology).
Bar-Hillel, Y. — A. Kasher — E. Shamir
   1963   "Measures of syntactic complexity", *Technical Report* 13 (The Hebrew University of Jerusalem)
Bar-Hillel, Y. — M. Perles — E. Shamir
   1961   "On formal properties of simple phrase structure grammars", *Zeitschrift for Phonetic, Sprachwissenschaft und Kommunikationsforschung* 14: 143—172. [Reprinted in Yehoshua Bar-Hillel (1964), *Language and information.*]
Bloomfield, L.
   1933   *Language* (New York: Holt).
Bohnert, H.
   1961   "Project LOGOS", International Business Machines (unpublished).
   1962a   "Formation rules for LAMB", International Business Machines (unpublished).
   1962b   "An Englishlike extension of an applied predicate calculus", International Business Machines (unpublished).
   1962c   "The logic of the relative pronoun 'that'", International Business Machines (unpublished).
   1962d   "A system of grouping for Englishlike languages", International Business Machines, NC-122.

1963   "Englishlike systems of mathematical logic for content retrieval",
            Proceedings of American Documentation Institute 2: 155–156.
Carnap, R.
1937   *The logical syntax of language* (New York: Harcourt, Brace and Company).
1942   *Introduction to semantics* (Cambridge: Harvard University Press).
1947   *Meaning and necessity: A study in semantics and modal logic* (Chicago).
1952   "An outline of a theory of semantic information", *Technical Report* 247
            (Research Laboratory of Electronics: Massachusetts Institute of Technology).
1958   *Introduction to symbolic logic and its applications* (New York: Dover).
Chomsky, N.
1955   "Logical syntax and semantics – their linguistic relevance", *Language* 3:
            36–45.
1957   *Syntactic structures* (The Hague: Mouton).
1965   *Aspects of the theory of syntax* (Cambridge: Massachusetts Institute of
            Technology Press).
Church, A.
1956   Review of Wundheiler, L. and A. (1955), *Journal of Symbolic Logic* 21:
            312–313.
Cook, S.
1965   "Algebraic techniques and the mechanization of number theory", (The
            RAND Corporation, RM-4319-PR).
Cooper, W. S.
1964   "Fact retrieval and deductive question-answering information retrieval
            systems", *Journal of the Association for Computing Machinery* 11.
Darlington, J. L.
1965   "Machine methods for proving logical arguments expressed in English",
            Mechanical Translation 8: 41–67.
Farber, Griswold, and Polonsky
1964   "SNOBOL, a string manipulation language", *Journal of the Association
            for Computing Machinery* 11: 1.
Floyd, R. W.
1963   "Syntactic analysis and operation precedence", *Journal of the Association
            for Computing Machinery* 10: 316–333.
Fodor, J. A. and J. J. Katz (eds.)
1964   *The structure of language: Readings in the philosophy of language* (Engle-
            wood Cliffs, New Jersey: Prentice-Hall).
Harris, Z. S.
1951   *Methods of structural linguistics* (Chicago: University of Chicago Press).
Gorn, S.
1962   "The treatment of ambiguity and paradox in mechanical languages",
            Reprinted from "Recursive function theory", *Proceedings of Symposia
            in Pure Mathematics* 5, American Mathematical Society.
Jespersen, O.
1927   *Analytic syntax.*
Postal, P. M.
1964   "Underlying and superficial linguistic structure", *Harvard Educational
            Review* 34: 246–266.
Quine, W. V.
1940   *Mathematical logic* (Harvard Press).
1950   *Methods of logic* (New York: Holt).
1960a   "Logic as a source of syntactical insights", *Structure of language and its
            mathematical aspects*, ed. by R. Jakobson, American Mathematical Society,
            1961.

1960b   "Variables explained away", *Proceedings of the American Philosophical Society* 104, 3.

1960c   *Word and object* (Cambridge: Massachusetts Institute of Technology Press, and New York: Wiley).·

Reed, A. — B. Kellogg

1888   *Higher lessons in English* (New York: Clark and Maynard).

Reichenbach, H.

1947   *Elements of symbolic logic*, Chapter 7 (New York: Macmillan).

Sillars, W.

1953   "An algorithm for representing English sentences in a formal language", *National Bureau of Standards Report* 7884. (U. S. Department of Commerce).

Wang, H.

1960   "Toward mechanical mathematics", *IBM Journal of Research Development* 10: 2–22.

Williams, T.

1956   "Translating from ordinary discourse into symbolic logic", ACF Industries.

Wundheiler, L. and A.

1955   "Some logical concepts for syntax", *Machine translation of languages* (eds.) W. Locke and D. Booth, 194–207 (New York: John Wiley and Sons).

Appendix

A: English II syntax rules collected for reference

In the following rules, *any* letters (or strings of them) may be used as meta-linguistic variables ranging over strings, their role being made explicit in each rule. Symbols of English II (see Table I in text) appearing in the rules refer to themselves in an obvious way.

It is assumed that "name" and expressions of the form "P is a predicate of category C with demand D" have been defined by an input dictionary list. One null placer (symbol beginning with PO.) will be said to be *less than* another if its place number (following the period) is less. E. g., PO.2 is less than PO.4.

1. Names are terms.

2. If a and b are terms, then so are:
Na, Ba.b, Eavb	(grouped forms)
a.b, avb	(ungrouped forms)
a.*b, av*b	(low precedence forms).

3. If P is a predicate of demand D and category C then it is also a fragment with the same demand and category.

4. If t is a term and F is a fragment whose demand contains PO.1 then
tF, t does not F	(if F is a verb fragment)
t is F, t is not F	(if F is an adj fragment)
t is a F, t is not a F	(if F is a noun fragment)

   are fragments whose demands are obtained by deleting PO.1/ and whose category remains that of F in each case, provided that such deletion does not leave the demand null; if null demand does result, the "filled" fragment is assigned the category of sentence.

5. If t is a term, p a non-null placer, F a fragment whose demand contains p then Fpt is a fragment whose demand is obtained by deleting p/ from the demand of F, and whose category is that of F, provided that such deletion does not leave the demand null, otherwise, a sentence.

6. If t is a term, F a fragment in whose demand a lowest null placer, p, exists but with $p \neq PO.1$ then Ft is a fragment whose demand is obtained from that of F by deleting p/, and whose category is that of F, provided that such deletion does not leave the demand null, otherwise, a sentence.

7. If t is a term, F a fragment whose demand does not contain PO.1, p the lowest null placer in the demand of F, then tF is a fragment whose demand is obtained from that of F by deleting p/ and whose category is that of F provided that such deletion does not leave the demand null, otherwise, a sentence.

8. If t is a term, p a non-null placer, F a fragment whose demand contains p but not PO.1 then ptF, Fpt are fragments whose demand is obtained from that of F by deleting p/ and whose category is that of F provided that such deletion does not leave the demand null, otherwise, a sentence.

9. If F and G are fragments of identical category and demand, then
   NF, BF.G, EFvG, F.G, FvG, F.*G, Fv*G
   are fragments of the same category and demand, provided that this does not result in a final term of F being separated from a first term of G by a connective. In such a case, the same compounds may be formed but with a comma preceding the connective.

10. If d is a determiner and N is a noun fragment whose demand consists just of PO.1/ then dN is a term.

11. If w is a relative pronoun and F is a fragment whose demand consists just of PO.1/ then
    wF, w does not F   (if F is a verb) ⎫
    w is F, t is not F   (if F is an adj) ⎬ is a relative
    w is a F, t is not a F   (if F is a noun) ⎭ clause.

12. If w is a relative pronoun and F is a fragment whose demand consists just of p/, $p \neq PO.1$, then
    pwf   (if p is not a null placer) ⎫
    wF   (if p is a null placer)   ⎬ is a relative clause.

13. If R and S are relative clauses then
    R.S, RvS are relative clauses.

14. If d is a determiner, n a name, F a fragment of the noun category whose demand is just PO.1/, and R a relative clause, then dFR, nR are terms.

15. If F and G are sentences, then IF ⊃ G is a sentence.

B: Sample translations English II to English I

The first two examples are shown with all four output versions. Thereafter, fewer are shown.

1. Positive Universal

INPUT IN ENGLISH II
    EVERY MAN IS MORTAL.

        THE TRANSFORMED SENTENCE

IN ENGLISH I
    FOR EVERY Z1 IF Z1 MAN THEN Z1 MORTAL

IN PARENTHESIS NOTATION WITH ATOM DISPLAY
    A Z1 (Z1 MAN =∗ Z1 MORTAL)

IN PARENTHESIS NOTATION
    A Z1 (H26. Z1 =∗ H27. Z1)

IN POLISH NOTATION
    A Z1 I H26. Z1 H27. Z1

2. Negative Universal

INPUT IN ENGLISH II
    NO ELECTRON DECAYS.

        THE TRANSFORMED SENTENCE

IN ENGLISH I
    FOR EVERY Z1 IF Z1 ELECTRON THEN NOT Z1 DECAYS

IN PARENTHESIS NOTATION WITH ATOM DISPLAY
    A Z1 (Z1 ELECTRON =∗ N Z1 DECAYS)

IN PARENTHESIS NOTATION
    A Z1 (H12. Z1 =∗ N H10. Z1)

IN POLISH NOTATION
    A Z1 I H12. Z1 N H10. Z1

3. Positive Existential

INPUT IN ENGLISH II
    SOME PRIME IS EVEN .

        THE TRANSFORMED SENTENCE

IN ENGLISH I
FOR SOME Z1 BOTH Z1 PRIME AND Z1 EVEN

IN PARENTHESIS NOTATION WITH ATOM DISPLAY
E Z1 (Z1 PRIME . Z1 EVEN)

4. Negative Existential

INPUT IN ENGLISH II
SOME SENTENCE IS NOT DECIDABLE .

THE TRANSFORMED SENTENCE

IN ENGLISH I
FOR SOME Z1 BOTH Z1 SENTENCE AND NOT Z1 DECIDABLE

IN PARENTHESIS NOTATION WITH ATOM DISPLAY
E Z1 (Z1 SENTENCE . N Z1 DECIDABLE)

5. Rule for *every*

INPUT IN ENGLISH II
IF EVERY GUEST DECLINES THEN THEPARTY FAILS .

THE TRANSFORMED SENTENCE

IN ENGLISH I
IF FOR EVERY Z1 IF Z1 GUEST THEN Z1 DECLINES THEN THEPARTY FAILS

IN PARENTHESIS NOTATION WITH ATOM DISPLAY
(A Z1 (Z1 GUEST =∗ Z1 DECLINES) =∗ THEPARTY FAILS)

6. Rule for *any*

INPUT IN ENGLISH II
IF ANY GUEST DECLINES THEN THEPARTY FAILS .

THE TRANSFORMED SENTENCE

IN ENGLISH I
FOR EVERY Z! IF Z1 GUEST THEN IF Z1 DECLINES THEN THEPARTY FAILS

IN PARENTHESIS NOTATION WITH ATOM DISPLAY
A Z1 (Z1 GUEST =∗ (Z1 DECLINES =∗ THEPARTY FAILS))

7. Rule for *a* in direct object

INPUT IN ENGLISH II
EVERY FRIEND OF A BOOKIE IS A FRIEND OF A GANGSTER .

THE TRANSFORMED SENTENCE

IN ENGLISH I
FOR EVERY Z1 IF FOR SOME Z2 BOTH Z2 BOOKIE AND Z1 FRIEND OF Z2 THEN
FOR SOME Z3 BOTH Z3 GANGSTER AND Z1 FRIEND OF Z3

IN PARENTHESIS NOTATION WITH ATOM DISPLAY
A Z1 (E Z2 (Z2 BOOKIE . Z1 FRIEND OF Z2) =∗ E Z3 (Z3 GANGSTER
. Z1 FRIEND OF Z3))

8. Rule for *some* (certain) in direct object

INPUT IN ENGLISH II
EVERY FRIEND OF A BOOKIE IS A FRIEND OF SOME GANGSTER

THE TRANSFORMED SENTENCE

IN ENGLISH I
FOR SOME $Z3$ BOTH $Z3$ GANGSTER AND FOR EVERY $Z1$ IF FOR SOME $Z2$ BOTH $Z2$ BOOKIE AND $Z1$ FRIEND OF $Z2$ THEN $Z1$ FRIEND OF $Z3$

IN PARENTHESIS NOTATION WITH ATOM DISPLAY
E $Z3$ ($Z3$ GANGSTER . A $Z1$ (E $Z2$ ($Z2$ BOOKIE . $Z1$ FRIEND OF $Z2$) =*
$Z1$ FRIEND OF $Z3$))

9. Two cases with *every* and *any* equivalent

INPUT IN ENGLISH II
JOHN READS EVERY BESTSELLER .

THE TRANSFORMED SENTENCE

IN ENGLISH I
FOR EVERY $Z1$ IF $Z1$ BESTSELLER THEN JOHN READS $Z1$

IN PARENTHESIS NOTATION WITH ATOM DISPLAY
A $Z1$ ($Z1$ BESTSELLER =* JOHN READS $Z1$)

INPUT IN ENGLISH II
JOHN READS ANY BESTSELLER .

THE TRANSFORMED SENTENCE

IN ENGLISH I
FOR EVERY $Z1$ IF $Z1$ BESTSELLER THEN JOHN READS $Z1$

IN PARENTHESIS NOTATION WITH ATOM DISPLAY
A $Z1$ ($Z1$ BESTSELLER =* JOHN READS $Z1$)

10. Two cases with *every* and *any* not equivalent

INPUT IN ENGLISH II
JOHN DOES NOT READ EVERY BESTSELLER .

THE TRANSFORMED SENTENCE

IN ENGLISH I
NOT FOR EVERY $Z1$ IF $Z1$ BESTSELLER THEN JOHN READS $Z1$

IN PARENTHESIS NOTATION WITH ATOM DISPLAY
N A $Z1$ ($Z1$ BESTSELLER =* JOHN READS $Z1$)

INPUT IN ENGLISH II
JOHN DOES NOT READ ANY BESTSELLER .

THE TRANSFORMED SENTENCE

IN ENGLISH I
FOR EVERY Z1 IF Z1 BESTSELLER THEN NOT JOHN READS Z1

IN PARENTHESIS NOTATION WITH ATOM DISPLAY
A Z1 (Z1 BESTSELLER =∗ N JOHN READS Z1)

11a. Short Scope *a*

INPUT IN ENGLISH II
JOHN DOES NOT READ A BESTSELLER .

THE TRANSFORMED SENTENCE

IN ENGLISH I
NOT FOR SOME Z1 BOTH Z1 BESTSELLER AND JOHN READS Z1

IN PARENTHESIS NOTATION WITH ATOM DISPLAY
N E Z1 (Z1 BESTSELLER . JOHN READS Z1)

11b. Long Scope *some*

INPUT IN ENGLISH II
JOHN DOES NOT READ SOME BESTSELLER .

THE TRANSFORMED SENTENCE

IN ENGLISH I
FOR SOME Z1 BOTH Z1 BESTSELLER AND NOT JOHN READS Z1

IN PARENTHESIS NOTATION WITH ATOM DISPLAY
E Z1 (Z1 BESTSELLER . N JOHN READS Z1)

12. The short scope determiner *no*

INPUT IN ENGLISH II
JOHN READS NO BESTSELLER .

THE TRANSFORMED SENTENCE

IN ENGLISH I
FOR EVERY Z1 IF Z1 BESTSELLER THEN NOT JOHN READS Z1

IN PARENTHESIS NOTATION WITH ATOM DISPLAY
A Z1 (Z1 BESTSELLER =∗ N JOHN READS Z1)

Three Examples of Relative Pronouns

13. Example 1

INPUT IN ENGLISH II
EVERY PRIME WHICH IS ODD IS GREATER THAN TWO .

THE TRANSFORMED SENTENCE

IN ENGLISH I
FOR EVERY Z1 IF BOTH Z1 ODD AND Z1 PRIME THEN Z1 GREATER THAN TWO

IN PARENTHESIS NOTATION WITH ATOM DISPLAY
A Z1 ((Z1 ODD . Z1 PRIME) =∗ Z1 GREATER THAN TWO)

14. Example 2

INPUT IN ENGLISH II
 EVERY CHILD TO WHOM GEORGE GIVES A TOY WHICH BUZZES IS HAPPY .

 THE TRANSFORMED SENTENCE

IN ENGLISH I
 FOR EVERY Z1 IF BOTH FOR SOME Z2 BOTH BOTH Z2 BUZZ AND Z2 TOY AND
 GEORGE GIVES Z2 TO Z1 CHILD THEN Z1 HAPPY

IN PARENTHESIS NOTATION WITH ATOM DISPLAY
 A Z1 ((E Z2 ((Z2 BUZZ . Z2 TOY) . GEORGE GIVES Z2 TO Z1) . Z1
 CHILD) =∗ Z1 HAPPY)

15. Example 3

INPUT IN ENGLISH II
 A WRITER THAN WHOM NO SAGE WAS WISER WROTE ISAGOGE .

 THE TRANSFORMED SENTENCE

IN ENGLISH I
 FOR SOME Z1 BOTH BOTH FOR EVERY Z2 IF Z2 SAGE THEN NOT Z2 WISER THAN
 Z1 AND Z1 WRITER AND Z1 WRITES ISAGOGE

IN PARENTHESIS NOTATION WITH ATOM DISPLAY
 E Z1 ((A Z2 (Z2 SAGE =∗ N Z2 WISER THAN Z1) . Z1 WRITER) . Z1
 WRITES ISAGOGE)

Compound Forms

16. Compound Subject

INPUT IN ENGLISH II
 GEORGE OR DONALD PLAYS .

 THE TRANSFORMED SENTENCE

IN ENGLISH I
 EITHER GEORGE PLAYS OR DONALD PLAYS

IN PARENTHESIS NOTATION WITH ATOM DISPLAY
 (GEORGE PLAYS V DONALD PLAYS)

17. Compound Direct Object

INPUT IN ENGLISH II
 ARNOLD PUSHES BETTY OR CHARLES .

 THE TRANSFORMED SENTENCE

IN ENGLISH I
 EITHER ARNOLD PUSHES BETTY OR ARNOLD PUSHES CHARLES

IN PARENTHESIS NOTATION WITH ATOM DISPLAY
 (ARNOLD PUSHES BETTY V ARNOLD PUSHES CHARLES)

18. Compound Indirect Object

INPUT IN ENGLISH II
    BETTY GIVES ROVER TO CHARLES OR DONALD .

        THE TRANSFORMED SENTENCE

IN ENGLISH I
    EITHER BETTY GIVES ROVER TO CHARLES OR BETTY GIVES ROVER TO DONALD

IN PARENTHESIS NOTATION WITH ATOM DISPLAY
    (BETTY GIVES ROVER TO CHARLES V BETTY GIVES ROVER TO DONALD)

19. Compound Fragment

INPUT IN ENGLISH II
    DONALD GIVES ROVER , OR GEORGE GIVES FIDO TO ESTELLE .

        THE TRANSFORMED SENTENCE

IN ENGLISH I
    EITHER DONALD GIVES ROVER TO ESTELLE OR GEORGE GIVES FIDO TO ESTELLE

IN PARENTHESIS NOTATION WITH ATOM DISPLAY
    (DONALD GIVES ROVER TO ESTELLE V GEORGE GIVES FIDO TO ESTELLE)

20. Abbreviating Power of Factoring

INPUT IN ENGLISH II
    IF ARNOLD AND BETTY AND CHARLES GIVE OR SELL ROVER OR FIDO TO FRANK
    OR GEORGE , THEN FRANK OR GEORGE SIGNALS OR WAVES TO DONALD OR ESTELLE .

        THE TRANSFORMED SENTENCE

IN ENGLISH I
    IF EITHER BOTH EITHER EITHER ARNOLD GIVES ROVER TO FRANK OR ARNOLD
    GIVES ROVER TO GEORGE OR EITHER ARNOLD GIVES FIDO TO FRANK OR ARNOLD
    GIVES FIDO TO GEORGE AND BOTH EITHER EITHER BETTY GIVES ROVER TO
    FRANK OR BETTY GIVES ROVER TO GEORGE OR EITHER BETTY GIVES FIDO TO
    FRANK OR BETTY GIVES FIDO TO GEORGE AND EITHER EITHER CHARLES GIVES
    ROVER TO FRANK OR CHARLES GIVES ROVER TO GEORGE OR EITHER CHARLES
    GIVES FIDO TO FRANK OR CHARLES GIVES FIDO TO GEORGE OR BOTH EITHER
    EITHER ARNOLD SELLS ROVER TO FRANK OR ARNOLD SELLS ROVER TO GEORGE
    OR EITHER ARNOLD SELLS FIDO TO FRANK OR ARNOLD SELLS FIDO TO GEORGE
    AND BOTH EITHER EITHER BETTY SELLS ROVER TO FRANK OR BETTY SELLS
    ROVER TO GEORGE OR EITHER BETTY SELLS FIDO TO FRANK OR BETTY SELLS
    FIDO TO GEORGE AND EITHER EITHER CHARLES SELLS ROVER TO FRANK OR
    CHARLES SELLS ROVER TO GEORGE OR EITHER CHARLES SELLS FIDO TO FRANK
    OR CHARLES SELLS FIDO TO GEORGE THEN EITHER EITHER EITHER FRANK
    SIGNALS TO DONALD OR FRANK SIGNALS TO ESTELLE OR EITHER GEORGE
    SIGNALS TO DONALD OR GEORGE SIGNALS TO ESTELLE OR EITHER EITHER
    FRANK WAVES TO DONALD OR FRANK WAVES TO ESTELLE OR EITHER GEORGE
    WAVES TO DONALD OR GEORGE WAVES TO ESTELLE

21. Three examples with General Terms in Compound Fragments

INPUT IN ENGLISH II
    EVERY SENTENCE IS TRUE OR FALSE .

        THE TRANSFORMED SENTENCE

IN ENGLISH I
    FOR EVERY Z1 IF Z1 SENTENCE THEN EITHER Z1 TRUE OR Z1 FALSE

IN PARENTHESIS NOTATION WITH ATOM DISPLAY
    A Z1 (Z1 SENTENCE =∗ (Z1 TRUE V Z1 FALSE))

INPUT IN ENGLISH II
    GEORGE PUSHED OR PULLED EVERY LEVER .

        THE TRANSFORMED SENTENCE

IN ENGLISH I
    FOR EVERY Z1 IF Z1 LEVER THEN EITHER GEORGE PUSHES Z1 OR GEORGE PULLS
    Z1

IN PARENTHESIS NOTATION WITH ATOM DISPLAY
    A Z1 (Z1 LEVER =∗ (GEORGE PUSHES Z1 V GEORGE PULLS Z1))

INPUT IN ENGLISH II
    GEORGE OR AN ASSISTANT PUSHED A BUTTON , OR PULLED A LEVER .

        THE TRANSFORMED SENTENCE

IN ENGLISH I
    FOR SOME Z1 BOTH Z1 ASSISTANT AND FOR SOME Z2 BOTH Z2 BUTTON AND FOR
    SOME Z3 BOTH Z3 LEVER AND EITHER EITHER GEORGE PUSHES Z2 OR Z1 PUSHES
    Z2 OR EITHER GEORGE PULLS Z3 OR Z1 PULLS Z3

22. Determiner, Simple Predicate, Relative Clause

INPUT IN ENGLISH II
    EVERY MAN OR WOMAN WHO APPLIES RECEIVES A COUPON FROM JONES .

        THE TRANSFORMED SENTENCE

IN ENGLISH I
    FOR EVERY Z1 IF BOTH Z1 APPLIES AND EITHER Z1 MAN OR Z1 WOMAN THEN
    FOR SOME Z2 BOTH Z2 COUPON AND Z1 RECEIVES Z2 FROM JONES

IN PARENTHESIS NOTATION WITH ATOM DISPLAY
    A Z1 ((Z1 APPLIES . (Z1 MAN V Z1 WOMAN)) =∗ E Z2 (Z2 COUPON . Z1
    RECEIVES Z2 FROM JONES))

23. Determiner, Compound Fragment, Relative Clause

INPUT IN ENGLISH II
    EVERY MAN OR EVERY WOMAN WHO APPLIES RECEIVES A COUPON FROM JONES .

        THE TRANSFORMED SENTENCE

IN ENGLISH I
FOR EVERY Z1 IF Z1 MAN THEN FOR EVERY Z2 IF BOTH Z2 APPLIES AND Z2
WOMAN THEN FOR SOME Z3 BOTH Z3 COUPON AND EITHER Z1 RECEIVES Z3 FROM
JONES OR Z2 RECEIVES Z3 FROM JONES

IN PARENTHESIS NOTATION WITH AROM DISPLAY
A Z1 (Z1 MAN =∗ A Z2 ((Z2 APPLIES , Z2 WOMAN) =∗ E Z3 (Z3 COUPON
. (Z1 RECEIVES Z3 FROM JONES V Z2 RECEIVES Z3 FROM JONES))))

24. Two Examples with Compound Relative Clause

INPUT IN ENGLISH II
EVERY ENTREPOT WHICH IS NOT STRIKEBOUND AND FROM WHICH COFFEE IS
EXPORTED TO FINLAND AND TO WHICH BEANS ARE SHIPPED FROM BRAZIL IS
WATCHED BY A DETECTIVE .

IN ENGLISH I
FOR EVERY Z1 IF BOTH BOTH NOT Z1 STRIKEBOUND AND BOTH COFFEE EXPORT
FROM Z1 TO FINLAND AND BEANS SHIP FROM BRAZIL TO Z1 AND Z1 ENTREPOT
THEN FOR SOME Z2 BOTH Z2 DETECTIVE AND Z1 WATCH BY Z2

INPUT IN ENGLISH II
EVERY CARBONATOM WHICH IS PART OF A WMOLECULE AND WHICH IS
SINGLYBONDED TO A HYDROXYL IS PART OF A RING OF WHICH A
MAGNESIUMATOM IS PART .

        THE TRANSFORMED SENTENCE

IN ENGLISH I
FOR EVERY Z1 IF BOTH BOTH FOR SOME Z2 BOTH Z2 WMOLECULE AND Z1 PART
OF Z2 AND FOR SOME Z3 BOTH Z3 HYDROXYL AND Z1 SINGLYBONDED TO Z3 AND
Z1 CARBONATOM THEN FOR SOME Z4 BOTH BOTH FOR SOME Z5 BOTH Z5
MAGNESIUMATON AND Z5 PART OF Z4 AND Z4 RING AND Z1 PART OF Z4

INPUT IN ENGLISH II
EVERY AGENT WHO CONTACTS A REPRESENTATIVE OF ANY NATION TO WHICH
EVERY KSHIPMENT IS SENT VIA SINGAPORE ALERTS EVERY MSTATION WHICH
CONTROLS A FLIGHT WHICH ORIGINATES IN ANY ZREGION IN WHICH TOBU
LIES .

        THE TRANSFORMED SENTENCE

IN ENGLISH I
FOR EVERY Z7 IF BOTH TOBU LIES IN Z7 AND Z7 ZREGION THEN FOR EVERY
Z3 IF BOTH FOR EVERY Z4 IF Z4 KSHIPMENT THEN Z4 SENT VIA SINGAPORE
TO Z3 AND Z3 NATION THEN FOR EVERY Z1 IF BOTH FOR SOME Z2 BOTH Z2
REPRESENTATIVE OF Z3 AND Z1 CONTACTS Z2 AND Z1 AGENT THEN FOR EVERY
Z5 IF BOTH FOR SOME Z6 BOTH BOTH Z6 ORIGINATES IN Z7 AND Z6 FLIGHT
AND Z5 CONTROLS Z6 AND Z5 MSTATION THEN Z1 ALERTS Z5